Kidd – the Search for his Treasure

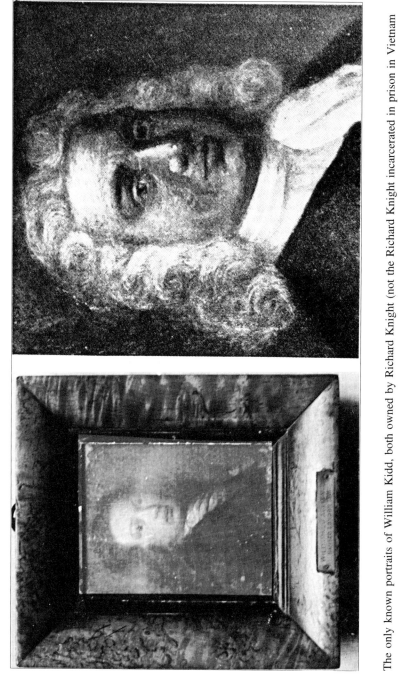

The only known portraits of William Kidd, both owned by Richard Knight (not the Richard Knight incarcerated in prison in Vietnam whilst searching for Kidd's treasure). The miniature is of Kidd aged 13 years, the other is a painting made from a sketch penned during his trial in 1701.

Kidd

The Search for his Treasure

George Edmunds

The Pentland Press
Edinburgh – Cambridge – Durham – USA

By the same author:
The Gower Coast (1979)

First published in 1996 by
The Pentland Press Ltd
1 Hutton Close
South Church
Bishop Auckland
Durham

ISBN 1-85821-357-6

Typeset by Carnegie Publishing, 18 Maynard St, Preston
Printed and bound in Great Britain by
Bookcraft (Bath) Ltd., Midsomer Norton, Somerset

For
My wife Coral
The treasure I sought and did find

Contents

Illustrations

Diagrams

Foreword

This is the stuff that dreams are made on. Pirate treasure on a remote island – secret charts in old sea chests – X marks the spot – it is all so redolent of Long John Silver and *Treasure Island* and romantic fiction of one's youth. When that undiscovered treasure, buried over three hundred years ago, is linked to one of the most famous of pirates, Captain Kidd, the lure is almost irresistible. Yet is it romantic day-dreaming, fiction or a hoax? Dozens of men and women have believed in it over the years. Many were rogues or optimistic dreamers, but by no means all: some were cautious, diligent and competent researchers and they were convinced as to its existence. It is a complex historical puzzle worthy of the attention of serious people who will take the trouble to disentangle the fables and distortions from the facts. The facts are there and they are highly persuasive: anyone who dismisses them out-of-hand merely reveals his ignorance of the evidence.

Hitherto these facts and the inferences to be drawn from them were scattered all over the place. It is to the credit of the author, George Edmunds, that he has gathered them together in this volume and assessed them carefully. As he himself says: 'I will not make such a bold statement as to say it is all here, but I would like to think of this as the definitive work . . . Nowhere else will you find all the information together and almost certainly there is nothing more to divulge about these charts.' I would agree unreservedly with that statement and I have had some experience in these matters.

My own part is described in the book, so I need not repeat much of it here. I appeared on the scene in about 1952 and had to start from scratch and check everything with the greatest care. The original charts had been discovered (between 1929-34) by Hubert Palmer of Eastbourne and I was able to locate a Mrs Elizabeth Dick, who had been his housekeeper for years and had inherited his property. She generously gave me *carte blanche* and full access to all his papers and other material, including the charts themselves. Mr Edmunds re-tells the story of my researches with complete accuracy. I continued the research until my friend Commander Baker died in 1969, then, largely owing to pressure of my professional work and the loss of a valued companion, I rather lost interest, although satisfied that the Palmer/Kidd charts were probably genuine. I think my own claim to any significance in this story is that I am now probably the last person to have examined the charts and their history in depth while the original records were in existence and while the sole eye-witness of the discoveries was still alive.

One thing that was borne upon me as the years passed was the needless secrecy which dominated many who had done some similar research, however superficial. Without taking into account the work done by one's predecessors, one is in grave danger of merely rediscovering the wheel and also of missing valuable points.

When the author Rupert Furneaux contacted me in 1968, I decided to help him and made available copies of the charts and most of my numerous and bulky files. Furneaux's published accounts were a disappointment, but his story is rightly told in this book. Then in 1985 George Edmunds got in touch with me and for the first time I was impressed with the thoroughness and tenacity with which a serious researcher pursued his subject. It was a rare pleasure to find him both very critical and well-balanced in his assessments, so I was happy to give him all my records and copies of those mysterious charts and co-operate to the full. His investigations have gone far further than anything I achieved and it is fascinating to read about his discoveries.

The best copies of all the charts are reproduced here. But that only scratches the surface: a myriad questions remain. For instance, did Kidd have any treasure that he could have hidden in 1669 as the charts indicate? We are given as accurate account as is possible of his life and movements, historical facts carefully separated from conjecture and fable.

Then there is the present-day identification of Kidd's island, an obvious starting-point and an appallingly difficult problem, which the author fully explores. It is true that I was originally attracted to the northernmost of the Sequerias Islands (said to be at 8°45′N 131°22′E), but I think now that I may have been unduly influenced by the fact that this was Palmer's identification, for it was the authenticity of his charts and his investigations with which I was primarily concerned at the time. However later research gave me grave doubts and I no longer hold this view: Mr Edmunds gives the pro and contra arguments.

If then we abandon any search for the elusive Sequerias Islands, what remains? A very great deal, involving matters of considerable technicality. The author thoroughly examines them all. He also considers the various expeditions which were formed to go in search of the treasure to see what others had thought. Most were just ridiculous fiascos or worse, but I think two are of particular interest – those by Rupert Furneaux in 1975 and 1976 and by Richard Knight in 1982 and 1983.

Rupert Furneaux was a strange man and a prolific writer of popular books. He was an industrious and indefatigable researcher, but his weakness lay in his interpretation of his material. He would ingeniously get a theory and then research the facts to support it but conveniently ignore facts which ran contrary to his conjectures. For instance, he casually dismissed the China Sea references on the Palmer/Kidd charts and totally ignored the latitude directions: everyone agrees longitude would have been wholly unreliable. He, as many others, looked for an island to fit the shape of Kidd's island no matter where it was: his choice fell on Providenciales Island (21°48′N 72°15′W) to the south of the Bahamas. He visited the island twice, found no treasure, but thought he had solved the mystery: he usually did on all the unsolved mysteries which he tackled. Mr Edmunds explains why he is sure that Furneaux had got the wrong island and I agree with him.

Richard Knight's solo expeditions in 1982 and 1983 are a real puzzle. As Edmunds says: 'I do not know what to make of Richard Knight.' He identified Kidd's Island as Hon Tre Long (formerly Isles des Pirates, now Hon Doc) 10°19′N 104°21′E) in the Gulf of Thailand. He claims to have found part of the treasure, but had to abandon it and, having been imprisoned by the Vietnamese, left the bulk of it still intact. But did he really find it? There is no evidence to support him and all indications are to the contrary. His book *Richard Knight's Treasure* was ghost-written for him by the journalist Glenys Roberts and tells a good readable yarn which, unless one knows the full Kidd story, seems convincing. Undoubtedly Richard Knight is a very colourful character, but Mr Edmunds explains his doubts about his claims and I fully support them.

Nevertheless, as I have said, the island identification is the starting point and all the facts are here for the reader to decide for himself. At the end of it all, Mr Edmunds suggests his own reasoned conclusion: he may well be right.

Until one has a convincing island identification, my personal view is that it is not much good worrying about treasure directions, though we have all had a dabble at untangling them. They are a nightmare to understand, but once again Mr Edmunds gives full details and tries to cover all the options – with marked ingenuity.

I have only picked out a few points upon which to comment here. The outstanding feature of this book is that it is comprehensive; everything the reader needs to know about Captain Kidd's treasure is here: it is definitive. If you are a treasure-seeker or merely interested in historical puzzles, you do not need the charts or supporting material: you just need this book.

A.D. Howlett
March 1996

Acknowledgements

Four people really stand out in their contribution to this book. First of all – Anthony D. Howlett. Without his original magazine article there would have been no book. After I had finally tracked him down, I found him most interested and helpful in what I was doing. Nothing was too much trouble to him and he was most kind in making available to me anything I required of his own original research material. He continues to be active in the world of mystery and is currently President of the Sherlock Holmes Society.

My wife Coral, without whose help, support and enduring encouragement the book would not have been possible. She has a rare unselfishness I find difficult to describe. No sacrifice would have been too great in her efforts to help me get the book published. An exceptional and very special lady.

Drusilla Furneaux, the daughter of Rupert Furneaux. Another person it took a lot of detective work to find. I must thank her in particular for entrusting me with her late father's notes. Were it not for her help the book would not be so complete.

The late Richard B. Knight, who kindly gave up his time for me when I visited him in Kent. He allowed me to photograph and examine his Kidd paintings and the Kidd workbox. When he was not rebuilding vintage racing cars he relaxed with his books – hundreds of them – and indulged in what he was expert at – Kidd and pirates.

Mr Arno, son of the (deceased) Mr Arno who originally purchased the 'Skull' or 'Morgan' chest. He and his family made myself and Mr Howlett very welcome and gave us every assistance in photographing and examining the chest, for which I am very grateful.

Other people and institutions I am indebted to are:

Philip Masters, marine research historian, my correspondent in America. Philip has been most helpful and useful with research and information. Mrs Irene Ungar, my most helpful correspondent in Canada. She keeps me up to date with newspaper cuttings and so on about Oak Island and has done so ever since I advertised in a Halifax newspaper many years ago. Mr D. M. Mann, (then) Curator at the Hydrographic Office, MOD Taunton. Mr D. Simpson, Head of Hydrographic Data Centre; also Fiona Bloor of the Geodetic Unit. Mr D. R. Barraclough of the Geomagnetism Group. British Geological Survey. The National Maritime Museum Department of Ships and Antiquities. The BBC TV programme 'Watchdog' (Nationwide) for information and help in tracking down Mr Howlett and for help in the Alan Marshall affair. The features editor of the *Star* newspaper. The late Mr John Bowman of the Ancient Britain Research Society (Dowsing); also Mr H. A. Snowdon. The Department of the Navy, Naval Historical Centre, Washington, USA. Oakden & Co. Eastbourne (Auction catalogue of the Palmer/Kidd effects). Bonaire Holiday Publications, the Netherlands Antilles. Dr David Koblick, University of Toronto, Canada. Mr Bagley, Curator, Rye Museum, Kent. *Treasure Hunting* and *The Searcher* detecting magazines, also *Treasure* magazine (USA). George Moore, another correspondent and metal detectorist in New York, who writes a good letter and has been very informative.

The Public Record Office, London.

Sally Gaminara of Penguin Books and Richard Knight for the story (Treasure). Victor Gollancz Ltd., publishers of *Castaway*; Lucy Irvine author and Ian Newsham map artist.

I have gone to great lengths to establish copyright ownership of certain material it was necessary to use, in particular that contained in H. T. Wilkins' books. Whilst a lot of the material is suspect, I nevertheless acknowledge the source and inspiration. He told a colourful story in his own style and I am grateful he recorded a lot of the Palmer/Kidd history – even if some of it is questionable. Without his words this book would not be so interesting. Most of the photographic material used in his books was not owned by Wilkins but by Mrs Dick who passed on copyright and authority to use to Mr Howlett. Furneaux's files contained a letter from Wilkins' son dated 1965. Attempts to contact him have proved unsuccessful.

Kenneth M. Clark for permission to use material from his book *Murder by Mistake*. Letters to W. S. Crooker, author of *The Oak Island Quest* and to his publishers have gone unanswered.

Many attempts have been made to contact Maurice Taylor, last known owner of the chart – or charts. Some of the charts have been reproduced many times in many different publications over the years. I am assuming that *if* the authors of those publications tried to contact the owner of the charts, then they had the same problem as myself, Furneaux and Howlett. The charts' whereabouts and that of their owner are a complete mystery. However, I wanted to tell him what I was doing and hoped to get his story. I also of course wanted to know where the charts are today and what condition they are in. I would very much appreciate therefore that if Mr Taylor is reading this, that he – or whoever has the charts – gets in touch.

Owing to the upheaval and changes in the publishing world in recent years – takeovers etc. – rights in some books have changed ownership sometimes several times. It is quite common for publishers not to be aware, even, of their rights in a particular book. All this has made it very difficult – sometimes impossible – to establish copyright ownership. Any copyright holders not contacted because of the aforementioned problems and the fact that most publications consulted are now long out of print, I thank in advance and ask that they contact the publishers so that proper acknowledgement can be made in future editions.

The chart extract on page 47 is reproduced from Admiralty chart 2101 by permission of the Controller of Her Majesty's Stationery Office. © Crown Copyright.

Introduction

As a teenager, I was fascinated by mysteries and the unexplained. I would put away and keep any article about which after reading I could say to myself, 'Now that is interesting.' That fascination for mysteries has remained with me and I now have voluminous files and books on subjects ranging from mysteries of the sea and shipwrecks (I am biased towards anything to do with the sea) to buried treasure, UFOs and ghosts and other phenomena.

One of the articles put away all those years ago (1958) appeared in a magazine called *The Wide World*. It has now ceased publication. The article was titled 'The Mystery of Captain Kidd's Treasure'.* I can remember thinking to myself at the time that it was the first time I had come across a story concerning real pirate treasure maps. My files were 'pruned' over the years but that particular article was always kept – I must have known somehow it would be needed one day.

I surprised myself (and a lot of other people) in 1979 when my first book was published. This was called *The Gower Coast* and dealt in detail with that particular part of South Wales. That book really started owing to my interest in diving (SCUBA) and the search for the Dollar Ship. However, the surprise was that I discovered I had a talent for writing. I was a design engineer by trade, hated English in school and still can't tell a verb from a noun.

I enjoyed writing that first book, so much so that during the next few years I decided it would not be my only book. I had a couple of ideas in mind but Captain Kidd kept coming to the fore. I had often wondered

---

* After much detective work, I was eventually able to track down the author of the *Wide World* article. His files on the subject had long since been put away but he was obviously still an authority on the subject and became most enthusiastic again after our first of several meetings. It is putting it mildly when I say I was quite pleased when he said, 'This [book] has to be the definitive work on the whole subject.'

if the author of the *Wide World* article had sailed off and dug up the treasure – as he had hinted at doing at the end of the story. I had even made efforts to contact him which proved almost impossible owing to the magazine having ceased publication some twenty years before.

Over the years I had of course kept any other references to Kidd and his treasure that I came across and was amazed by the differing opinions of various learned people. Some dismissed the charts out of hand; others had solved the directions and announced that they knew where the island was (all had different islands). But not until 1975 did someone put his money where his convictions were. He was the author Rupert Furneaux. He visited his (Kidd's) island on two occasions and claimed to have solved the mystery.

I decided then to write a book dealing with the searches for Kidd's treasure, and at the same time try to lay to rest the mystery of the charts (if any), the island and the treasure (if any). I was not going to set out to solve the charts myself but, unfortunately, once you get tied up in this business it gets at you and I found I had to attempt to solve them in order to complete my book.

This then is the background to the book. I believe all available data appertaining to the charts and treasure hunts appears here together for the first time.

I hope you enjoy reading it as much as I enjoyed putting it all together.

I will of course be more than happy to come along as adviser on any expedition you may care to organise!

Chapter 1

The Charts

Background

T he public had the first indication that Kidd had left any treasure maps in 1935. This was when Harold T. Wilkins' book *Captain Kidd and his Skeleton Island* was published. Besides giving a history and describing the life and travels of Kidd, the book tells for the first time of the discovery of the charts in the early thirties by a retired lawyer, Hubert Palmer.

We are of course in debt to Wilkins for putting it all down in writing, but unfortunately his writing style left something to be desired. The book can be said to be carelessly written: conjectures are represented as facts and the chapters on the charts and their discovery are particularly unreliable.

The actual charts are not reproduced, the reader being led to believe that those shown on the inside cover and within the book are the real ones. Indeed, under the chart drawing within the book is the caption 'Kidd's Skeleton or Pirate Treasure Island, found hidden in a sea-chest he gave in Newgate 1701 to his bos'n Ned Ward.' (See charts C1 and C2)

In fact, the charts shown are a complete fabrication and blatant fakes drawn by Wilkins himself, bearing no resemblance whatsoever to the actual charts. This was to get him in a little hot water later on, when hunters of the Oak Island treasure travelled to England to interview Wilkins, hoping to obtain information, and believing his charts depicted their island.

The person we owe our biggest debt to regarding the accurate story of the discovery of the charts is Anthony D. Howlett. He began looking into the matter in the early fifties and had to start from scratch. He was fortunate in having access to all of Palmer's private papers and notes, including Kidd relics as well as the original charts. His investigation into

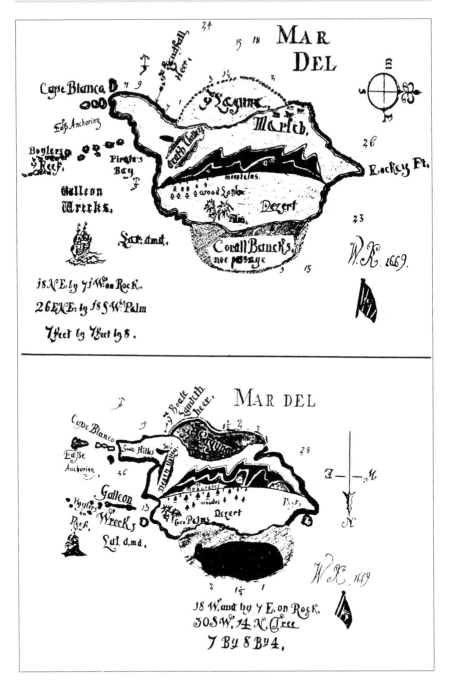

C1 & C2. The two composite charts from H.T. Wilkins' book *Captain Kidd and his Skeleton Island*, published in 1935. The bottom chart he said was found in the Hardy chest.

the charts lasted five years and, as he said, he investigated the whole subject with the greatest care, and initially with considerable scepticism, but became quite fascinated by it, declaring his belief that the charts were genuine.

> First of all I verified all the details of the discoveries from Palmer's own records and photographs and made numerous enquiries and checks of my own. I very thoroughly examined the charts themselves, together with enlarged photographs of them, taken by infra-red and ultra-violet light. In addition, I perused and checked written opinions of the British Museum, of eminent handwriting experts, cartographers and other leading authorities, deliberately seeking flaws. I was forced, nevertheless, to recognise the fact that the evidence indicated that the charts were genuine.

Howlett published his finds in the *Wide World* magazine in October 1958. Like Wilkins he did not publish the charts; tantalising the reader, in the last chapter he wrote: 'At last, in the sombre print of an ordinary Admiralty chart, in daily use at sea by hundreds of ships, was unmistakably indicated Captain Kidd's treasure island.'

For obvious reasons Howlett held back certain information and admitted to me in later correspondence that that paragraph was the only exaggeration in his article, and was on publisher's advice, implying that he had a positive identification of the island.

He was not certain of the identification, that being a very difficult task indeed, as we shall see.

First Discovery – The Bureau

The story starts in Eastbourne in 1929. Guy and Hubert Palmer lived there in retirement, both wealthy bachelors with a deep interest in the sea and maritime history.

Their collections included seafaring relics associated with famous ships and with Drake, Nelson and many other distinguished sailors. Hubert Palmer was a recognised authority on piracy, his collection of books and relics in his museum being probably unique and without rival in the world. He was very careful to accept into his collection only those items that had passed his rigorous tests to prove genuineness. The bureau he

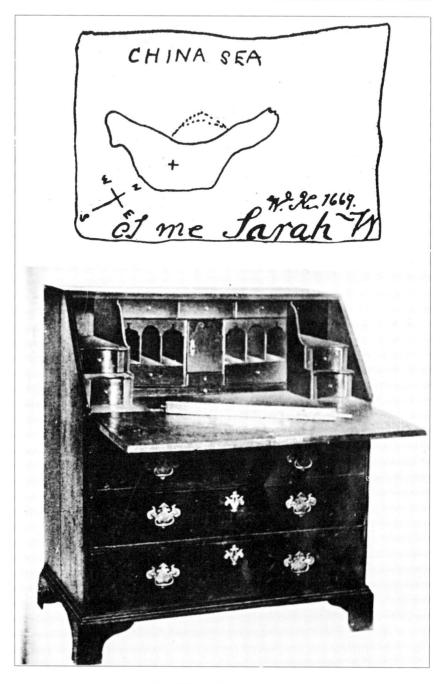

The first chart, found in 1929, and the bureau in which it was found.
Actual chart size is 4.75 × 3.1 ins (12 × 8 cm).

bought in 1929 was to receive the same intensive testing. It came from London and was a heavy seventeenth-century oak bureau bearing a much worn brass plate inscribed with the words 'Captain William Kidd, Adventure Galley 1669'.

Knowing that furniture of the period often contained secret compartments, Palmer subjected the bureau to his usual intensive examination and found three hiding places that had been unknown to previous owners: all were empty.

One day whilst using the bureau, one of the runners supporting the lid broke off. Carved upon it he noticed the barely decipherable words: 'William Kidd, his chest'. There was also impressed on one end, in wax, the insignia of a foul anchor. Guessing the runner to be hollow, he carefully broke the seal. Inside there was a brass tube, and tightly rolled around this was a small piece of parchment-vellum, yellow with age. He called his brother and, unrolling their find, they discovered they had before them (although they did not know it at the time) the first of the Kidd charts. It showed in red and black ink the outline of an island with an 'X' in the middle. At the top were the words 'CHINA SEA', and at the bottom 'W. K. 1669'. There was a compass north bearing and along the bottom, 'of me Sarah-W'.

Although 1669 appears on the chart, it was obviously drawn at least twenty-three years later, after Kidd had married Mrs Sarah Oort. This suggests that Kidd visited the island in 1669.

Subsequent scientific testing by experts confirmed that the wax, ink and parchment were of seventeenth-century origin. Further examination revealed nothing more, leaving Palmer with a mystery and wondering if there were any other Kidd relics in existence that might provide a clue to the map.

He now concentrated in particular on Kidd relics, hoping that perhaps he might find more clues to his mystery drawing. A thorough examination of Kidd relics already in his possession revealed nothing, so he started to advertise, without of course revealing his real reason. It was the start of a long search.

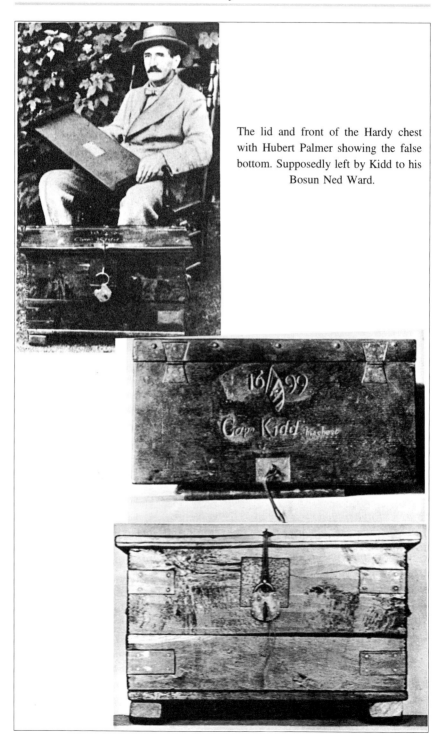

The lid and front of the Hardy chest with Hubert Palmer showing the false bottom. Supposedly left by Kidd to his Bosun Ned Ward.

The Hardy Chest

Towards the end of 1931, Palmer bought an old oak sea chest from his antique dealer friend, who also supplied a 'pedigree' as follows:

> Oak sea chest, 26¼ inches long, 13 inches wide and 16 inches deep, left by Captain William Kidd to his boatswain Ned Ward, with a threat that Kidd would haunt him forever if he broke the chest open after he was dead and gone. This chest was sold to Captain Thomas Masterman Hardy (of the famous warship HMS *Victory*, later Vice-Admiral Sir Thomas Masterman Hardy, author) by the great grand-son of Ward, the boatswain to Kidd. This chest came from the (late) Miss Pamela Hardy, great-niece of Captain Masterman Hardy. It was bequeathed to her by her father, John Hardy, brother of the said Captain T. M. Hardy. On the lid is a Black Flag, carved with date 1699. There is in it a cutlass also carved. Under the Black Flag is deeply carved the words: 'Capn Kidd his chest'.

Palmer gave the chest his usual thorough examination; he noticed that some nails on the bottom were really cleverly disguised screws. Removing these released a false bottom inside the chest which lifted out.

Secured by rusty nails to the false bottom was a slim book on the title page of which were the words: 'Carolus Redux or a sermon preach'd on May 29 1662 being the Anniversary Day of His Majesties Return, By Danial Cudmore Minister at Tiverton in Devon. London.'

Behind the book Palmer discovered a piece of ancient parchment. It was another map, but to his great disappointment it was more or less the same as that which he had discovered in the bureau, but with no reference to the China Sea, and told him nothing new. Scientific tests once again proved this map to be of seventeenth-century origin.

Palmer continued his search.

The Morgan 'Skull' Chest

In 1932, Palmer was introduced to a Captain Dan Morgan of Bristol by Mr Hill Cutler, his antique dealer friend. Cutler was, on behalf of Palmer, on the lookout for Kidd relics. He had received the following letter from Morgan:

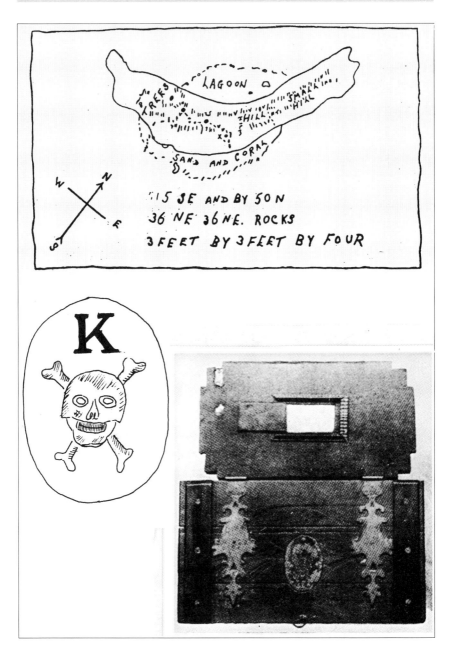

The third chart, found in the 'Morgan' or 'skull' chest. Photograph shows at the bottom, the lid – the chest is resting on its front – with the back of the false bottom lying on the top. The mirror slides out revealing a cavity in which was hidden the chart. The monogram on the lid is also shown. Actual chart size is 5.55 × 3.35 ins (14 × 8.5 cm).

Respected sir,

As you seem keen for pirate stuff i have dug something out of my attick wich may sute you it is a bit more Kidd stuff and hope you will like it i have been told Kidd was a kind gent and was murdered but when you see this thing i think you will say he was only a Bloody pirate and deserved all he got i will try and hoble down end of the week sir so heres to 15 men on the dead mans chest and dont forgit the rum ile hav som you bet after the deal.

> your obedant servant.
> D. Morgan.

Morgan claimed descent from the famous buccaneer Sir Henry Morgan. He explained that he had a sea chest that had once belonged to Kidd, saying that one of his ancestors had been head gaoler at Newgate Prison at the time of Kidd's trial, who after Kidd's death had 'removed' the chest. It had remained in his family ever since. Morgan carried on:

> My old dad told me when I was a boy that this was the same box that was brought in at the trial of Captain Kidd and used as evidence against him. The lawyers froze onto the skull in the box, which they said proved Kidd a pirate. It was Kidd's chest and used by him.

The chest had ornamental brass hinges, a plate engraved with the monogram 'K', and the skull and crossbones. Inside the chest was a plaster skull fixed to a bible, also in plaster, this item most probably used for the swearing in of pirate crews. The skull and bible were attached to a false bottom to the chest – something like a shallow tray about ½ inch from the real bottom; there was no attempt at concealment. When you lifted the skull out, the false bottom came as well.

After checking for the usual hidden compartments and finding none, Palmer turned his attention to a small mirror on the inside of the false bottom. On removing the beading and mirror a cloth was revealed. Carefully cutting this away he found a shallow well, inside which was parchment. To his great delight it proved to be the same island depicted in the previous maps but with a difference. This chart showed hills, a lagoon, reefs, four conspicuous looking 'dots' and a cross. A red zig-zag line joined the cross and the dots. A compass north and compass bearing with distance were also shown. Palmer was elated; it looked as though

A close-up of the skull, also the mirror with end-beading removed showing how the chart was hidden behind the mirror.

Kidd really had buried a treasure. He had the chart checked and once again its authenticity was proved.

So Palmer had the directions to a treasure, but still did not know where (except for a vague reference to the China Sea) this island was.

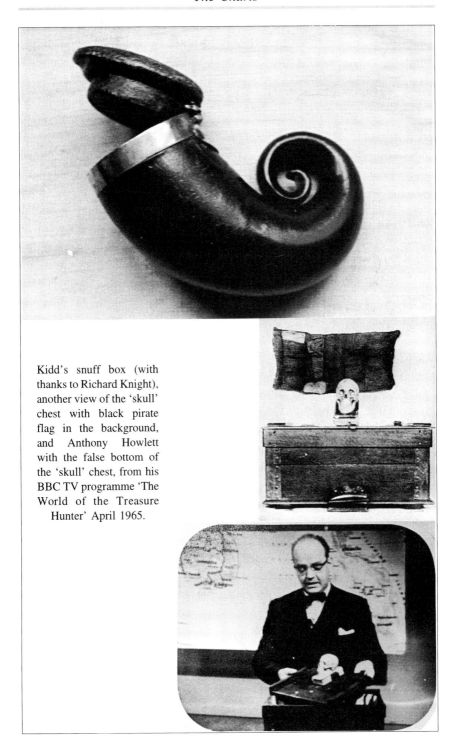

Kidd's snuff box (with thanks to Richard Knight), another view of the 'skull' chest with black pirate flag in the background, and Anthony Howlett with the false bottom of the 'skull' chest, from his BBC TV programme 'The World of the Treasure Hunter' April 1965.

Sarah Kidd's Workbox – The 'Key' Chart

In 1934 a small box believed to have been Mrs Kidd's workbox was located. It belonged to a retired naval officer living in Jersey and had previously belonged to his brother who had lived in America. It was a small box 12½ inches long, 7½ inches wide and 7 inches deep, bound and decorated with ornamental brasswork, with a brass plate on the top with the words 'William and Sarah Kidd, their box' engraved on it.

Careful measuring tests led Palmer to believe that the box was hiding a secret compartment. He withdrew four nails from the beading around the edge of the bottom of the box. This released the beading, revealing a narrow cavity. Probing inside he withdrew what appeared to be an old piece of leather binding. This turned out to be the backing of an oblong piece of yellow parchment. He realized straight away that this was 'the' chart – the key to all the others. The search was over.

Larger and more detailed than the 'skull chest' chart, there were additional directions around the margin but, most important of all, the latitude and longitude of the island was given. Palmer could hardly contain his excitement. He quickly had the chart tested by the experts who verified its seventeenth-century origin. The writing around the edge was compared with known specimens of Kidd's in the Public Record Office and it was declared that it could well have been Kidd's writing.

The next few years were spent researching the location of the island and planning an expedition.

John S's Rough Map

That same year (1934), Palmer heard that an old family in Guernsey possessed two old engraved horn drinking mugs. Palmer was able to examine these but, unfortunately, it is not known what his opinion was. Each horn is dated and initialled 'W. K. 1697'. One has engraved upon it a three-master in full sail, a flag with skull and crossbones, an open chest, a flintlock pistol and the head of a pirate with an eye patch.

The second horn has similar illustrations but with chest closed, a two-master in full sail and skull and crossbones. But what is interesting is that both horns also have a plan of an island remarkably similar to the existing charts.

As with the bureau chart it is basically an outline with an 'X' marked

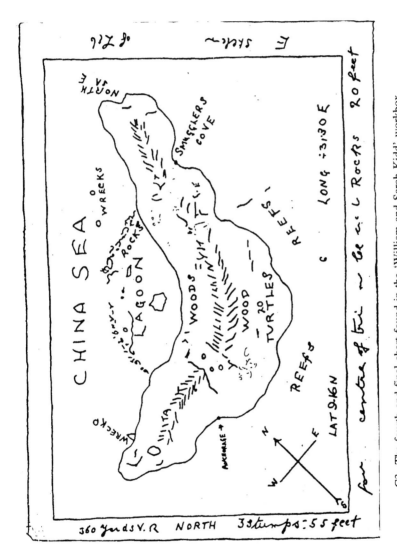

C3. The fourth and final chart found in the 'William and Sarah Kidd' workbox.
This, the 'key' chart, is shown slightly smaller than actual size, which is 8.3 x 5.8 ins (21 x 14.7 cm).

Palmer demonstrating how the fourth chart was hidden in a compartment behind the side beading of the workbox. (The lid retaining chain is a modern addition.)

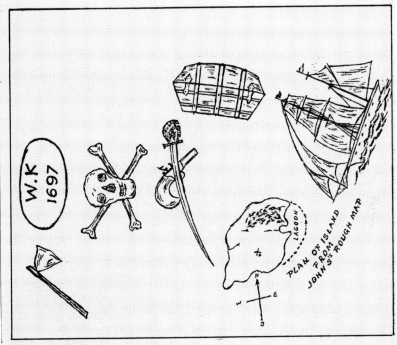

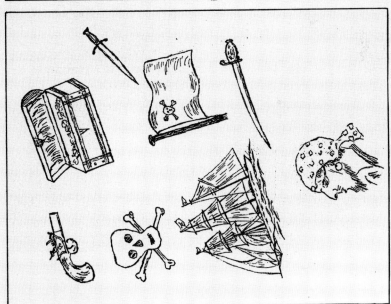

The engravings on the two old horn drinking mugs that came from a Guernsey family. The detail shows that some of the engravings must have been made *after* 1697.

with compass north pointing to it. A lagoon is also shown – albeit south of the island but then, sand and coral reefs are shown to the south of the island on the 'skull chest' chart. Underneath the engraving of the map are the words 'Plan of island from John S's rough map'.

John S, whoever he was, obviously had a rough map of a treasure island which was copied and engraved by someone onto the horns. Could this have been Kidd? Palmer also had an ivory tooth initialled 'W. K.'. It could be that Kidd enjoyed engraving and engraved these horns himself. The date of 1697 on the horn is something of a puzzle: some thirty years after the bureau chart. It suggests that, if engraved in 1697, John S was with Kidd or acquainted with him. Kidd was on the King's business at that time and during his trial he produced a list of the ninety-seven men 'that deserted the Adventure Galley at the Port of St Maryes in Mada-gascoe, Capt. Wm. Kidd Commdr. and went aboard the Moca Friggot a Pirate Shipp in the said Harbour, commanded by Robert Cullever' – Kidd's words.

One of the crew listed was named Jno Jonas; known by his surname it would sound like John S. So he could be one and the same. This could possibly corroborate the evidence of these horns and be further evidence that the Kidd charts are genuine. It does not explain though why, having drawn four previous charts, all obviously depicting the same island, i.e. with shape roughly the same as the bottom of a horseshoe or a banana, the horn island is not the same unmistakable shape. The shape is so distinct as to be unforgettable, but then, thirty years is a long time, the memory fades, and the engraving does after all say 'rough' map.

Later on I will show how the Kidd/Palmer charts and this map could relate to the same island.

The Yunnan Island Parchment

Some three or four years after Palmer had found the final 'key' chart, he purchased a very old oak framed mirror. It was about 15 inches square with a skull and crossbones and had the initials 'W K' carved on the frame. The mirror was thought to have been salvaged from a wreck near Eastbourne.

Palmer was not too happy about its supposed history and viewed it with some suspicion. However, the 'W K', for obvious reasons, intrigued

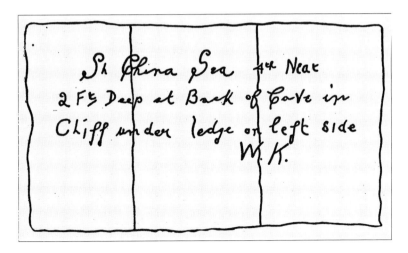

The Yunnan parchment, found in a cavity in the back of a mirror frame that had the initials 'WK' carved on it. Actual document size is 7.5 × 4.2 ins (19 × 10.5 cm).

him and he gave the mirror his usual close examination. He discovered a very small arrow carved on the front of the frame. After removing the back of the mirror he found a concealed shallow cavity: the arrow on the front had been pointing to this. Inside was a piece of folded parchment with a piece of thin wood as backing, and marked upon the wood, as though pricked out with the point of a pin, were the words 'Yunnan Island'. The parchment contained three lines of writing: 'Sh China Sea 4th NE at 2ft Deep at Back of Cave in Cliff under ledge on left side.' Underneath were the initials in block capitals 'W.K.'

It would at first appear that this document gives further instructions to the exact positioning of the treasure. Having arrived at the spot marked 'X' on the previous charts, and it may well do so, the 'China Sea' reference would seem to clinch it; also, as there is no reference to a particular island, with no latitude or longitude, then the document obviously has to be used in conjunction with some other – such as those already found.

Assuming this parchment is genuine – and we do not know if it is because Palmer never had it tested as he did the other charts – it would after all not make sense to create treasure instructions without some reference to a precise location. What is the significance of 'Yunnan

Island'? No such island exists. Yunnan is a large inland province of China and its latitude position is nowhere near that stated on the 'key' chart. What is interesting is that the South China Sea can be said to be at latitude 9° 16′N, as shown on the 'key' chart. The reference to the South China Sea appears only on this document.

I would suspect that although China in those days was a mysterious – probably avoided – country, Yunnan province was known to Kidd. He had to call his island something, maybe to remind himself in years to come, and China Island wouldn't sound right so he called it Yunnan Island. It is also possible, of course, that a Yunnan Island did exist three hundred years ago but is now known by some other name.

With reference to the picture shown of the parchment you can see that within the group of letters 'NƐ at', I have assumed that '&' is the correct interpretation of the symbol that appears in its place. Whether or not the symbol shown was used in the seventeenth century as an abbreviation for 'and' I do not know but my interpretation of 'NƐat' as being 'North and at', seems to me to be the only one that makes sense.

What does '4th' refer to? Is this the fourth document relating to the treasure instructions or instructions for the fourth cache? There are, after all, four significant looking 'dots' on the 'skull chest' chart.

The reference to a cave also only appears on this parchment. It is of course possible that a cave is mentioned on the 'key' chart, where the gaps appear in the directions around the border.

A very clever hoax?

So we have six items of evidence, all giving clues to a buried treasure or treasures:

1. The first basic outline chart, found in the bureau.
2. The second basic outline chart, found in the Hardy chest.
3. The third chart, found in the 'skull chest', giving island details and directional instructions.
4. The fourth 'key' chart, found in the workbox, giving more detailed information, together with latitude and longitude.
5. The two drinking horns with John S's rough map.
6. The Yunnan Island parchment.

It has been suggested that it is all a great big con by a skilled forger with a very clever brain, possibly Palmer himself or Wilkins and Palmer together. After all, we only have Palmer's word that the charts were found as described; there were no independent witnesses. We will never know for certain unless the island of the charts is positively identified and the treasure recovered. If, however, one was going to perpetrate a pirate treasure hoax, I would have thought a more acceptable location would be in the West Indies or Caribbean, areas where one would expect a Westerner's treasure island to be, certainly not somewhere in the China Sea.

Some people have also remarked on the remarkable coincidence of these charts all being found after over three hundred years within just over three years. Well, of course it was not a coincidence. Palmer collected anything piratical, and after finding the first chart in the bureau, he put all his efforts into finding and collecting anything to do with Kidd, advertising and travelling widely. His efforts were finally rewarded, but it took some years. Except for this collaboration with Wilkins he kept his findings to himself. He didn't set out to con the public by advertising his finds; indeed, it was not realised what he had until after his death.

One must also not forget that the leading expert of the day, Mr R. A. Skelton, Superintendent of the Map Room at the British Museum, pronounced the charts genuine.

I believe the charts to be genuine: they have that 'air' and indecisiveness about them. It is difficult to describe, but you feel and know they are for real. Besides, Anthony Howlett of course examined the original charts and checked Palmer's claims; he has no doubt that the charts are genuine.

The Charts and Relics – Epilogue

The charts first really hit the headlines – making the general public aware of them for the first time – in 1949. Hubert Palmer died in July of that year aged eighty-five. He left his huge collection of pirate relics and books to Mrs Elizabeth Dick, his companion and nurse for eleven years. When Mr Palmer's will was declared, Mrs Dick gained world wide publicity. Interviews with newspapers and magazines in this country, in France and in America were followed by newsreel and television appearances.

Within a few days she had received more than a thousand letters and had to engage two secretaries to answer them. Many contained proposals of marriage for this grey-haired lady. Many more contained offers to buy the treasure maps. Soldiers, sailors and airmen sent photographs, identity cards and even birth certificates, and asked to be included in any expedition that was arranged. A Frenchman wrote: 'Send me the map and I will send you 15 dollars.' An American wrote: 'Send me the maps, I will organise an expedition and if we locate the treasure we will give you half of all we find.' Mrs Dick replied: 'When you send me half the treasure, I will send you half the map.'

At that time, Mrs Dick, to whom the relics and curios meant as much as they did to Palmer, said she would never part with any of them. But a year later, alone in a large eighteen-room Victorian house, heavy taxation and rates forced her to change her mind. She decided that all the relics had to go and so an auction sale was arranged over two days at the house. As she said at the time: 'I don't want to part with anything, but what else can I do? I would like the museums to have many of the pieces, but they won't pay for them, and I just can't afford to give them away.'

So almost everything was sold, cutlasses, vicious looking swords, jewelled daggers, pistols, pieces of eight, hundreds of books about pirates, a wicked looking dirk – the property of Ann Bonney the woman pirate, a long-handled axe supposed to have been used by Captain Teach to behead treacherous crew members, sea chests, the oak bureau and of course the maps.

'Why don't you keep the maps and go out and see if you can find the treasure yourself?' she was asked. 'I can't afford it,' she replied, 'In any case it would cost thousands to mount an expedition, besides, at my age I am too old to go gallivanting about the China Seas.'

The appropriate pages of the auctioneer's catalogue (see p 23–26) list the particular items we are interested in as follows:

LOT 129. The 'skull' chest. This was bought by a gentleman (since deceased) and is still with his family who asked me not to reveal their address. They very kindly allowed me to examine the chest and photograph it.
LOT 165. The Sarah Kidd workbox. This of course originally contained the 'key' chart and was purchased by Richard Knight* (not of Vietnam

---

* Now sadly deceased.

MISCELLANEOUS ITEMS, CURIOS, ETC.

LOT
123 A 16in. miniature dressing chest, a 6in. inlaid nest of two drawers, a small easel and two wall plaques
124 A 10in. games box containing four sets of playing cards and a number of mother-of-pearl counters
125 An old offertory box, a mahogany writing box, a book rest and sundry ornamental items, etc.
126-127 An old oak inn sign, "Ye Jolly Roger"
128 A duelling sword alleged to have been presented to Sir George Middleton by Prince Rupert in 1680
A sword and a pair of spurs alleged to have been once the property of Prince Rupert, Governor of Windsor Castle
129 An 18in. mahogany chest reputed to be originally the property of Captain Kidd containing model skull on Bible
130 An old six-chamber pistol inscribed "J. R. Cooper's Patent"
131 An old dagger in box inscribed "Ann Bonny her dagger 1726"
132 An old seaman's dagger in sheath inscribed "Ann Bonny"
133 An old flint-lock blunderbuss
134 A brass-mounted ditto
135 An old long pistol reputed to be once the property of the pirate "Blackbeard"
136 An old silver-mounted pistol inscribed "Captain Avery his barker"
137 An old gold decorated long pistol
138 An old silver-mounted pistol inscribed "J. R."
139 An old iron-mounted powder horn
140 Three pirates' old masks and a pair of old iron spurs
141 A sailor's knife, a stadiometer, two old locks and an old iron spear
142 A belt and a collection of small articles in cabinet reputed to be once the property of Captain Kidd
143 Five old daggers
144 An Oriental sword and sheath
145 An old flint igniter and two powder horns
146 Two old iron locks, two powder flasks, an old gunpowder pouch and an old pistol (butt broken)
147 An old flint igniter, the mechanism of an old pistol, an old cross dagger and three old oak mementos
148 An old oak knocker and two pieces of Captain Kidd's black flag
149 A copper and brass pistol reputed to have been the property of Emperor Christophe of Haiti
150 An Oriental dagger with jade hilt and a brass and silver mounted powder horn
151 A telescope in leather case inscribed with the initials and crest of Admiral Boscawen
152 An old naval telescope
153 An engraved steel and brass sword reputed to have been worn by the Dauphin during the French revolution
154 Two old model cannons and sundry ornamental items, etc.
155 A mantle clock in elephant design case and a pair of companion candelabra (1 f)

"STAINCLIFF"
22, GRANVILLE ROAD
Eastbourne

CATALOGUE
OF THE
ANTIQUE AND MODERN

FURNITURE
AND EFFECTS

including

Antique Mahogany Bow-front and other Chests of Drawers, Georgian Mahogany Secretaire Bookcase, Oak and Mahogany Dower Chests, Old Oak Bible Boxes, Sheraton Secretaire Chest, Chippendale Bureau-Bookcase, Sheraton Serpentine-front Sideboard, Old Dutch Mahogany Sea Chest, Mahogany Bergere Suite, Sheraton Mahogany Card Table, Two Gilt Convex Mirrors, Chippendale Wall Mirror, Chippendale Piecrust-top Table, Library of Old and Modern Books, Sheffield-plated Items, Upright Pianoforte by Collard & Collard, Oil Paintings and Water Colours, many Items of Historical Interest, including a Brass Studded Sea Chest, an Oak Bureau and other articles reputed to be originally the property of Captain Kidd

Which Messrs.

OAKDEN & CO.

Will Sell by Auction on the Premises on

Thursday & Friday, 20th & 21st July, 1950

Commencing at 2.30 p.m. each day

On View:
Tuesday and Wednesday prior to Sale days, from 10 a.m. to 4 p.m. each day.

Copies of this Catalogue (price 3d. each) may be obtained from the Auctioneers' Offices:—
24, CORNFIELD ROAD, EASTBOURNE.   Tel.: EASTBOURNE 1234/5.

Strefield & Day Ltd., Eastbourne—9037

LOT
156 A 12in. imitation bronze cherub figure and sundry ornamental items, etc.
157 An old pottery bottle
158 An old Spanish rapier and an old cutlass
159 A cutlass reputed to have been presented to Captain Kidd by King William III
160 An old cutlass inscribed "Tom Crocker his winger"
161 An old pirate's boarding axe
162 A South Sea island totem pole
163 A sword and whip reputed to have been the property of Napoleon I
164 An old walking stick with negro's head handle
165 A 13in. old oak box inscribed "Wm. and Sarah Kidd—Their Box 1699," and two old boxes
166 A 16in. old mahogany tea caddy with interior compass
167 Ten small pictures and sundry curios, etc.
168 A carved wood book rest, a 12in. lacquered nest of drawers and sundry curios, etc.
169 Two artist's boxes of paints
170 A violin in mahogany case
171 A ditto with two bows in ebonised case
172 A miniature dressing chest and sundries
173 An old lacquered writing box, a ditto trinket box, two oval table mats and a ditto blotter
174 An old Spanish painted and lacquered dressing case
175 Thirty-one carved wood chessmen in box and three small trinket boxes
176 An old brass ship's lamp and two old lanterns
177 Six old glass wine bottles and sundries
178 An 11in. mahogany writing box and a 9in. old inlaid mahogany tea caddy
179 A 12in. old ivory-mounted trinket box
180 A 16in. brass tray, a 12in. old brass tazza
181 A walking stick with inset measure and level
182 A ditto with glass flask and small drinking cup
183 A stereoscope, a quantity of slides and sundries
184 A plaster figure, a toby jug and sundry ornamental items
185 A quantity of photographic equipment
186 Ten scrapbooks containing a collection of cigarette cards
187 Nine ditto
188 An album containing a collection of cigarette cards mostly complete sets
189 A similar lot
190 A similar lot
191 Two albums containing a collection of cigarette cards, mostly complete sets
192 Two ditto
193 Two ditto
194 Three ditto

LOT
195 A collection of unmounted silk ditto in box
196 Three small albums of cigarette cards, a collection of unmounted cigarette cards, and eight albums and scrapbooks
197 Two 10in. embossed brass trays and a small oval mirror on metal stand
198 A 12in. antique oak tea caddy with lead lining
199 An 8in. brass-bound mahogany trinket box and an 11in. carved wood bowl
200 Three carved Oriental figures and sundry ornamental items
201 A collection of thirty-four Coronation and other china mugs
202 A collection of china and other figures
203 A Sheffield-plated two-handled urn with tap
204 A Sheffield-plated table epergne with four branches
205 A 10in. old pewter alms dish, two ditto plates and a circular pewter tobacco box, a pewter measure, a ditto jug and a ditto tankard
206 An old pewter communion jug and a copper alms dish, a 12in. copper tray and an 8in. brass ditto
207 A 9in. brass inkstand, a 7in. brass vase, a 15in. oval copper tray and a plated tankard
208 Six plated cups and a ditto tankard
209 A 6in. Sheffield-plated tea caddy, a pair of candle snuffers on tray, a candlestick, a circular plated pot pourri bowl, a mustard pot and a silver-mounted table mirror
210 An oval fluted plated teapot and a circular ditto
211 Sundry china and glass
212 Model sailing ship in bottle
213 An old ships lantern, alleged to have been used on Capt. Kidd's ship "Adventure Galley"
214
215 Three swords and two harpoons
216

END OF FIRST DAY'S SALE

SECOND DAY'S SALE—FRIDAY, 21st JULY, 1950
Commencing at 2.30 p.m.

GROUND FLOOR
HALL

LOT
217 Two coir door mats
218 A 2ft. 4in. folding card table with baize top
219 A wall mirror, 2ft. 6in. by 2ft., in heavy carved oak frame
220 A 2ft. 3in. antique oak side table having drawer and four turned legs
221 Three occasional chairs with wood seats
222 An aneroid barometer in 11in. circular gilt frame
223 An antique mahogany lacquered and brass-studded chest, 4ft. by 1ft. 9in., fitted with three drawers and mahogany stand (reputed to be once the property of Henri Christophe, the Negro King of Haiti)
224 A magic lantern, a large quantity of slides and screen
225 A Chippendale mahogany framed wall mirror, 2ft. by 1ft. 4in., having gilt eagle mount
226 A 3ft. 6in. walnut kidney-shaped side table with carved stretcher support
227 A bronze gong with beater on mahogany stand
228 A small old oval portrait oil painting and three small oil paintings
229 A small portrait oil painting attributed to *Hogarth*
230 A large panel oil painting, 4ft. by 3ft., reputed to be once the property of Captain Kidd
231 A pair of small circular panel oil paintings and a small portrait oil painting
232 A small oval portrait oil painting, a small panel oil painting, "Lock," and a ditto, "Seascape"
233 A Georgian portrait oil painting, canvas 2ft. 6in. by 2ft. 2in.
234 A portrait oil painting, canvas 24in. by 18in., and a landscape, canvas 21in. by 18in.
235 An oil painting, canvas 24in. by 18in., "Shipping," attributed to *C. Stanfield*
236 An oil painting, "Horse in Stable," and an oval portrait
237 A gallery oil painting, 6ft. by 4ft., "The Well," signed *John H. Sylvester*
238 An old oil painting on panel, 28in. by 22in.
239 An oil painting, canvas 3ft. by 2ft. 4in., "Children," by *G.K.Palmer*
240 An old oval portrait oil painting
241 A small pencil drawing by *P. Potter*, a small water colour by *P. Potter* and two small oil paintings
242 A small oval pencil drawing by *J. Walter West*
243 A pastel drawing, "Mother and Child," and two portrait oil paintings
244 An oil painting, "Mill," and a ditto landscape and seven prints and paintings (various)
245
246
247

10

MORNING ROOM

LOT
248 The 7ft. mahogany pedestal sideboard having mirror back, drawer and two cupboards
249 A 3ft. 6in. Old English mahogany bureau bookcase having upper part fitted with adjustable shelves and two doors, fall front with interior fittings, four long drawers and bracket feet
250 The mahogany framed three-piece Bergère suite with loose cushions and comprising settee and two easy chairs
251 An ebonised mahogany pole screen with square embroidered bannerette in ebonised frame, glazed
252 A Sheraton inlaid mahogany 3ft. semi-circular card table with baize lined interior and four tapered legs
253 A Moorish ivory inlaid X-shaped armchair
254 A Georgian circular convex mirror in 18in. gilt frame with eagle surmount and candle branches
255 A ditto in 18in. ball-mounted gilt frame with eagle surmount and candle branches
256 A 3ft. 6in. old mahogany and oak lined secretaire chest of four drawers
257 A pastel drawing, 3ft. by 2ft. 3in., "Edwardian Lady," attributed to *John Russell, R.A.*
258 A ditto, 2ft. by 2ft. 6in.
259 A ditto, 2ft. by 2ft. 9in.
260 An old oil painting, 8in. by 9in., after *A. Vandyck*
261 An old oil painting, canvas 2ft. 6in. by 1ft. 4in., after *J. M. W. Turner, R.A.*
262 An oil painting, canvas 21in. by 15in., "Sophie Jennings," after *Angelica Kauffman, R.A.*
263 An oil painting, panel 14in. by 10in., of "Neptune and other figures," and six other paintings and sketches
264 An oval portrait oil painting, panel 15in. by 13in., after *Sir Henry Raeburn, R.A.*
265 An oil painting, canvas 15in. by 12in., "The Cameo," by *Hal Hurst, R.I.*
266 An oil painting, canvas 16in. by 14in., "Portrait of a Child," and an old panel oil painting
267 An oil painting, canvas 2ft. 9in. by 1ft. 10in., and an oil painting, "Harbour Scene"
268 An oval portrait oil painting after *Sir Thomas Lawrence*
269 A Chart reputed to have been made by Capt. Kidd showing the location of his buried treasure
270
271

DINING ROOM
272 A Sheraton mahogany pole screen on square base with oval bannerette
273 A 3ft. 6in. pierced brass fender
274 A 3ft. Sheraton mahogany Serpentine-front card table having folding top, polished interior and four tapered legs

11

LOT
275 A carved oak frame cheval screen with old tapestry panel
276 An antique oak mule chest, 4ft. 9in. by 1ft. 9in., having carved frieze and front panels and two drawers
277 An old carved mahogany easel
278 An oak four-fold screen with carved panels
279 A Jacobean oak chair with cane-panelled seat and back
280 A Chippendale mahogany 2ft. 9in. circular piecrust-top table on carved pillar and tripod support with claw and ball feet
281 A Portuguese 21in. panelled and brass-bound rosewood money chest with three interior drawers and original lock and key, on brass-mounted stand
282 A Sheraton 6ft. mahogany and satinwood-banded Serpentine-front sideboard having cupboard, centre drawer and cellarette on six tapered legs with tapered shoes
283 An 18in. old oak spice cupboard with eight interior drawers
284 An Old English mahogany two-pillar dining table, 5ft. 6in. by 4ft., having reeded quadruple supports and brass-capped feet
285 A suite of six Stuart chairs with carved bird figure mounts, carved seats and backs and carved stretchers
286 A 3ft. old walnut two-division corner cupboard, 7ft. 6in. high, enclosed by two panelled doors
287 A small oval coloured engraving by G. Gogain after I. Northcote and seven small paintings, etc.
288 An oil painting, canvas 30in. by 24in., attributed to Pietro F. Mola
289 A pair of oval coloured engravings after Sir Jos. Reynolds, a small old oval portrait oil painting and a small hexagonal oil painting
290 An oil painting, 2ft. 6in. by 2ft., "The Death of General Wolfe," *£5-5* attributed to Benjamin West
291 An old oil painting, 4ft. 3in. by 1ft. 8in.
292 A small panel oil painting in carved gilt wood frame after Corregio
293 Five oil paintings and water colours
294 Five ditto
295 The portrait oil painting, "Captain Wm. Kidd," in frame made *£5-5* of wood from his ship, "The Adventure Galley"
296 An oil painting, canvas 24in. by 18in., attributed to George Morland
297 A water colour, "The Birth of Christ"
298 A small portrait oil painting and three others
299 A small oil painting attributed to G. Sartorius
300
301
302

12

LIBRARY

LOT
303 A Turkey pattern Axminster rug, a wool rug and a mohair rug
304 An 18in. lacquered and inlaid nest of drawers on mahogany stand
305 An old wall mirror in oak frame reputed to be originally used on *£2* Captain Kidd's ship, "The Adventure Galley"
306 A Sheraton mahogany 3ft. 6in. secretaire bookcase having upper part enclosed by latticed glazed panelled doors, interior fittings and three long drawers and bracket feet
307 A 3ft. 6in. mahogany bookcase enclosed by two glazed doors
308 An old inlaid mahogany 3ft. 3in. cupboard enclosed by two doors
309 A 20in. walnut Wellington chest of six drawers
310 A 5ft. mahogany two-division bookcase fitted with two drawers
311 A 21in. nest of three drawers on stand
312 A 3ft. seven-tier open bookcase
313 An antique iron bullion chest, 24in. by 13in.
314 A 15in. old iron-bound elm chest inscribed "Wm. and Sarah Kidd—Their Box"
315 A 21in. oak Bible box containing a Bible with inscription "Kidd's Family Bible"
316 A 20in. antique oak Bible box with carved sides and front
317 A Spanish antique iron bullion chest, 2ft. 6in. by 1ft. 6in. *£4-15* with original locks and key
318 A 4ft. 3in. antique oak bureau having fall-front fitted interior and two long and two short drawers reputed to be originally *£33* the property of Captain Wm. Kidd and used on his ship, "Adventure Galley," in 1669
319 A carved mahogany easel
320 A 2ft. 9in. oak open bookcase
321 A 3ft. rosewood four-tier bookcase enclosed by four drop glazed doors
322 An electric fire, an iron fender and an old iron coal cauldron
323 A 6ft. 6in. stained wood bookcase enclosed by glazed doors
324 A 3ft. 6in. ditto enclosed by two glazed doors
325 A 4ft. oak open bookcase
326 An antique elm spindle-back armchair with rush seat
327 An antique oak coffin stool
328 A 2ft. 3in. oak iron-bound sea chest inscribed "Captain Kidd— *£11* his chest, 1699"
329 A 4ft. mahogany cabin table with two drop leaves, drawers and cellarette
330 Oil painting, canvas 24in. by 20in., "Pirate Ship attacked by *£1* Man-o'-war," attributed to Butterworth
331 Oil painting, canvas 24in. by 18in., "Naval Officer"
332 Oil painting, panel 30in. by 22in., "Royal Reception"
333 Oil painting, canvas 20in. by 19in., "Knitting Lesson," by J. G. Patten, 1865
334 Oil painting, canvas 32in. by 28in., "Portrait of Lady"
335 Two small portrait oil paintings

13

fame) for £3 17*s*. 6*d*. He still has it in his possession and allowed me
to examine and photograph it. I had a very pleasant and useful day with
him; there is no doubt he is an authority on piracy and an expert on
Kidd.

LOT 269. A chart reputed to have been drawn by Kidd. Failed to reach
its reserve price.

LOT 295. Portrait oil painting of Kidd in frame made of wood from
his ship *Adventure Galley*. Sold to the aforementioned Mr Knight for
£5 5*s*. 0*d*.

LOT 305. The Yunnan Island mirror. Sold to a Mr Thorn for £2; efforts
to trace him have failed.

LOT 318. The bureau. The first chart was found in this. It was purchased
for £33 by a furnishing firm in Eastbourne and subsequently sold by
them to an unknown buyer.

LOT 328. The 'Hardy' chest. The second chart was found in this. Purchased by a Richard Butler of Eastbourne for £11. He has moved from
his last known address and efforts to trace him have failed.

LOT 314. Another Kidd chest; it contained no secret compartments and
was not pursued.

The chart (which one is uncertain) as we know was withdrawn, after
only one bid of £25. Mrs Dick said, 'I would rather give it to a museum
than sell it at such a ridiculous price; the treasure – gold, silver and
jewels – is worth more than £100,000.' She said she had already turned
down an American syndicate's offer of £3,000 for it and wanted at least
this amount before she would sell it.

June 1952 saw Mrs Dick in the news again, commenting on the
Japanese expedition that had recovered a £100 million treasure off the
island of Yokoate south of Japan. 'I doubt if the treasure is the one
shown on my map,' she said. 'It is nearer the South China Sea, a different
place altogether. He took only one treasure ship all the time he was
sailing, and valued it at £120,000.' The Caribbean was a popular 'hide-
out' for pirates who, under cover of the numerous islands, used to prepare
themselves for plunder, added Mrs Dick. 'The Japanese treasure if it
has been found is more likely to be the loot of another pirate.' (see
p 189)

A year later, a treasure expedition, with Mrs Dick's authority, set
sail for the China Seas. Following the wreck of the ship off the

Isle of Wight, she decided to have nothing more to do with any expedition. 'So far as I am concerned, the matter is ended,' she told a reporter. 'I am tired of the whole business; it has brought me nothing but expense and worry.'

Mrs Dick died in July 1965, but the charts had been sold in 1957. Apparently a Maurice Taylor of Toronto, Canada, had contacted Mrs Dick in June of that year. He was acting for (and part of) a syndicate of Canadian and American sponsors who wished to purchase the charts. Mrs Dick sought the counsel of Anthony Howlett who advised that she should do nothing except through her solicitors and on their advice.

Taylor's group wanted to sponsor a Kidd treasure hunting expedition and Howlett accompanied him to Eastbourne to discuss the matter with Mrs Dick. Taylor returned with an option to purchase within the next six months.

In December, one of the syndicate, a Mr Alex Freeman of Winnipeg, arrived and finalised the deal. The four charts, Yunnan Island parchment and various photographs of them were handed over to a representative of the solicitors acting for the syndicate. Howlett was not involved with the sale of the charts so had no idea how much was paid for them.

Early in 1958 Taylor wrote to Howlett to say that for various reasons

Mrs Dick examining Palmer's scrapbook.

the planned expedition was shelved and the charts were in a bank vault; he hinted that they might possibly resell the charts.

In July 1959 Howlett was able to contact Taylor again through his solicitors and was told that he (Taylor) had bought out the interest of all the original members of the syndicate and that he was the sole owner of the charts. He was also of the opinion that the charts had a great commercial value and therefore if Howlett wished to make an offer, it would have to be a substantial one.

That appears to be the end of the line regarding the original charts although I believe Furneaux was able to contact Taylor during his research and was told the charts were very badly faded. Efforts to trace Taylor (1986) have failed and to my knowledge nothing more has been seen or heard of the original charts.

This of course does not pose any problem to us as we have copies which are better than the originals and anyway for our purposes the originals would not be of any use – except to verify that our copies are genuine. Fortunately Howlett had copies of the original negatives which were given to him by Mrs Dick. I was able to examine these and can say quite categorically that the reproductions in this book are accurate.

Chapter 2

Where?

Meridian Madness

O ne would think that with the charts and information therein available, we could sail straight off to our treasure island. After all, we know it is in the South China Sea and we have a latitude and longitude: what more could we want? Unfortunately, of course, it is not that simple. If it was, why for example did Rupert Furneaux go to an island nowhere near the China Sea?

The answer lies really in the longitudinal position of the island. The chart gives (we assume) 131° 30′ East. The '1' in front of the 3 could be viewed with suspicion, because the marks there do not resemble a '1'. However, the '1' could have faded leaving palimpsest (marks of the original erased writing) marks. Obviously 31° 30′ E is nowhere near the China Sea, and that position would in fact put us in the Sudan.

So 131° 30′ E it has to be. But navigation up to the mid-eighteenth century was very much a hit and miss affair, particularly regarding one's longitudinal position.

The finding of latitude has always been relatively simple by comparison because it is the arc of meridian north or south of the equator. All celestial bodies culminate on every meridian during the 24-hour rotation of the earth, and provided the angular height of one of those bodies (usually the sun) above the equator was known, and its altitude above the horizon could be observed at culmination, a ship's latitude could be found.

No such facility existed for the finding of longitude, but, knowing that the earth rotated a full 360° in every 24-hour period, navigators appreciated that the determination of longitude depended on their ability to measure the time difference between one meridian and where they were.

The prime meridian, or position from which the measurement is made (i.e. the place through which the imaginary line passes from north pole to south pole), has varied greatly over the centuries.

As early as 150 AD Ptolemy was using Alexandria as a reference point, also the 'Fortunate Islands', now known as the Canary Islands, because they were then the most westerly land known. For fifteen hundred years, the western world made little progress. In 1492 Behaim of Nuremburg constructed a globe of the world with the prime meridian passing through the Canaries. Mercator in 1541 followed suit using one of the easternmost islands. Ortelius, a Dutch cartographer, used in 1570 the most eastern of the Cape Verde Islands. Later the Dutch went back to the Canaries and chose Tenerife, because the mountain there was believed to be the highest in the world ' . . . and from the meridian of this mountain they judge the numeration of longitude, because they think fit that a famous durable place for all ages may be best chosen for this purpose.'

In 1634 Louis XIII of France decreed that the prime meridian be that through Ferro, or the western part of the Isle of Fez (Hierro), one of the Canaries. John Davis the Navigator used St Michael's, one of the Azores. The reason for the Azores being used was that there was no magnetic variation there.

Even so, we find that on later voyages Davis also used London. The French changed again in 1680; as a result of a scientific enquiry they chose Paris.

Charles II took an active interest in navigation and in 1675 founded the Greenwich Observatory as a step towards helping the navigator find the longitude at sea. After that date and for about a hundred years, English map makers tended to use London. The Nautical Almanac, started in 1767, used the Greenwich meridian and encouraged its use. But it was not until 1884 that an international conference, after long and bitter debate, finally decided to adopt the Greenwich meridian.

So, by the mid-seventeenth century, a dozen or more meridians were in use, most nations choosing their own. However, up to the end of the seventeenth century, the period we are concerned with, an English sailor would probably have used the Canaries, Azores, London (St Pauls), or the Cape Verde Islands. To add to the problem, it was also not uncommon for a navigator to have several different meridians on one chart.

This then was the navigational state of affairs for Europeans and those sailing around Europe. We do not known where Kidd was or from where he was sailing in 1669, the only date to appear on any of the charts and the date we must assume he visited the island.

In addition, because of the aforementioned problems of longitude, one of the most frequently used navigational methods was that of parallel sailing, that is, following the latitude of the intended destination until it is reached. For example, a vessel sailing from an east coast American port for the West Indies would sail by compass towards the south-east, keeping track of her position by log and compass (dead reckoning) and observations of latitude, until the trade winds were reached, at which time the vessel would head in a more westerly direction, find the appropriate latitude of the intended island and then follow it until a sighting was made. If the destination was for the extreme end of the Windward Islands, say Barbados, such a voyage might take a ship as far to the east as longitude 55° or 50°, that is 250 to 500 miles to windward of the islands, leaving plenty of leeway for error in dead reckoning which might be as much as 100 to 200 miles, because of the currents and inaccuracies in method.

However, a figure of longitude appears on the chart so Kidd did use a meridian. The fact that he gives it to within ½° is surprising, to say the least. He must have been confident of his position and dead reckoning and/or was in sight of land.

One can now see the treasure hunter's problem. Which meridian did Kidd use? It is unlikely he was in European waters during the 1660s: more likely the West Indies, Caribbean or the West Pacific. Even so, a check with the Navigational Department of the National Maritime Museum reveal that even if Kidd was based in the Colonies, because he was British, he would probably have used St Paul's. But of course we do not know definitely.

A book that I read during my research shows that even the Greenwich meridian *could* have been used. Writing about a journey at the end of the seventeenth century, the narrator says:

> . . . and entered in the ship's position at noon, which was in about 21 degrees south latitude, and about 10 degrees west of the longitude of Ferro, or *28 degrees from our new position of Greenwich.*

However, if you do not want to rely on that, we still have the options of the Azores, Canaries or Cape Verde Islands.

Navigation Today

Whilst not relevant to our particular problem, it makes sense to supplement this chapter by bringing you up to date with the present state of affairs regarding position fixing. It is interesting and you would be forgiven for thinking that, with today's satellite navigation and computer systems, there would be no problems with position fixing. This is still far from the truth. We have accuracy today, yes, but as with the problem of charts of hundreds of years ago of which we ask, 'Which meridian?' Today we have to ask, 'Which datum?'

The subject is of course by its nature complicated, technical and very specialist. To understand even basic navigation for maritime purposes takes many hours of study. We are not all technically minded: who knows what a 'Breton Plotter' is, or that there are two norths, true and magnetic? As I said, it is a specialist subject. However, I will attempt to explain in simple terms where possible.

First of all the abbreviations and definitions. There are a lot used in this field (or should I say ocean?) common to the profession but not to us. If I explain them first you will know what is meant as you read through. They are;

1. Spheroid. Also referred to as an ellipsoid. A mathematically defined figure which also provides a practical earth model upon which positional computation can be based. To explain further: The 'true' shape of the solid earth is its topographical surface which includes mountain peaks and ocean trenches. It approximates to an oblate, or flattened (at the poles), spheroid but, because of its irregularities, it departs from a spheroidal shape by as much as about 9,000 metres on land and 11,000 metres in the oceans. This topographical surface is much too complicated to be described mathematically and to use as a reference surface for positioning.

2. Geoid. In simple terms a surface approximating to an averaging out of the land masses and ocean floor. It equates approximately to Mean Sea Level (MSL). In technical terms it is defined as that equipotential gravity surface which equates to MSL. This surface line varies around the earth from the true spheroidal form by only 100 metres. To be technically correct: globally, the geoid differs from the WGS 84 spheroid by a maximum of about 100 metres.

3. The Datum. The relationship of a particular spheroid to the geoid.

4. GPS. Global Positioning System.

5. WGS 84. World Geodetic System 1984.

6. ED 50. European Datum 1950.

7. NAD 27. North American Datum 1927.

8. WGS 72. World Geodetic System 1972.

9. ECDIS. Electronic Chart Display and Information Systems.

10. OSGB 36. Ordnance Survey of Great Britain 1936.

11. DGPS. Differential Global Positioning System. (See explanation on pp. 35–6)

If you understand the definitions of geoid and spheroid then you will have a good idea of what this is all about. Basically, the problem today is that if you are using a chart produced say just twelve years ago and you obtain your position fix by means of a satellite navigation system, then before plotting your position you should adjust it by an amount specified on the chart. For example, a note on the chart might read: 'SATELLITE DERIVED POSITIONS – Positions obtained from satellite navigation systems are referred to WGS 72 Datum. They should be moved 0.03 minutes SOUTHWARD and 0.11 minutes EASTWARD to agree with this chart.' The amount quoted will vary with the Datum being used, and where on the earth's surface you are.

Many different spheroids have been developed to provide a 'best fit' to the geoid for local and more extensive areas of the Earth's surface. The OSGB 36 Datum, which is used for charts covering the coastal waters of England, Scotland and Wales, is based on the Airy spheroid and is within about 4 metres of the geoid in that region. ED 50 was developed for military mapping in central Europe after the Second World War. Its potential as a means to reference positions to a single datum over large areas was soon recognised. There was pressure to extend the network but this introduced errors. ED 50 is not the same in the Suez region as that defined in central Europe. Similarly NAD 27 when extended into the Caribbean introduced errors which became apparent when comparing the differences between satellite global datums such as WGS 84.

What it boiled down to is that local region datums were very accurate for that region but not for another part of the globe. For example ED 50 provides close approximation to the shape of the Earth over Europe but becomes progressively poorer the further you go away.

In the 1960s, satellite technology provided the means of defining a global datum based on the Earth's centre of mass and this resulted in the development of the WGS 72 Datum, which relates the satellite-derived spheroid to the geoid. WGS 72 has been superseded by the current WGS 84 Datum. The shift between these datums reaches a maximum of about 17 metres at the equator, being zero at the poles. It is therefore significant for charts of about 1:50,000 scale and larger, especially in low latitudes. WGS 84 is a global system adopted internationally and is now the standard. Obviously it is going to take many years before all charts conform; WGS 84 is after all a recent development. To date, the shift values which relate the local datum to WGS 84 have been calculated and are quoted for nearly half of the BA (British Admiralty) series.

Many charts have significant inherent positional weaknesses resulting from the antiquity and inadequacies of some of the source material used in their compilation. Thus, a mariner may be tempted to make use of his apparent 10 metre navigational accuracy provided by DGPS to skirt dangers whose charted positions could be many hundreds of metres from their real location, rather than give them a suitably wide berth. So there are problems in having a navigation system which can be many more times accurate than the charts on which positions are plotted. The problem becomes more significant as we enter the ECDIS era where users may increase scale inappropriately and fail to realise the significance of poor positional accuracy. This important topic is receiving the attention of the International Hydrographic Organisation.

So, even with the majority of modern charts, it is still not a simple matter to fix accurately your position on a chart. You must know what datum that chart is using. Or to be more precise: you must ensure that the horizontal datum of the chart is compatible with the datum to which the observed positions are referenced.

An explanation of DGPS for those students of navigation who may be interested: As the name implies, DGPS makes use of comparisons between GPS observations. In the navigational sense, DGPS makes use of a second GPS receiver which is located at a fixed known point or reference station. Because the position of this reference station is known it is possible to work the positioning equations in reverse and calculate what the errors were in the signals received from the GPS satellites. Corrections to these errors can then be transmitted and applied to observations at the mobile – the yacht or vessel whose position is required. The system relies on the errors being experienced similarly at both the fixed reference station and the mobile. However, providing the corrections are transmitted within seconds of their determination the distance between reference station and mobile can be several hundreds of kilometres without significant loss of accuracy.

In brief: The principle of DGPS is that if a GPS receiver is located at a known position it is possible to calculate errors contained in the satellite data and transmit this information, as error corrections, to the GPS receiver on the platform whose position is required.

Putting the technical stuff behind us, one can see that for navigators it is routine that one has to be very careful about the chart datum appropriate for the chart being used, but these datums are supplied on the majority of modern charts and have to be fed into the ship's GPS (Global Positioning System) set which then makes the corrections automatically. If one is uncertain or has not got the appropriate chart datum, there are several ways of getting round the problem; as a last resort, the navigator could and should revert to the old, time-honoured sextant method, if only as a check.

With regard to accuracy, GPS navigation is unbeatable in terms of great precision and consistent accuracy – anywhere and at any time. GPS is based upon a number of satellites so placed that at least four are 'visible' anywhere in the world at any time. To protect military interests, the GPS system has been degraded for civilian users by the addition of Selective Availability (SA), but nevertheless accuracy should still be at least within 100 metres. In practice it is usually within about 65 metres. During the Gulf War when SA was switched off, accuracy was plus or minus 5 metres!

Any competent navigator today should have little difficulty in finding any island, anywhere in the world, with or without satellite navigation.

Now back to the Kidd business.

Possible Positions

To find where our island may lie, we now have to relate the seventeenth-century longitude meridians to today's Greenwich meridian as follows:

Present Positions

Cape Verde Islands	23°W of Greenwich
Azores (Del Corvo Isle, most westerly)	31°W " "
Azores (St Michael's Island)	26°W " "
Canary Isles (Tenerife)	17°W " "
Canary Isles (Hierro)	18°W " "

London of course would be 0° for this exercise, Greenwich being only 0° 05′E can also assumed to be zero.

Kidd's Island: Actual position relative to Greenwich

1. Cape Verde Islands,   131° 30′ – 23° = 108° 30′E
2. Azores (Del Corvo),   131° 30′ – 31° = 100° 30′E
3. Azores (St Michael's),   131° 30′ – 26° = 105° 30′E
4. Canary Isles (Tenerife),   131° 30′ – 17° = 114° 30′E
5. Canary Isles (Hierro),   131° 30′ – 18° = 113° 30′E
6. London,   131° 30′ – 0° = 131° 30′E

The next question is, how accurate were the sightings made in the seventeenth century? Again, a check with the National Maritime Museum revealed that a good navigator should be within ± 1° of actual, or approximately ± 70 miles. If within sight of land he should be more accurate. (See chapter on accuracy, page 51)

So we now have six possible locations for Kidd's island.

At position 1 and with reference to Map M1 on p. 38 there are no islands at longitude 108° 30′E on the latitude line of 9° 16′N. The nearest can be said to be Poulo Sapate at 9° 56′N, 109° 06′E some 40 miles to the north.

Position 2 (100° 30′E) is 500 miles from the South China Sea and is in the Gulf of Thailand. For these reasons I think we can ignore this position.

Position 3 (105° 30′E) puts us high and dry in South Cambodia.

Position 4 (114° 30′E). There is nothing there. The nearest island is Spratly Island some 200 miles to the west.

Position 5 (113° 30′E) puts us about 70 miles closer to Spratly Island.

Position 6 (131° 30′E) i.e. the 'key' chart position, puts us right out in the West Pacific Ocean, to the east of the Philippines, some 1,300 miles from the middle of the South China Sea. It would appear that there are no islands there, but more about that later.

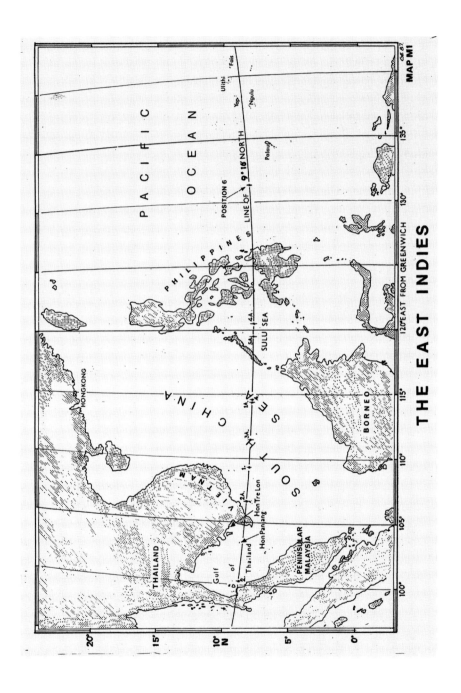

Of the coordinates now plotted, positions 1, 4 and 5 can be said to be in the South China Sea, but there are no islands there, so is this the end of the trail? In fact, if we ignore the longitude for the moment, there is only one island in the South China Sea area that is almost exactly on the line of latitude of 9° 16′N. That is the island of Hon Panjang* at longitude 103° 30′E, about 140 miles to the west of our nearest plotted position 3. Unfortunately, this island is in the Gulf of Thailand, albeit the South China Sea end. It could be, of course, that in Kidd's time he knew all this area as only the South China Seas.

What is interesting about this island is that Maurice Taylor (who bought the original charts from Mrs Dick) planned and mounted a (failed) expedition to this island. See p. 55.

Vanishing Islands?

Knowing Kidd came from the British Isles, why not look at the obvious? He would more than likely have used London as his prime meridian. We must recall also that the National Maritime Museum suggested London (St Paul's).

Using London puts us at position 6, i.e. at 131° 30′ in the Pacific Ocean. Nothing there, you say, and of course, looking at any modern chart or map, there is nothing shown there (See Map M1). This poses a mystery to us, because at one time there were islands shown on charts at this approximate position. They were known as the Sequeiras Islands. It is these islands that Anthony Howlett is hinting at in his *Wide World* article, as is Wilkins in his book *Captain Kidd and his Skeleton Island*.

To understand the mystery of these vanishing islands, one needs to look at the cartographical history of them as follows:

On his journey north in 1525, the Portuguese Diego de Rocha discovered in latitude 9° or 10° north a group of small islands close together. He named them the Islands of Gomez de Sequeira after his pilot. He was reported to have spent four months there amongst the 'simple and friendly people' whilst waiting for favourable winds.

---

* Poulo Panjang on old Admiralty Charts.

On 1 January 1528, on his voyage west across the Pacific, Alcaro de Saavedra sighted a group of islands which he named 'Los Reyes'. These were apparently the Sequeiras Islands, but he, being Spanish, did not know that they had already been discovered.

For over two centuries after this sighting there are several reports of islands sighted in this area but, owing to the difficulty of positioning longitude, no islands are positively positioned and identified. For example:

1543. On western passage across Pacific sighted small island – perhaps Fais. Three days later found larger island with reef and named it Arrecifes – perhaps Yap.

1565. Stood off an island, perhaps Sorol, next day another low island to the west, possibly Nugulu.

1625. Dutch fleet sighted an island three days out of Guam at 10½°N, either Fais or Ulithi. Next day sighted a high island, probably Yap.

1686. Spanish vessel from Manila sighted an island to the south of Guam, possibly Yap or Ulithi.

1711. Spanish vessel from Manila sighted four tiny islands that may have been Nugulu.

Not until 1802 do we have another 'positive' sighting of the Sequeiras Islands. This was by Don Lafita of the Spanish navy. He very carefully positioned three islands at 8° 45′N and 131° 22′E, identifying them as the Sequeiras Islands. He made a report which was subsequently published 19 June 1804 in the *Gazeta de Madrid*.

In 1827, in his *Atlas de L'Océan Pacifique*, Krusenstern shows the islands in the same position and named 'Is Sequeiras'. This is the largest scale chart to show these islands (see p. 41) and Krusenstern in his *Recueil des Mémoires Hydrographiques* stated: 'These islands are indisputably the Sequeiras Islands of Diego de Rocha.'

The Discovery of the Pacific Islands (1960) disagrees, stating that 'it is probable that the islands of Sequeira were those of Yap Atoll.'

However, Lafita's report is interesting and is as follows:

Lieut. Commander D. Joaquin Lafita, in command of the packet-boat *Principe de Asturias*, sailed from Manila for New Spain (Mexico) on the 25th September 1802. Leaving the Strait of San Bernadino, he set course for the Palau Islands and the Carolines, through whose

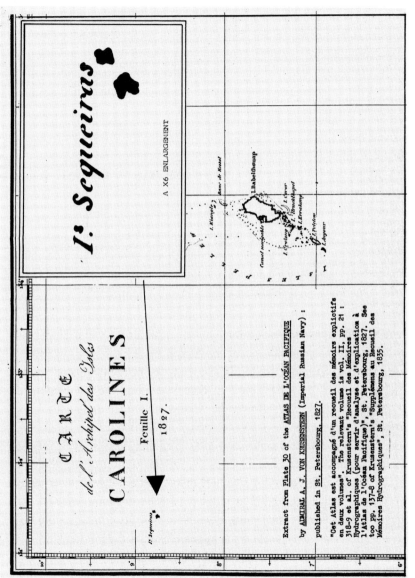

Map 2: Sequeiras Islands

dangerous seas he gained the longitude necessary to return north-wards and pass to the east of the Marianas. After a month, which elapsed between losing sight of the Philippines and sighting the Carolines, he found his estimated position to be 14° in error to the west of his fix. This voyage has restored to geography the islands of Martires, Matalotes and Catritan, discovered in former times, which foreigners have with little justification removed from modern charts. Lafita, who has actually seen them, has determined their positions as follows:

	Lat N.	*Long E. of Cadiz*
Martires and Matalottes (very clearly),	8° 45'	137° 42'
Catritan,	8° 25'	137° 42'
Valientes (the most westerly),	6° 00'	164° 24' 2"

It is interesting to note that the Spanish were using Cadiz as their prime meridian in the early nineteenth century. Cadiz is at 6° 20'E which puts Lafita's islands at 137° 42' – 6° 20' = 131° 22'E, which is in fact where they are shown on Krusenstern's chart. Krusenstern was obviously using the Greenwich meridian before it was established as the prime meridian.

Arrowsmith's (1832) and Laurie's (1847) Pacific Ocean charts both show the islands in position, probably copied from earlier publications.

In 1859, the Admiralty (probably copying earlier publications) shows the islands in position and named on their chart No. 2683, edition A1. In 1872, edition A9 still shows the island but with the symbol '?' underneath.

In 1875, the Admiralty published chart 781, the largest scale of the area. The Sequeiras were *not* inserted in this issue, indicating that the Admiralty were satisfied that the islands did not exist. Subsequently they were removed from chart 2683 at its next major redrawing in 1887.

The second edition of the Admiralty's 'West Pacific Pilot', published in 1890, was the last Navy reference to these islands. Thereafter they are not mentioned in any Admiralty Pilot or chart.

One day Palmer confided to an old friend his problem of identifying the island. His friend, Captain Harold Orchard, was a retired naval officer who said he had landed on a island remarkably similar to that described by Kidd on the charts and in the area where Palmer deduced the island to be. Captain Orchard, who was very familiar with the China Seas, also related to Wilkins and Palmer a strange story:

In the late 1890s, about the time when China was defending Formosa against the attacks of Japan, I had returned from a cruise in which we were keeping watch on blackbirders and gun-runners attempting to run the blockade of the Chinese forts under our control, and of our own naval patrol. In the port of Yokohama I was in a shore tavern listening to the roaring of a long shanty, with many staves, by a set of old shellbacks who have long since vanished from the oceans. I recall a verse about 'Kidd's angels, eyeless and 'airless, keeping watch in a valley', and then there was something about a treasure buried 'five fathoms deep'. When I saw the chart of the island which Kidd hid in his sea-chest, and noted the topographical features of 'Death Valley', which he or some buccaneering friend of his marked on the treasure island chart, this old shanty came back to my mind.

I think Wilkins probably added a bit of colour to that transcript; certainly the last part is pure imagination as we know there is no Death Valley on the Kidd charts. However, Captain Orchard's comments convinced Palmer that he had correctly identified Kidd's island as being one of the Sequeiras Islands.

Unfortunately, the name of the island that Captain Orchard recalled is now lost. Howlett says that Palmer's notes on this matter were stolen after his death and that anyway, they were incomplete and unintelligible to an outsider.

I was interested to learn the opinion today of the Admiralty, now the Hydrographic Department of the Ministry of Defence at Taunton. A letter from them confirmed the previous Admiralty chart information regarding the Sequeiras with the following added statement:

'The islands do not appear on the current charts published by Japan and the USA, both of whom chart the area on a larger scale and in more detail than ourselves.'

So do we ignore or accept the learned advice from the MOD? I should think common sense must prevail and we accept it. The Sequeiras Islands do not exist. What we must accept is that a small group of islands obviously do exist in an area to the east of the Philippines at something like latitude 8–10° N, and that owing to the already mentioned problems of navigation all those years ago, the Sequeiras were obviously mistaken for one of a group of islands that are now known to exist east of the Philippines.

Henry Stommel in his book *Lost Islands* comes to the same conclusion. He relates how Lafita reported north-west of the Pelew Group three islands, two of which he named the Martyros and the third twenty miles south of the former Citritan. Since that time these were believed to be the 'Sequeiras' of Rocha. Stommell goes on to comment that although the islands were placed by Lafita in a much frequented channel, they have not been seen since; also that their description answered remarkably well to the Gulu or Matelotas (the Lamoliork or Freyeinet) near the same latitude but 6° east of the assumed position of the Sequeiras.

His final comment was that it was very probable therefore that no islands exist where the Sequeiras are shown on charts.

The Sequeiras Islands are by no means unique. For example, ship after ship was sent out by the Dutch East India Company at the Cape in the late seventeenth century to search for St Helena Nova, a lovely island supposed to lie somewhere between St Helena and the African coast. Portuguese charts showed this island – hence the Dutch expeditions. Saxemburgh, which was supposed to lie halfway between South America and South Africa in latitude 30°S was another one. First reported in 1670, it was sighted several times over the centuries since, the last time in the early 1800s. The old South Atlantic charts showed Isla Grande in latitude 45°S 'a very large pleasant island', discovered by Anthony la Roche. Other sailors searched for this island and found indications of land: discoloured water, driftwood and kelp, but the island has never again been sighted.

If the Sequeiras Islands really did exist, then probably some undersea volcanic eruption destroyed them. This is not unusual; as we know, volcanoes do create and destroy islands.

Island Groups in the West Pacific Ocean

Yap	Approx.	9° 30′N,	138° 20′E
Ulithi	Approx.	10° 00′N,	139° 30′E
Fais	Approx.	9° 80′N,	140° 40′E

| Palau | Approx. | 7° 20′N, | 134° 30′E |
| Ngulu | Approx. | 8° 30′N, | 137° 40′E |

When looking at the longitudinal positions, the obvious question is: how can one relate these longitudes to that of 131° 30′E? Surely Kidd can not have been 3°– 9° out? Probably not, so we must look for another explanation, and it could be this: we have already seen that the Kidd charts have faded badly, giving numerous omissions on the 'key' chart and possibly introducing palimpsest marks. For the same reasons it could be that our 131° 30′ is not that at all but 137° 30′.

This now brings it all into perspective. Allowing for errors of the time, any one of the groups can qualify, the obvious contenders being Ngulu and Yap.

What makes Captain Orchard's remarks particularly interesting is his reference to 'Kidd's Angels'. This is a very odd description and does not make sense at all until you realise that the Ngulu Islands were at one time known as Angeli.

The description of these islands is also interesting to us and with reference to Meinicke the German cartographer in 1869 is briefly as follows:

They number six small islands and that Ngulu or Angeli is one, they are flat wooded islands near a very dangerous reef. The two largest islands 3 miles apart are on the southern edge of the reef and seven miles to the north-west is another conspicuous islet. The group extends for about 22 miles north and south. Ngulu, the southmost island is inhabited and has on it coconut palms, the tops of which are about 100 feet above high water. A reef extends north-east of the group for a distance of about 3 miles. Between Ngulu and North island the reef is in detached patches and does not break during westerly winds. The islands have only a small population.

The Pacific Islands Pilot Vol. 1 gives the following description:

Is 98ft high to the tops of the trees, is densely covered with coconut palms, it lies at the southern extremity of the atoll and is the only inhabited island of the group.

The Pilot locates this atoll at 8° 30′N, 137° 30′E.

I spent some time at the Hydrographic Department studying the largest scale charts available of the islands so far mentioned, Ngulu was one of the first to be looked at; unfortunately it is not the flat 'U' or 'banana' shape we are looking for. (see Chart C4) But it does have similarities in shape. One must also remember that the state of the art of cartography in the seventeenth century was very primitive compared with today's satellite photography. A rough drawing had to be made on site; there was no way of getting an accurate plan view; it might have been drawn in a hurry or from memory at a later date. Another point is that today's island shape – particularly of a coral island – is likely to have changed anyway in three hundred years. So dissimilarities between modern chart shapes and Kidd's island chart should not put the treasure hunter off too much.

It is interesting to note that John S's island outline is similar to that of Ngulu.

A note in one of Palmer's scrapbooks reads as follows: 'I do not agree that the Ngulu Islands are those seen by Lafita or that one of them is Kidd's nameless island.'

Having decided that 137° 30′E is the longitude, we must of course once again relate it to the other five possible prime meridians as follows:

1a. Cape Verde 137° 30′ – 23° = 114° 30′E.

2a. Azores 137° 30′ – 31° = 106° 30′E.

3a. Azores 137° 30′ – 26° = 111° 30′E.

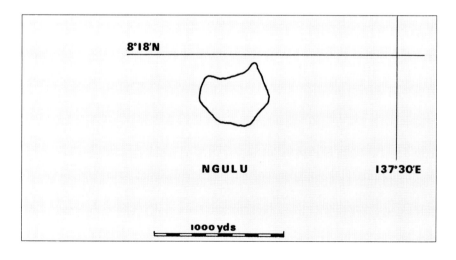

Chart C4. Ngulu

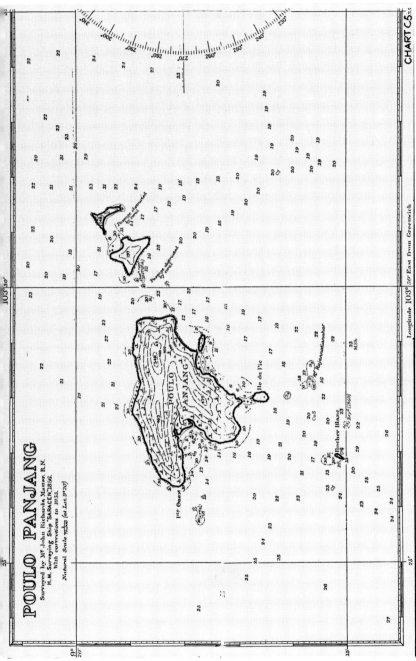

C5. Paulo Panjang (Reproduced from former Admiralty Chart 2101 with the permission of the Controller of HM Stationery Office and of the Hydrographer of the Navy. Crown Copyright.)

CHART C5.

4a. Canary Isles137° 30′ – 17° = 120° 30′E.

5a. Canary Isles137° 30′ – 18° = 119° 30′E.

This set of figures of course puts us 6° to the east of the last set. The width covered by the longitude tolerance band of 106° to 120° certainly puts us in the South China Sea at the latitude of 9° 16′ and just about covers the width of the South China Sea at this point. It also takes in part of the Sulu Sea west of Mindanao in the Philippines.

At position 1a (114° 30′E), the nearest island is Sin Cowe at 9° 40′N, 114° 20′E. This island bears no resemblance to Kidd's island and is only a couple of hundred yards across. Further north are the Tizard bank and reefs; these are what they say they are: reefs and a couple of very small sand covered islands.

At position 2a (106° 30′E), the nearest island is Con Son at 8° 40′N, 106° 35′E. It could be a contender, the shape is close, but the island needs to be reversed to be seriously considered.

At position 3a (111° 30′E), the nearest island is Spratly at 8° 38.5′N, 111° 55′E. It is less than half a mile long, 8ft high and surrounded by numerous reefs. The shape bears some resemblance but does not have the qualifying features.

At positions 4a and 5a (Sulu Sea), we have the Tubbataha Reefs to the south of line 9° 16′ and Cagayan Islands to the north; none of them bear any resemblance whatsoever.

Single System of Navigation

Unfortunately the problem of longitude continues because of another system in use at the same time and so that we can say that we have covered all possibilities, we must look at it too.

A mariner may have fixed his position from a given meridian using the full 360° available rather than the dual system of 180°E or W. For example, in 1725, the man-of-war *Elisabeth* arrived at a latitude of 44°. Its logbook read: 'Lat. 44°, long. 327° 30''. This single system did not disappear until the late eighteenth century. This means that taking into account fading and palimpsest marks, the longitude on the chart could be:

231° 30′E

237° 30′E

331° 30′E

337° 30′E

Assuming London were the meridian used, then today's position relative to Greenwich could be as follows:

1. 360° − 231° 30′E = 128° 70′W.

2. 360° − 237° 30′E = 122° 70′W.

3. 360° − 331° 30′E = 28° 70′W.

4. 360° − 337° 30′E = 22° 70′W.

Positions 1 and 2 are in the middle of the Pacific Ocean, the nearest island (Clipperton) being over a thousand miles away.

Positions 3 and 4 are about six hundred miles off the west coast of Africa, the nearest island being the Cape Verde Islands about five hundred miles to the north.

If Kidd used the single system, he obviously did not use London as his meridian. We can also see that even if any other of the five meridians were used we will always get a longitude *West* of Greenwich. The China Seas are *East* of Greenwich, so should we not dismiss the single system out of hand? Not if we are to look at all location possibilities. After all, a lot of people believe the island to be in the West Indies, the reference to the China Sea being put on the chart deliberately by Kidd to put people off the trail. So although tedious, we must calculate all the positions to cover all the possibilities.

We have already obtained a set of figures assuming London were the meridian used. Island locations for the remaining meridians will be as follows:

Assumed, chart figure	*Deduct from 360 to give westerly (W)*				
231° 30′,	Island Posn = 128° 70′W	(*of Cape Verde*)	+ 22°W	(to Greenwich)	= 150° 70′W.
237° 30′,	Island Posn = 122° 70′W	(" " ")	+ 22°W		= 144° 70′W.
331° 30′,	Island Posn = 28° 70′W	(" " ")	+ 22°W		= 50° 70′W.
337° 30′,	Island Posn = 22° 70′W	(" " ")	+ 22°W		= 44° 70′W.
231° 30′,	Island Posn = 128° 70′W	(*of Del Corvo*)	+ 31°W	(to Greenwich)	= 159° 70′W.
237° 30′,	Island Posn = 122° 70′W	(" " ")	+ 31°W		= 153° 70′W.
331° 30′,	Island Posn = 28° 70′W	(" " ")	+ 31°W		= 59° 70′W.

337° 30′,	Island Posn = 22° 70′W	(" " ")	+ 31°W		= 53° 70′W.
231° 30′,	Island Posn = 128° 70′W (*of St Michaels*)		+ 26°W	(to Greenwich)	= 154° 70′W.
237° 30′,	Island Posn = 122° 70′W	(" " ")	+ 26°W		= 148° 70′W.
331° 30′,	Island Posn = 28° 70′W	(" " ")	+ 26°W		= 54° 70′W.
337° 30,′	Island Posn = 22° 70′W	(" " ")	+ 26°W		= 48° 70′W.
231° 30′,	Island Posn = 128° 70′W (*of Tenerife*)		+ 17°W	(to Greenwich)	= 145° 70′W.
237° 30′,	Island Posn = 122° 70′W	(" " ")	+ 17°W		= 139° 70′W.
331° 30′,	Island Posn = 28° 70′W	(" " ")	+ 17°W		= 45° 70′W.
337° 30′,	Island Posn = 22° 70′W	(" " ")	+ 17°W		= 39° 70′W.
231° 30′,	Island Posn = 128° 70′W (*Hierro or Ferro*)		+ 18°W	(to Greenwich)	= 146° 70′W.
237° 30′,	Island Posn = 122° 70′W	(" " ")	+ 18°W		= 140° 70′W.
331° 30′,	Island Posn = 28° 70′W	(" " ")	+ 18°W		= 46° 70′W.
337° 30′,	Island Posn = 22° 70′W	(" " ")	+ 18°W		= 40° 70′W.

The lower longitude figures, i.e. those between 39° 70′W and 59° 70′W, would locate the island in the Atlantic Ocean, off the north-east coast of South America. There are no islands at the positions indicated or anywhere near. The closest position to land (59° 70′W) is just 70 miles off the coast of Venezuela, the nearest island being Tobago about 170 miles to the north-west at 11° 12′N 60° 40′W, and whose shape is nothing like that of Kidd's island.

The higher longitude figures, i.e. those between 139° 70′W and 159° 70′W, would locate the island in the middle of the Pacific Ocean. There are no islands at the positions indicated or anywhere near. The nearest island at approx. 6°N, 162°W is Palmyra some 220 miles to the south-west. This island, on what is known as the North-West Christmas Island Ridge, bears no resemblance whatsoever to Kidd's island; neither do the other islands on the ridge further south, i.e. Fanning and Christmas Island.

In conclusion, the reader must really make his own mind up about whether or not Kidd used this single system. I think however that this investigation shows that he used the dual system.

The only remote possible way one could favour the single system is by the fact that Tobago is the only island that can be said to be in the Caribbean (south-west corner), but that really is grasping at straws.

Accuracy of Latitude and Longitude in the 17th Century

Latitude

Several instruments such as the astrolabe, the cross-staff, the English quadrant (back staff) and the graphometer made astronomical surveys possible. Using these instruments navigators were able to calculate their line of latitude to a fairly accurate degree. They determined either the sun's position in relation to the horizon at noon each day or the position of the pole star and then made the necessary corrections according to marine almanacs.

Whereas today a navigator would use a sextant to take the observed altitude, his seventeenth century counterpart would have had to use a cross-staff or more probably a back-staff. The back-staff, or Davis' quadrant as it was sometimes called, was perfected about 1590 and was a greatly superior instrument; nevertheless, with the conservatism of sailors, some mariners still continued to use a cross-staff well past the seventeenth century. It seems unlikely though that a cross-staff would have been used in our case, as it would have been known to give only comparatively rough-and-ready results. The instrumental error would be a high and probably unknown factor and the personal error, even with an experienced operator, would be considerable: errors of about 3° would be quite possible. Furthermore, with angles over 20° the cross-staff became extremely tricky to use and a meridian altitude of the sun in a latitude around 9°N would clearly involve a high angle.

By comparison, it was found that the back-staff gave astonishingly good results and in conjunction with the National Maritime Museum, Anthony Howlett carried out a wide series of experimental observations made with a back-staff and compared with simultaneous sextant readings.

Taking into account the appropriate tables, Almanacs and time differences etc. his findings on the possible and probable *maximum* error was as follows:

Error in true altitude (dip correction)	± 20′
Error caused by refraction semi diameter and parallax	± 16′
Error in declination	± 10′
Personal error	± 14′

It can be seen therefore that the total error is plus or minus 1 degree. It must be emphasised that this is the absolute maximum error for a latitude obtained in the mid-seventeenth century. Navigators frequently obtained their latitude to within 30′ or less.

Longitude

Whereas the finding of latitude was fairly straightforward, the finding of one's longitude position was just about impossible.

We have already examined the meridian problem earlier in this chapter and even if a longitude were shown on a seventeenth century chart it would be hopelessly inaccurate. Precise determination of longitude could not be made until the perfection of marine chronometers by John Harrison in the latter half of the eighteenth century. Because the earth rotates 15° every hour (360° every 24 hours) the difference between local time and the first meridian made it possible to calculate the longitude reached.

A seaman happening upon an island in the seventeenth century had no means of knowing or finding out his longitude other than by guesswork of his vessel's reckoning, usually estimated in leagues from his point of departure. A position at this time would have been given as so many leagues east of the departure point or as a compass bearing and distance from presumably somewhere in the Philippines.

A chart such as ours therefore with a longitude marked on it (which is surprising anyway) would be useless to a navigator of the seventeenth

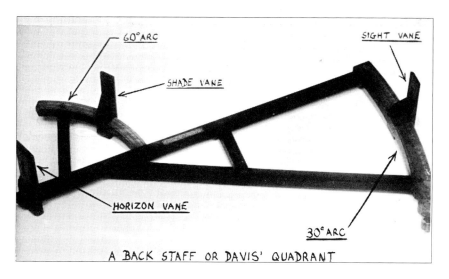

A BACK STAFF OR DAVIS' QUADRANT

century as (a) he would have no means of finding his longitude with any accuracy and (b) the coasts of Asia and outlying islands depicted on globes and world maps at this time were in error by some 10° to 20°, even allowing for the various prime meridians used.

As I say, the fact that a longitude is shown is most surprising and that it should be to within ½° even more surprising. If genuine it suggests Kidd must have been very confident and likely to have been in sight of land whose position in relation to a meridian was known accurately. Even so, and for that reason only I think we can work on an error of ± 5°. For more general work the error would be ± 10° for this period.

Chapter 3

The Searchers

The Challengers

Quite a few people have had no doubt whatsoever about these charts and their authenticity. Palmer himself of course: he and his brother spent some years before the war planning a expedition. The war intervened, Guy Palmer died during the war and Hubert Palmer died in 1949.

Then there is Anthony Howlett, the gentleman who is indirectly responsible for me writing this book. He was a barrister – now retired – and a naval officer during the war (admirable qualifications for researching this Kidd business) and was probably the last person to have examined the charts and their history in depth whilst the original records were in existence and while the sole eye-witness of the discoveries was alive. With a colleague, Commander Baker RN (who had been in the Hydrographic Service of the Royal Navy) he carried out extensive research for many years into the island's identity culminating in a twenty-minute television programme in 1965. Research continued but when Commander Baker died in 1969, Howlett admitted he lost interest.

Rupert Furneaux's interest started when he was writing his book *Money Pit: The Mystery of Oak Island*. His story follows later (see p. 57).

Richard Knight – there are two Richard Knights mentioned in this book: one the author, collector and expert on all things piratical; and Richard Knight who was imprisoned in Saigon in Vietnam whilst looking for Kidd's treasure. More about that later (see p. 114).

Maurice Taylor of Canada, who bought the original charts from Mrs Dick, subsequently mounted an expedition (see p. 55) and Alan Marshall, a somewhat dubious character who borrowed a lot of the public's money to finance his treasure hunt (see p. 100).

Expeditions

The publicity that the charts produced during the mid-1950s promoted four expeditions over the next two years. Various newspaper reports of the time said that the treasure was supposed to consist of coin to the value of about £60,000 and many bales of costly silks hidden in different parts of an uninhabited island, about 5 miles long and 3–4 miles wide, in the South China Seas, about 700 miles off the nearest shipping lane and about 600 miles south of Siam.

The Discoveries Ltd. Expedition

The first (known) Kidd treasure expedition hit the headlines in grand style in November 1951 when their ship was wrecked off the south Hampshire coast.

It all started in January of that year when Mr James Brownlie, works manager of the Rock Channel Shipyard, Rye, Sussex, announced that he was organising an expedition to seek Kidd's treasure using the charts provided by Mrs Dick. The expedition was expected to cost £12,000 and to consist of fifteen men. A 65 ft. motor trawler was being hired for the trip to Singapore with Capt. Jack Mumford as skipper.

Later it was announced that two women were joining the expedition and in May that they were all to sail in the 150-ton motor yacht *La Contenta*. Copies of the charts were being flown to a Singapore bank from where they would be sent by sea to north Borneo. The whole expedition was being organised by means of a private limited company – Discoveries Ltd.

In August it was reported that the owner and master of *La Contenta*, Capt. W. J. Studdard, was under arrest in consequence of a writ issued by Mr Shepherd (leader of the expedition) because Capt. Studdard wanted the boat to go on a scientific cruise.

Two months later it was reported that the expedition was now sailing on the schooner *Lamorna* with Capt. Athanasios Coumandaraes as skipper. Thirteen people were now in the expedition including Herman Brandes, a thirty-year-old ex-Luftwaffe pilot, as engineer, John Wishart, Geoffrey Taylor, Maurice Taylor, and George Shepherd as leader. It was stated that precautions were being taken against pirates known to operate in the vicinity of the island.

The *Lamorna* sailed from Gosport on 1 November 1951 and four days later it was reported she was wrecked in a Channel gale 20 miles south of the Needles. The crew were rescued by the Isle of Wight lifeboat and the frigate *Radpole* sent from Portsmouth took the *Lamorna* in tow, but the tow parted and the *Lamorna* was driven ashore in Christchurch Bay.

The leader of the expedition stated that everything was lost and the expedition would have to be abandoned.

Pinney–Brownlie–Sinclair Expedition

A few days after the 'Discoveries' disaster, it was reported that another expedition was being planned to go to Kidd's Island and search for the treasure. It was intended to seek other treasures *en route*, to combine the enterprise with commercial exploitation (especially in America) of film, book, newspaper and magazine rights in the story, and also to advertise the sale of British goods overseas. The proposed route was Shoreham, Marseille, Tangier, Salvage Islands, Cape Verde Islands, West Indies, Panama, San Pedro (near Los Angeles), Honolulu, Manila (base), and South China Seas.

The expedition members were to be: Mr Richard W. Pinney of Shrewsbury (leader), James Brownlie, Miss Valerie Sinclair (Mrs McCulley), and Thomas Palmer; also associated with the project were Lord Glenarthy, Miss Goldie Beldam, Mrs Bacon, John Comey, and in America, Derek Palmer, Mrs Joan Nash and Earl Jermyn (6th Marquis of Bristol).

For the purposes of the expedition, it was intended to purchase the 75-ton motor yacht *Barra* (the purchase was never completed) and Commander Baker RN (Anthony Howlett's colleague) was to be invited to go in command. He was also the expedition's nautical advisor – though in no way connected with the fiasco into which the expedition apparently deteriorated. The promoters, it seems, proved wholly unreliable and had no detailed knowledge of Kidd's charts. Nothing further was heard of this expedition which is understood to have been abandoned.

The Shepherd–Phillips Expedition

In December 1951 it was reported that a rival expedition was being planned by Major G. T. Phillips, landlord of the Swan Hotel, Forest Row, and it was intended to use aircraft in the search. The leader was to be George Shepherd who had made three previous attempts.

Nothing further was heard of this expedition.

The Pinney–Bacon Expedition

In January 1952 it was reported that another expedition was being planned by Mrs Alice H. Bacon, a forty-two-year-old retired business woman and Brighton property owner. A 140-ton twin-screw diesel yacht had been purchased at Worcester and it was hoped to sail in April 1952. The expedition was being organised by Richard W. Pinney and it was also intended to seek other treasures.

Nothing further was heard of this expedition which is understood to have been abandoned.

The Furneaux Expedition

I am very familiar with Rupert Furneaux's books; the introduction to this book tells of my fascination for mysteries. My bookshelf holds several titles by Furneaux including: *Great Treasure Hunts*; *The World's Most Intriguing Mysteries*; *The World's Strangest Mysteries;* and *Money Pit: The Mystery of Oak Island*, published in 1972.

Furneaux first heard of the existence of the Kidd/Palmer charts in 1965 when Anthony Howlett spoke of them on a BBC2 TV programme and told the story of their discovery. Furneaux contacted Howlett and discussed the charts and their possible origin. Whilst researching his book he was convinced that the charts depicted Oak Island and deals at length in his book with the remarkable similarities.

Many other people had connected Kidd with Oak Island believing it was he who had buried his treasure in the Money Pit – a shaft over 200 ft. deep connected to the shore 500 ft. away by two tunnels. The engineering genius who created the Money Pit certainly was not Kidd, as Furneaux discovered, and as far as I know nobody has yet solved that particular mystery. (See also p. 163.)

One Gilbert Hedden, excavating Oak Island in the 1930s, believed that the charts in Wilkins' book depicted Oak Island. He was convinced that a crude drawing of an island in the book *Captain Kidd and his Skeleton*

Island was that of Oak Island. Wilkins had of course loosely based his island on the Palmer charts which he had briefly seen; he had never seen an outline of Oak Island.

Having discounted the Kidd connection with Oak Island, Furneaux's curiosity about the charts revived in 1974 after he had published the *Money Pit Mystery*, and he devoted most of his time and energies to solving the charts. He was convinced that the date 1669 on the bureau chart was the key to the problem.

This was about the time the Buccaneers fled from the Caribbean. They went northwards to the Bahamas from where they carried on their piratical depredations for another fifty years. Kidd, Furneaux believed, had concealed the loot from his buccaneering days on some island which he had carefully charted: probably the nearest uninhabited island to the north of the Caribbean.

Wisely or unwisely, Furneaux chose to ignore the latitude, longitude and China Sea reference on the charts as it had, he learned, been decided that no islands now existed (the Sequieras) at the only possible longitude, i.e. 131° 30′E. He decided there was no point in further examination or research into that area.

Author's note: The following story of Furneaux's treasure hunt is copied from his own draft manuscript on the venture. A shortened version appeared in the Christmas 1977 issue of the *Illustrated London News*. The full story also gives the prospective treasure hunter an idea of the pit-falls and ups and downs of trying to organise and carry out such a venture, also the problems created by clashes of personality. Some passages which were not essential to the story have been omitted, as had they been left in they might have left me open to libellous action owing to Furneaux's not too flattering remarks about certain people his expedition brought him into contact with. Whilst they are not my words, I am not taking any chances!

First Expedition

I searched atlases and maps seeking an island which resembled the island of the charts. I obtained large scale maps and photographs.

The huge 5 ft. long air photograph of one particular island matched the island depicted in remarkable detail.

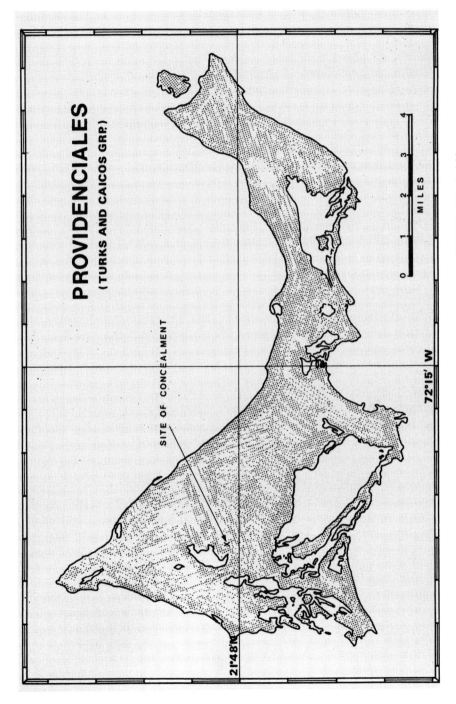

C6. Providenciales, the island where Rupert Furneaux convinced himself Kidd had buried his treasure.

Providenciales Island, one of the Turks and Caicos group at the southern tip of the Bahamas, lies 150 miles north of Tortuga. Its general outline conforms to Kidd's island, bearing in mind the changes that may have occurred in three hundred years and the difference between rough seventeenth century charting and the precision of modern air photography.

The Turks and Caicos Group remained a British Colony following the grant of independence to the Bahamas in 1970. They are governed by an elected Executive Council presided over by an English Governor. They comprise six small islands and innumerable tiny cays rising barely above sea level. Providenciales is the odd one out, rising to a considerable height in its centre.

I held, I believed, the clues which could lead to the discovery of Kidd's famous and long sought treasure, or at least I might find confirmation that it had once existed.

Of one thing I was convinced. Treasure hunting, even in the comparative safety of a British colony, is not a game to be played alone. I sought allies, energetic partners to share the hazards of exploration. The story of how I found partners at this time of gloom and despondency is a modern fairy tale, complete with its horrid nightmares.

Most treasure hunts end in failure for a variety of reasons. The partners quarrel, or run short of money, or the clues are inadequate, the scent having gone cold, or the treasure never existed, or was removed following its concealment. High hopes end in disappointment. Should I find partners I was determined that they should understand these unpalatable facts.

I knew Bennie Gray slightly. He operated an antiques supermarket in London and had become a journalist, being nominated in 1974 'Campaign Journalist of the Year'. He was young, energetic, and easy to get on with. I made an appointment and spread my charts and air photographs on his desk. Bennie accepted my general identification of the island. He was astonished to learn that Kidd had been a real person rather than, as he thought, the fictional hero of boys' stories.

Bennie suggested bringing in his friend Douglas Villiers. He owned a large ocean going yacht based in American waters in which we could travel and live. Douglas came to our next meeting, arriving in his chauffeur-driven Jensen complete with radio-telephone. He had flown in from somewhere and was off again in a few days. Getting hold of Douglas is like chasing a rainbow or clutching a piece of quicksilver. He gets bored easily and seldom stays long in one place. His friends say that, although he cruises his yacht in tropical waters, he never gets sunburnt. He is not in one spot long enough. Like the Queen, and only her, Douglas sends his yacht ahead and flies in between. Douglas, needless to say, is a 'last minute man'. Vital decisions are left until the point of no return is almost passed. Then he starts telephoning all over the world, regardless of cost. It astonished him that I did not adopt that method of doing business. 'So much better than writing letters,' he thought.

Douglas enthusiastically agreed to join the expedition. An excited Douglas is even more dangerous than a bored one. Everything must be of the best, the most expensive. Anything cheap, and possibly more useful, is inferior, viewed with suspicion. Take, for example, the question of metal detectors. I told Douglas that the best models were recommended by the Laboratory for Archaeological Research at Oxford. I showed him photographs of their proton magnetometers. He denounced them as 'hoovers'. Somewhere in the world, most probably in America, someone had invented the perfect device. At his request and cost I telephoned Massachusetts Institute of Technology whose Professor Eggerton had developed a sonar depth sounder. His assistant explained that it was designed for use underwater and advised me to consult the world re-nowned expert, Dr Hall of the Oxford Laboratory. Douglas ordered two models, for the detection respectively of ferrous and non-ferrous metals. Bennie went to Oxford to learn to use them.

Douglas, his friends said, has flair and luck – likely advantages on a treasure hunt.

Early on, Douglas made it a condition of his participation that we obtain a television contract to pay part of the cost of running his yacht which he estimated at £1,000 a week. He and Bennie made an agreement with ATV who put up, in addition to the cost of the programme, a considerable sum to defray expenses. Their interest was aroused by Douglas's and Bennie's friend Francis Megahy, a television producer-director. ATV, he told me, saw the programme as a romantic adventure story, just what the viewers wanted in these dreary times.

I disliked the idea of such a programme. I feared, and was proved right, that the expedition would develop into a programme about a treasure hunt, which would perforce take second place. It meant also that another 'Chief' had been introduced into an enterprise which had too many already. But no programme, no yacht, and Douglas's large yacht seemed an important ingredient, though it proved to be a hindrance rather than a help. It was too big for the job.

Francis filmed the preliminaries before we left England, Bennie, Douglas and I examining the charts, air photographs and maps of Providenciales Island and discussing our plans. I obtained the loan of two of the pieces of furniture, the skull chest and the William and Sarah Kidd box in which Palmer had found the two chief charts and was filmed with them at home. Francis also filmed us, engaged in our private activities and sports, Douglas and Bennie playing tennis, and myself playing golf.

I corresponded and spoke on the telephone with the Governor of the Turks and Caicos Islands, Mr A.G. Mitchell, advising him of our visit, and discussing the English Law and Practice of Treasure Trove. English Common Law operated in the colony. This, according to the British Museum circular, provides that treasure trove, meaning articles of gold and silver concealed with the intention of recovery, and of which no known owner can be traced, belongs to the Crown which may reward the finders with whole or part of the treasure.

I learned that these islands of 'perpetual June' enjoy an enviable climate, with an average temperature of 80°F tempered by a constant breeze from the Atlantic Ocean. They are formed of coral and limestone and are covered by scrub. How high, thick and matted was this scrub I had yet to learn. Douglas, from his knowledge of the more northerly Bahaman islands, described it as low and sparse. It could be cut down with machetes, to enable us to run the metal detectors over the selected sites. That seemed easy. Equipped with picks and spades and professional metal detectors, and with ample money to recruit local labour, we would uncover the treasure quickly, or at least identify its one-time places of concealment. But I emphasised to my partners that people who may have buried treasure may have returned to recover it. Only in story books do the pirates sail away never to return. I would be content to confirm my identification of the island and to find physical corroboration of my interpretation of the sites indicated on the charts.

'D' Day was set for 10 January 1975. Everyone was packed and ready to go, when Douglas telephoned from Nassau or Dallas, Texas, I cannot remember which for he was all over the place, that his yacht, the *Piscator*, had been struck by heavy seas off Cape Hatteras and had been forced back to port for repairs. The damage was not serious. Douglas returned to London full of ideas. He wished to talk with an archaeologist and make sure we had the best equipment. I gave him a name to telephone. The archaeologist suggested that we take a water-diviner who might be able to detect metals underground. He suggested a man living in Ayrshire, Scotland. Douglas wished to bring him along until it was pointed out that the yacht would be filled to capacity by us three and the television team of six.

We flew to Nassau on 31 January. Bennie went separately flying via Miami and taking his wife and three small children to stay at the island's hotel. This led to complications, the necessity for collecting and depositing him at the start and finish of our various forays by car and voyages by motor boat, and denied us his advice at evening conferences.

The *Piscator* reached Nassau the same day. She is a small ship, built in 1962 as a Norwegian trawler and converted as a luxurious yacht. She is 110 ft. long with a draft of 10 ft. Captain Tim Hickman, ex-Royal Navy, had a crew of three: engineer, deck-hand and cook, the glamorous blue-eyed blonde, Patty Soutar, an English girl from Sussex who had been 'crewing' in the Caribbean for six years. She proved to be a first-class cook, and provided the television team with endless opportunities for colour photography.

Douglas discussed the sailing course with Tim Hickman, the 500 miles journey to the islands. This was more difficult than it appeared from the map. Before we could start work I needed to seek the Governor who lives on Grand Turk Island, 80 miles beyond Providenciales, but at least 150 miles by sea owing to the reefs and shallows by which the island group is surrounded. To overcome this difficulty it was decided that the yacht should go direct to Providenciales, three days sailing time, while Douglas and I flew ahead.

Douglas and I stayed in Nassau, he on Paradise Island where I joined him next day to go over the charts and maps. A chance remark from his host set Douglas off on another wild goose chase, a temporary nightmare. Why not get the famous Hollywood medium who had identified the Boston strangler? Holding Kidd's charts he might be able to sniff out the treasure. In a flash Douglas was on the telephone. Alas, or fortunately, there was no reply. He traced the man to New Mexico where the trail went dead. Two wild geese, the water-diviner and the medium, had escaped. Hopefully, I thought, the flock was spent, though far worse was to come.

Douglas and I sat all day at Nassau airport waiting for a flight that failed to materialise. In desperation we flew to Miami, where we took the scheduled flight next day, I to Grand Turk and he to Providenciales.

At Grand Turk I found a car waiting to take me to the Governor's office. His Excellency A.G. Mitchell received me with the government's legal adviser, Mike Jennings, and the newly appointed District Commissioner of Providenciales Island, Nathaniel Robinson. Recent constitutional changes, explained Mitchell, had made the Executive Council responsible for decisions affecting the islands. Fortunately the Council met next day. Prior to its meeting I told my story to one of its members, Headley Durham, who with Jennings and Robinson later explained it to the other members. The Council accepted my suggestions and Jennings was instructed to draw up an exclusive licence authorising me to search for treasure on Crown lands. Whilst this was being typed I visited the Land Office where I learned that both my sites were situated on Crown land. That obviated the need to trace and placate individual soil owners. Following lunch at the Governor's residence, I flew to 'Provo', as the locals name it, with Robinson by the 'Islander' plane, half an hour's flight.

We were met at the airport by Douglas, Bennie and the television team filming my arrival. Alighting from the aircraft, carrying my licence, I felt like Mr Chamberlain returning to Munich waving his 'peace in our time' message from Hitler. Douglas ignored the licence, in his opinion a superfluous document, to procure which had wasted a day.

At last I stood on Kidd's island. As we drove to the yacht's anchorage, I observed the scrub lining the road and cloaking the hills. It was far thicker and higher than I had expected. Provo island is now covered by dense, impenetrable underbrush formed by aloes, myrtles, century plants, salt-grass, cacti and other spiny shrubs interlaced with ankle-high creepers. There is no soil. These plants grow from rock. I cannot believe that it was always so dense.

Providenciales was first settled in 1790 by Georgian Loyalists who fled there following British recognition of American Independence. They established plantations and built stone houses which were destroyed by the hurricane of 1816. I saw their ruins. It is inconceivable that these people would or could have hacked their way through such scrub and have lived and farmed on these stony hills.

It seemed equally incomprehensible that Kidd would have penetrated two miles inland to make caches, as the charts indicate, on the spiny slopes of the central ridge. I believe that the present absence of trees and woods, marked on the charts, may account for this anomaly. From 1689 onwards the island was visited by Bermudians who came to collect salt and fell trees for boat-building. The tradition lingers that the island was once covered with trees. Their removal would have burned up the soil, exposing it to the full heat of the sun and reducing moisture, allowing the latent scrub to develop in their place. Lacking trees to shelter the soil from the scorching rays of the sun and without roots to hold humidity near the surface, every drop of rain sank into the arid ground.

On my return to England, I raised this question with the Keeper of Botany at the Natural History Museum. Mr R. Ross replied:

> It is perfectly true that in tropical countries the felling of forest and the exposure of the soil to the sun results in the oxidation of the humus in it which is no longer replenished by the fall of leaves etc. This is often followed by erosion both by wind and water during heavy storms, which occur from time to time even in areas where the rainfall is very low. These processes result in the area being only able to support a very different type of vegetation from that which it had originally.

I remark this point now in order to overcome the suggestion that no pirate or buccaneer would or could have penetrated inland in 1669 to conceal treasure near the central ridge. The scrub did not exist then in its present form.

The previous existence of trees was only one of the fourteen points of similarity I found between the island and the charts. As my local knowledge increased, so did my absolute certainty that Providenciales is the charted island. The chart-maker depicted that island with remarkable accuracy.

The overall 'boomerang' shape of Provo's northern shore line confirms the charts, and the resemblances between its two extremities, its north-western and north-eastern promontories, and those depicted, are striking. The lozenge-shaped north-western point suggests the coral outcrop which disguises the dangerous 'false cut' through the reef. It is strewn with ancient wrecks, one significantly at the spot where a WRECK is positioned on the chart. I was shown colour photographs of the coral-encrusted cannon and anchors which lie there, but which cannot be raised for detailed examination. They provide a tourist attraction and a means of livelihood for the island's diver-guides. Two more wrecks are shown on the 1669 chart. I was unable to identify them amongst the four hundred reputed wrecks which litter the reef.

The charted north-eastern point of the island shows precisely the peculiar shore line forming two slight indentations joined by a jutting point with slightly accentuated extremities at each end. A striking point of identification came several days after our arrival. Tim Hickman announced that he was moving the yacht from its off-shore anchorage on the southern coast to the 'only safe anchorage' on the island at the north-easterly point – the passage marked on one chart as NORTH SA(F)E.

Both charts indicate a reef enclosing a lagoon along the island's northern coast. The modern survey map names the central stretch of water as REEF HARBOUR. But there is inconsistency. The modern reef extends the whole length of the coast and is clearly visible from the foaming line of breakers. Thus, either the reef has extended since 1669 or the chart maker may have been content to demark only the area enclosed by the lagoon or harbour. Once again, local knowledge confirmed the ancient chart maker. An old resident, the American Tommy Coleman to whom I showed my charts, pointed to the round rock depicted within the lagoon. 'That's High Rock,' he exclaimed. It had been used for years by the island's boys as a diving platform until it became submerged by the sand as the beach extended. The spot is still known as High Rock.

Travelling round the island's south-eastern shore I noticed, which is so evident in the air photograph, the deep inlet which the ancient chart-maker depicted and named SMUGGLERS COVE. Its name is not the anachronism it may seem, and may help to confirm the date of the charts. The English Navigation Acts of 1643 and later prohibited trade with the American colonies other than in English ships. This enactment fostered smuggling with the connivance of the Colonists. It became a lucrative trade for the one-time Buccaneers who were forced by the Treaty of Madrid to become lone pirates and smugglers.

Further round the southern shore and towards the jutting promontory, the chart maker had indicated an ANCHORAGE. It conforms approximately to the position of Sam's Bay which is named on the modern maps and marked by an anchor. We landed on several stretches of sand in this area. But it was difficult to decide which might have been chosen as an anchorage. These 'bays' would have provided an anchorage only for vessels of limited draft owing to the shallows which extend several hundred yards seawards.

The present southern shore does not conform accurately to the chart maker's ideas. He depicted and described it as an area of SAND and REEFS, whereas now it is a confused mass of sandy shoals and inlets, covered and obscured by mangrove swamps. They may have developed since 1669, or the chart maker may have ignored their detail. Providenciales, like all West Indian islands, has been devastated by hurricanes many times during the last three centuries. It would be surprising if its 'soft' southern shore had not changed its shape.

It is on this shore that the chart maker noted the presence of 20 TURTLES. That could have been true in 1669. Professor J. J. Parsons (*The Green Turtle and Man*, University of Florida Press, 1962) states that these islands were great breeding grounds of turtles before they were exterminated. Since he wrote, the turtles have returned and I saw several swimming along the shore.

Other marks on the charts relate to places on the island, for example, the pond indicated near the north-western point. I failed to find the inverted triangle, indicated by the 'V', round that point, nor could my local guides locate it, except by suggesting that it may have represented an outcrop of rock jutting seawards. Nor did I identify the tiny half-circle indicated on the southern shore.

The most convincing point of the charts' accuracy came from my survey, from the heights and shore level, of the spiny ridge shown running through the island. The charts indicate the contours, with four elevations at the western end of the island, and the shallow gap in the island's waist, and the high hill extending to the small hill towards the eastern end. The chart maker noted accurately the division of the western ridge into two arms, a feature invisible from the shore. These many points of similarity convinced me that he knew the island intimately.

There are also points of divergence between the island and the charts.

The statement on one chart that the island is located in the CHINA SEAS is not the stumbling block it may appear. This name could have been added to prevent identification and to serve as a decoy. It is improbable that Kidd could or would have sailed halfway round the world to conceal treasure on a remote island in a sea then virtually unknown to European seamen. Kidd's reference to the 'Indies' in his appeal for mercy to the Speaker of the House of Commons applied in those days in greater likelihood to the 'West Indies' rather than to the East Indies which were still known as the Spice Islands.

The values of latitude and longitude (9° 16′N and ?31° 30′E) on one chart are difficult to interpret, particularly in the matter of longitude, an extreme uncertainty at that date, depending upon the point (prior to 1695 when longitude became reckoned from Greenwich) from where it was determined. Longitude in the mid-seventeenth century was usually reckoned eastwards round the globe from some fixed point, such as the Azores. Thus, the values marked on the chart would approximate to an island in the Caicos Group, if the numbers read, before the first numeral became lost, '313'.

The value of latitude, 9° 16′N, given is way out. Providenciales Island lies at 72° 20′ W and 21° 40′ N. Possibly the '9' may have been preceded by an '1' which has faded, thus giving the value of 19° N, not an unlikely approximation for that period.

The compass bearing noted on both charts seemed reasonably accurate, bearing in mind the march of the compass since 1669. The western declination since has been about 7° as the northern magnetic field swung that way. The compass needle in 1669 would have pointed 2° East of True North, whereas it now points 5° West. The Geomagnetism Unit of the Institute of Geological Sciences at Herstmonceux, Sussex, told me that the errors on the charts might be not more than ½° or 1°. On the spot I found the compass bearings to be far less accurate. The chart maker's north appears to have been some 25° east of present north.

These many resemblances between the island and the charts could hardly be coincidental. It would be remarkable if Providenciales Island is not the island depicted on the charts. It is a coral island situated in exactly the right place to fit my theory of the charts' origin.

Kidd drew accurate charts of Providenciales Island. It is a reasonable assumption that he did that to indicate places of concealment, as certain marks and the direction on the charts suggest. They appear to indicate two sites, both situated near the spiny ridge where its elevations provided prominent landmarks. The directions are difficult to interpret owing to the loss of certain words and figures and the obscurity of the legends.

Presumably they would have made sense to the man or men who had treasure to hide. On one chart, that found in the William and Sarah Kidd Box, he has written round the edge: '360 yards V. R. North 3 stumps 55 feet' and continues with a word which may be 'from', to 'centre of tri(angle) be . . . Rocks 20 feet E. Skele(ton) of LEB'.

This chart shows three small circles placed in what seems to be a cutting or valley through the central ridge. But it is difficult to reconcile these marks with the directions. Do the '3' stumps indicate the three circles, possibly small mounds, outcrops of rock, or elevations? If so, from where should the 360 yards be measured? No starting point is indicated. The 'V. R.' could be interpreted to mean a 'valley running north'.

The second chart, that discovered in the Skull Chest, appears to be more helpful, though its directions seem meaningless. The four black dots conform with remarkable accuracy to the four summits noticeable on the spiny ridge, the heights of 125 ft., 125 ft., 75 ft. and 75 ft. Their spacing apart conforms to distribution of the dots on the chart. Alongside and below the fourth dot an 'X' has been placed.

But the directions on the chart appear to have no relevance. They read:

515 SE AND BY 50 N
36 NE 36 NE Rocks
3 FEET BY 3 FEET BY FOUR.

Should I seek the spot marked 'X', and was that the starting place from where to follow these directions?

Examining these charts in England, I had imagined that it would be possible to find the places by walking over the ground in order to locate landmarks and relate them back to the charts. The large scale Ordnance Survey map gave us no hint of the difficulties and in fact, by indicating several areas, incorrectly as I found, as 'scattered cultivation', it suggested that at least we should find many clearings in the scrub. The map reference, however, was a relic of the past and merely indicated areas where the American Loyalists had once tried to grow cotton, a few bushes still surviving amongst the tangle of scrub. Once the selected areas had been found, I thought we would be able to run over the ground with our metal detectors. The widespread scrub shattered this hope, for nowhere was the ground visible. From each elevation we reached we could see only a sea of scrub effectively cloaking and preventing access to either area. It took several days for us to realise the terrible handicap we faced.

The Scrub

We decided to make an extensive reconnaissance in order to view the western end of the island from several angles. We set out on our first 'walk' on the day following my arrival. It was brilliantly sunny and the temperature rose to the usual 80°F as we left the yacht at 8.30 a.m., an hour later than intended. This morning delay became standard practice. The portable 'igloo' carrying drinks packed in ice needed to be prepared, sandwiches cut and equipment brought on deck. Everything and everyone had to be lowered into the boats lurching in the swell at the yacht's quarter. The heavily laden speed-boats raced to the landing place where Bennie was waiting with the ten-seater air-conditioned Chevrolet hired by ATV. Transferring the crew, the cameras and sound gear caused further delay. We drove to the Blue Hills settlement on the northern coast to collect guides and helpers.

The modern map shows a faint track leading from behind the houses into the hills. Algernon and James Deane, our guides, knew it well. It may have been made by the American Loyalists who, so unaccountably, built their stone houses and animal corrals on the ridge. I saw the ruins, flat stones piled one upon another.

None of us had any inkling of the horrors of the climb. They became apparent as we plunged deeper and deeper into the thorny, matted scrub, tripping and stumbling on the rocky, uneven, foot-wide, twisting track, clutched by creepers and spiky branches. Algernon, carrying a machete, led the way. I followed. Behind came Douglas and Bennie, preceding the television team, weighed down by the heavy cameras and sound recorders.

Every few minutes Francis Megahy called a halt for the unit to get ahead to film and record our struggles and discussions. He had a passion for spontaneity and a lamentable lack of forethought. He beseeched us, the treasure hunters, to refrain from discussion except in front of the camera and he resented my often expressed wish to be told what he wished to film next. He preferred to 'let it happen'. That created an unhappy situation on an expedition which required considerable forethought, planning and friendly co-operation, and led to several squabbles. Megahy insisted that the expedition arose only from television backing and filming was all-important. I asserted that the expedition was the main consideration and that filming must take second place. This disagreement expressed the difficulties of a situation to which far too little thought had been given and which resulted, in my opinion, in a programme less interesting than it might have been.

As our search progressed the film became a desert island 'Highway Patrol' in which the principals were filmed again and again getting in and out of boats, setting off and returning to the yacht, and boarding and alighting from aircraft. It might make good television, but it made poor treasure hunting. Francis needed to justify his support for the programme of which he had sold the idea to ATV – an enterprise which might, and probably would, end in failure.

Francis saw it as a romantic adventure story involving three incongruous partners: the volatile Douglas Villiers, the millionaire property owner; the cool Bennie Gray who, with no need for monetary gain, had created a career in journalism, campaigning for individual rights against the callousness of property developers; and me. Francis called me the 'indispensable man', the leader of the search, the individual who must be filmed at every stage whether or not I wished to be. Francis irritated me. 'He irritates everyone,' Bennie responded.

An hour's exhausting struggle brought us to the summit of the 125 ft. elevation at the western end of the ridge, Conamurry Mountain as the locals name it, a bare expanse of rock enclosed by vicious scrub. The view to the south-east, where I needed to look, was obscured by another scrub-clad summit. I saw other elevations stretching away in the distance, possibly those portrayed on the second chart.

Our initial foray was intended to find the area in which lay Site 1, that indicated by the chart which carries the legend beginning '360 yards V. R. North', and which shows a distinct cleft or valley between the hills. This valley appeared to lie somewhere to the north of the place marked on the modern map as 'Pigeon Pond', and two miles inland from the indentation on the shore identified by the chart-maker as the AN-CHORAGE. In England I had picked on this pond, clearly visible on the air photograph, as a likely land-mark.

From the summit of Conamurry Mountain I could not see Pigeon Pond. The Deane brothers assured me that it lay to the right beyond another hill and could be reached by cutting our way through the scrub. Slightly to the left and beyond another summit I saw what appeared to be a shallow valley which seemed to run northwards from the Pond.

We were groping in the dark. The scrub made it impossible to see the ground in any detail. To reach Pigeon Pond would take another hour's exhausting walk. Someone, I forget who, suggested the possibility that we could far more easily find it by navigating the sea inlet on the southern shore which appeared to run close to the Pond. We decided to try this water-route.

The return march provided me with opportunity to peer into the many 'caves' with which the hills are honeycombed. These vertical shafts varied from three to six feet in width and from four to ten feet in depth. They are formed in solid rock and may be 'solution caverns', a feature of limestone and sandstone formations.

These caves could have provided ideal hiding places. No one in 1669 or now could have dug holes in the island's rocky terrain. The narrow entrance of one of these caves could have been disguised by rocks levered off the surrounding expanse of sandstone. This theory seemed to be enhanced by the three tiny circles, possibly the entrances to caves, within the valley on the chart showing Site 1, and by the mention of ROCKS on both charts. The final numbers in the directions provided in the charts which appear to point the way to Site 2, THREE FEET BY THREE FEET BY FOUR, may have indicated a cave of these dimensions.

My discovery of these caves seemed adequate recompense for our tiring climb to the ridge. We had seen much of the island and had, we hoped, discovered an easier route to Pigeon Pond.

So off we went next day, Douglas leading the way in the Lyman 'long-boat', a speed-boat with an outboard motor, and Tim Hickman piloting the 'whaler', a flat-bottomed boat also propelled by a powerful outboard motor. First Douglas looked for the ANCHORAGE. This appeared to conform to the place named SAM'S BAY on the map. But which was SAM'S BAY? There are several shallow indentations on that shore. Which had Kidd chosen? To his request for information I told Douglas that he probably owned a small vessel with shallow draft to enable them to slip into creeks and inlets when pursued by more powerful ships. Even so, he would have found it hard to navigate the shallows on the southern shore. We could not get the deep-keeled Lyman close in. To land we had to transfer to the shallower draft whaler, propelled by oars or by the television boys wading and pulling, with its motor hoisted inboard. We landed on a beach which may or may not have been the right one and after a quick look round re-embarked.

Tim led us to the opening of Well Creek which seemed likely to provide access through the mangrove swamps to Pigeon Pond. Again we transferred to the whaler, leaving the non-essential members of the team resting on the sand spit where a government fishery hut provided shade and shelter. We had gone only a few hundred yards when the whaler stranded on a sand bar, the passage being unnavigable at low tide. Tim thought we might make it at high tide at 8.00 a.m. We returned to the yacht, for Douglas needed to catch a flight that afternoon.

He flew to Miami on the first leg of his long flight to Rio de Janeiro where he wished to photograph the annual Carnival for the book he intended to publish, and he was away for a week. I think we both lost and benefited by his absence. Douglas's exuberance can be stimulating or frustrating. Thus far he had been keenly interested, full of ideas and determined to get on with the job. But I foresaw the danger that he might become bored by my intention to carry out first a full reconnaissance – in other words to 'think first and dig later'.

Tim took us back to Well Creek next day. Leaving the Lyman at the entrance we crept through the narrow channel in the whaler. But we were forced to give up after a mile because even at high tide the water was only two feet deep. Our hopes of finding an easier route to Pigeon Pond were dashed. We turned back along the coast to try to get into Chalk Sound. This route could take us to the shore from where I might be able to get a closer look at the range of hills and spot the fourth summit, which seemed to correspond to the fourth 'black dot' on the second chart.

Tim succeeded in getting the whaler into Chalk Sound. Bennie stood at the prow carrying the modern map and gazing ahead to recognise the twists and turns through the mangrove swamps. The television crew took it in turns to wade ahead and pull us over the shallows. We reached the place named John Caperon Bight. Beside it rose a steep hill. We struggled to its 100 ft. summit capped by a cairn of stones and a marker post – one of the several survey marks at this end of the island. To the east lay the air strip. To the west and north ran a range of summits, four in number. The fourth summit seemed to be the one the chart maker had identified by his final dot. Bennie disagreed. He thought that these elevations were those which we had seen in reverse from our previous view point on Conamurry Mountain. I think both of us may have been right, but our disagreement emphasised the difficulty in identifying these low scrub clad hills from different angles. Whether I was right and he was wrong, the aspect ahead was dismal. Between us and the likely hill lay a dense tangle of scrub a mile wide. Some sort of path ran from the end of the air strip to the head of the Bight. But having got so far, should we decide to use it, we would need to cut a path to the hill.

Tim was anxious to leave the Sound before the tide turned, so we went back to the entrance, all of us, I think, somewhat discouraged. There was no easy way to get into the hills. Should we succeed, we would be faced with the prodigious task of cutting a huge area in our search for either site before we could attempt to use our metal detectors. They, as well as the cameras and sound equipment, food and drink, would need to be carried by herculean labour to our starting point. Each day we would be faced by more than an hour's journey in stifling heat before we could begin the real work. The job would require stamina and perseverance. There were no easy solutions, no miraculous gimmicks. I had come 5,600 miles to identify the two sites and I was determined to do so as long as my partners would support me.

We rested the next day, Sunday, as Tim Hickman wished to move the yacht from the exposed roadstead on the southern shore to the 'only safe anchorage' on the island, off its north-eastern point. Owing to the shallows guarding the south-eastern entrance of the passage, that required the partial circumnavigation of the island. Tim set off at 8.00 a.m. guided by a local pilot. He took the *Piscator* round the north-western promontory and well outside the guarding reefs. This enabled me to view the island's contours from slightly above sea-level. We hove-to after four hours voyage in the narrow channel between the eastern end of Providenciales Island and the next, mangrove covered cay. That location left us 20 miles by road, and further by sea, from the western end of the island where the sites lay. The

Piscator was still too deep in the water to come alongside the reef. Traffic with the shore was by boat alone.

My reconnaissance was not yet complete. I needed to reach Pigeon Pond to find the dark area so conspicuously discernible on the air photograph. Examining the photograph in England, I had thought that this dark patch might represent an area of once-disturbed earth disclosed by air photography.

It seems an attractive theory. Someone had dug at that place, either to bury, or, horrible thought, to recover treasure. This belief developed long before I had seen the scrub, which I believed to be low and sparse. Another, even more exciting, thought came. The dark patch, I learned by use of my dividers, measured 360 yards in length – the exact measurement given at the start of the legend written around the edges of the chart which appeared to indicate Site 1. I was eager to find that dark patch.

Again I led the party on our third attempt to reach Pigeon Pond. Guided by the Deane brothers we ascended the narrow, steep, twisting path to Conamurry Mountain. After a short rest for refreshment we descended its southern slope, cut through more scrub and finally emerged onto a large, dry salt-flat, the one time Pigeon Pond. It had taken two hours to reach it. 'Your black patch lies beyond that hill,' remarked Bennie pointing to another ridge in the distance. We trudged across the salt-flat, our feet sinking into the soft sand, and struggled up the scrub clad ridge. But the high scrub obscured any view from its summit, so we forced our way to one side from where we were able to see the ground below, yet another sea of scrub cloaking what appeared to be a shallow valley between the hills – possibly the valley I had seen on the charts. But there was nothing resembling the dark patch, no open ground where soil might have been disturbed. Then it happened. A dark shadow rolled across the landscape – a cloud shadow – as had appeared when the air photograph had been taken. I had been deluded by a phantom. The mistake was unimportant for it neither confirmed nor denied the whereabouts of Site 1. But it discouraged Bennie whose waning interest became increasingly apparent. Lacking the black patch and with no obvious valley or cleft in the hills, there was nothing to guide us to Site 1.

We needed to hurry back to the yacht because we were expecting a visit from Governor Mitchell who was touring the island that day with an official from the British Commonwealth Office. We had little time to clean up and change our stained and torn clothes before he came aboard with Mr Duff, District Commissioner Robinson and the Chief of Police of the Colony. My recently acquired friend Mike Jennings, the government's legal adviser, visited us on another occasion. Throughout our activities I received the most complete help from everyone concerned, official and otherwise.

I was invited that evening to a party at the District Commissioner's house. There I had a fortunate meeting with the stalwart blond Swedish engineer and surveyor, Bengt Söderqvist, who is in charge of development in the centre of the island. He thought he might be able to help me and suggested a meeting at his office at the Third Turtle Inn. I had been unaware of his existence, as Bennie, who was staying at the inn, had omitted to tell me about the one man who could help us most.

Next morning, to the consternation of Francis who was eager to be off filming something, somewhere, irrespective of its importance, I insisted we call first on Söderqvist.

I showed him my chart and he produced large-scale double enlargements of sections of the air photograph I already possessed. He put these under the spectroscope. It brought up the contours in sharp relief. He indicated a 95 ft. hill at the end of the ridge, suggesting it might be the summit conforming to the fourth dot in the range of hills, the key to Site 2. It could be reached from Blue Hills by the well defined track he had cut with a bulldozer. It was wider and clearer than the one we had previously ascended, and Söderqvist offered to guide us part of the way.

Our revived enthusiasm led us into error. We began our walk at noon, at the hottest time of day. We would have been wiser to have postponed the journey until 6.00 a.m. next day, the time I vainly beseeched we should begin these excursions into the scrub. By the time we reached the summit, after an hour's climb, I was completely exhausted as was everyone else. There was nowhere to sit and little room to stand. The vast scrub screened the view into the low ground where I believed that 'X' marked the spot. Bennie shinned up a slender tree. He reported a sea of scrub extending in every direction. 'No one, not even to bury the body of the man he had murdered, would have penetrated that terrible jungle,' Bennie thought. No pirate or buccaneer would have cut his way through such an obstacle to bury treasure amidst the ridge when he could have done so close to the shore. Bennie's argument seemed plausible. This was before I had concluded that the scrub could not have been dense in 1669. Had the island been covered by scrub surely the chart maker would have indicated it, if only to deter would-be robbers?

We went back to the yacht to await Douglas's return. I wished to make a mass attack on Site 2. I hoped that Douglas's tremendous enthusiasm and energy would turn defeat into victory. We met Douglas at the airport and drove him to the yacht. Douglas had another idea, a new wild goose to chase. From someone he had heard of the 'local historian', Bertie Sadler who lived on Grand Turk Island. I had spoken with Sadler on my visit there to learn, as I had expected, that he knew nothing of the history of Providenciales Island in the seventeenth century, because it had no history then. 'We must interview Sadler,' Douglas insisted. He chartered a private aircraft and flew to Grand Turk Island with Bennie, Francis and part of the film crew. I stayed on the yacht.

Douglas, on his return, agreed that Sadler could tell us nothing we did not already know – other than the intriguing theory that one island of the group had been Columbus's original landfall on his historical first Atlantic crossing in 1492. But, and this was Douglas's final and wildest goose, Sadler had suggested that Kidd might have landed on Providenciales in 1699 on his final voyage to Boston, prior to his arrest. He may have called there, according to Sadler, to secrete part of the treasure he had gained from the *Quedah Merchant*, the rich prize he had taken in the Indian Ocean. Douglas accepted this unconvincing theory. Kidd would have hidden his treasure close to the shore, near the ANCHORAGE, and that was where we should seek it, he insisted.

I knew the details of Kidd's career, which Douglas did not. On his return from the Indian Ocean in 1699, he had abandoned his rich prize, with its bulky cargo, in the West Indies and had sailed in a fast schooner for New York and Boston, carrying the gold and silver bullion and the transportable loot, worth some £20,000. He called at Charleston, South Carolina on the way. It was vital to his safety to bring to Lord Bellomont at Boston, his principle backer, as much booty as he could to satisfy the influential politicians who, and only who, could save him from condemnation as a pirate. Had Kidd stopped to hide treasure on Providenciales Island, it is likely that the three members of his crew who were hanged with him would have tried to buy their lives with this interesting information. Bennie took the point. Douglas did not.

Nor could Douglas comprehend that Sadler's theory referred to a mythical treasure concealed thirty years *after* the charts found in Kidd's furniture had been drawn. Douglas dismissed this anachronism as being totally irrelevant. 'We must search the area 360 yards from the ANCHORAGE,' he announced. But where was the ANCHORAGE? That had yet to be determined.

While dismissing Sadler's theory, and Douglas's fervent advocacy, as totally irrelevant to our quest, its discussion stimulated a new thought in my mind. Had Kidd intended that the searcher should find a starting point '360 yards' inland from the ANCHORAGE, from where he could see the cleft in the hills, the area where the three tiny circles, possibly three caves, were marked?

With this possibility in mind I agreed to accompany my partners in what I believed otherwise to be complete folly. We spent a whole day on the beach, at or near Sam's Bay, dividing our forces and penetrating inland through the scrub as far as we could. I managed to penetrate less than 150 yards inland, an expedition from which I returned torn and bleeding. The others, entering the scrub further down, progressed no further. No one had been able to get a view above the scrub, far less identify a cleft in the hills.

'We must measure the distance 360 yards inland and cut a line parallel to the beach,' decided Douglas. I pointed out that, as we did not know the true location of the ANCHORAGE, this track would need to be at least a mile long, a task requiring a month's work. Douglas was unconvinced. On his flight over the island he had seen a valley or cleft in the hills, and he was determined to pursue his pet theory, the most elusive of all his wild geese.

Douglas went in the whaler next day, with Cameraman Ernest Vincze, to photograph the underwater cannon and anchor off the north-western point of the island, an expedition on which he was guided by Art Pickering, the diver who conducts tourists to the site of the ancient wrecks. The rest of us followed later in the Lyman, joining Douglas in yet another fruitless search for the ANCHORAGE. Francis wished to take a number of film shots on the beach. To return to the yacht before darkness fell at 6.00 p.m. we needed to leave the beach by 3.30 p.m. at the latest. The filming went on and on well past the deadline. It was close on 5.00 p.m. before Francis was ready to leave.

We could return to the yacht either along the southern shore where the heavily laden boats might ground on shallows, or round the north coast by skirting the reef. Douglas elected to go northwards. He, Bennie, Francis, Ernest and I were in the Lyman. The others followed in the whaler piloted by Graham Whitaker, the assistant cameraman, a small-boat expert. Douglas cut the corner too sharply, and we found ourselves within the reef, surrounded by foaming breakers and threatened by jagged pinnacles of coral.

The situation was frightening. Darkness would fall within the hour and we might be trapped and possibly wrecked. Francis leaped up insisting that he was getting out the life jackets stored beneath the seat. I fully agreed with him. 'You don't have to be . . . dramatic,' Douglas screamed at him. Francis refrained from retorting that Douglas, by his inexperience and impetuosity, had endangered our lives. Neither Francis nor I are good swimmers. Only Bennie remained calm. He lay flat in the bows, guiding the boat through the jagged reefs. The angry surf pounded the careering vessel and nearly threw him overboard. He clung on while Douglas manoeuvred through the swell. The whaler followed in our wake. I saw it tossed high by the huge waves. We did not get through the reef. Nor as far as I could see did we emerge from it. In that area, apparently, there are several banks of coral extending over several hundred yards of sea. I saw large brown discolorations in the water, coral patches rising from the sea bed. Douglas, relying on Bennie's eyes, steered round them, trying to manoeuvre towards land. But unknown to us, the whaler caught the reef, losing two blades of its propeller. This slowed her progress and she fell behind, dropping out of sight amidst surf and breakers.

Happily we spied ahead a small fishing boat. Cruising gently up to it, Douglas enquired from its astonished crewmen for a safe course to the yacht basin at the Third Turtle Inn on the coast about two miles distant. Steer direct for the high hill, they told him. Moving at greater speed Douglas brought the Lyman into the basin where Francis, Ernest and I leaped ashore in order, as I hastened to explain, to lighten the boat so that Douglas and Bennie could put to sea again in search of the whaler, and to give room in case they needed to rescue the crew. Donna Wolfe, the manageress of the Inn, drove Francis, Ernest and me to the quay where the *Piscator* was moored. By now darkness had fallen. I scrounged a lift from the crew of a diesel delivery barge who deposited me on the

Piscator. Then Tim Hickman took the return trip to go in search of the survivors. I was able to reassure Mrs Gray and her children who had spent the day on board that Bennie was safe. It was an hour at least before the others returned, having left the two boats at the Third Turtle Inn.

That was the end of the expedition as far as I was concerned. Douglas and Bennie, supported by Francis, rejected my suggestion that we should launch a final attack on Site 2. I went by myself to recruit our guides for a lone assault. I found Algernon and James Deane diffident. Next day was Sunday and they led the service at the Baptist Chapel. They could not start before noon. That was far too late as I wanted to begin the climb at sunrise, to reach the summit before the heat of the day.

By Monday it was too late for the others had plans for the car and boats. The unit set off early to film Douglas and Bennie measuring 360 yards from the beach and starting to cut a line parallel to it. I refused to go when I learned that it was 'pretend' only. They went to an easily accessible part of the shore, far distant from the ANCHORAGE, in order to stage a demonstration. They took with them, but did not use, the metal detectors which had cost £500 to hire. Douglas had the grace to say, on his return, that I had been right and that to cut such a path would take months. I refrained from saying that it would also have been futile.

I may sound over-critical of my two partners. As events transpired they were unsuitable for such an adventure. For them it was a 'bit of a lark', a mid-winter holiday in the sun, which might possibly succeed. Bennie never failed in courtesy and in paying tribute to the physical stamina of the partner nearly twice his age. He agreed that Douglas had misled us about the size of the scrub, but he failed to curb his old friend's eccentricities. From the early days of the discussion in England he left me to cope with Douglas alone, omitting to attend most of our many meetings.

For me Douglas was a new and shattering experience. In my career as an author I had become accustomed to dealing with educated people whose minds think logically and progressively. Douglas left school at sixteen to start a career which, entirely by his own genius, made him a millionaire at thirty-seven. Logical, progressive thought is foreign to his nature. As a result, the expedition which needed to be well organised became a shambles. Matters that needed careful consideration and decision were left undecided. For example, early on I suggested that we three partners should draw up and sign some form of Agreement. Douglas was enthusiastic and got his lawyers to provide its text. But he could never bring himself to sign it. Whenever I brought it up he prevaricated, insisting that there were more urgent matters to discuss, most of them irrelevant. He never did sign it, though it was in his interest to do so. I overcame the difficulty by arranging for the licence to search for treasure to be accorded to me alone.

Yet, despite his irritating ways, one cannot help liking Douglas. His manners are appalling, his language ultra-modern. His is happy as he is and has no wish to change. His is kind, generous, honest and genuine. Our failure to get on resulted, in my opinion, from our dissimilar racial characteristics.

The long-planned and expensive expedition had ended in frustration and disappointment. But not for me. I had achieved two of the things I had set out to prove or discover. I had completely confirmed my identification of the charted island and I had experienced the difficulties which I could never have learned from home. I looked back on the expedition as a first reconnaissance, my initial exploration of the island. I was determined to return to Providenciales to finish the job.

A Wild Goose Chase?

Before they left for Providenciales, the principle expedition members were interviewed. One paper quoted Frances Megahy, the TV producer in charge, as saying: 'Furneaux says he knows where the treasure is, but I am dubbing the film "The Biggest Wild Goose Chase of the Year".' Maybe Mr Megahy had a premonition, for after they came back and the resulting documentary called 'Three Characters in Search of a Treasure' was screened (July 1975), the preceding paragraph to the TV write-up guide said: 'Dead men tell no tales – neither it seems do their charts. Captain Kidd's faded parchments certainly lead Three Characters in Search of a Treasure on a wild goose chase in Tuesday's documentary.'

A critic said of the programme: 'It fizzles out when their rather ill-organised expedition does.'

Another: 'It appealed to some of mankind's lowest instincts. Foremost among them was the one making most of us grin or splutter with laughter disguised as a sympathetic cough. Much of the programme was a deadpan shamefully amusing chronicle of the fiasco.' Other comments included:

'A faintly malicious tale of disillusionment . . . '

'A work which ended up drenched in calamity . . . '

'Within minutes of landing on Providenciales, it must have been clear to the producer that he had a first class catastrophe on his hands' and so it goes on.

Back in England, Bennie Gray admitted, 'It was a failure, but nice as failures go.' He went on to say, 'I think in our enthusiasm we were beguiled by the excitement and romance of the whole thing. I admire Rupert's determination but I wouldn't go back.'

Neither would Douglas Villiers, who said: 'This was something I wanted to believe in, I was in a daze – like a schoolboy. It was a fantasy – with all the Yo-ho-ho feelings about pirates and treasure. I still believe the charts are right and it was the right island. But I'm not going back. Rupert Furneaux is a smashing guy and if he goes again I wish him luck.'

Even Furneaux called the expedition 'an amusing fiasco', but go again he did.

Second Expedition

Within a few months of my return to England I had arranged my second expedition. This was due to my book about Oak Island. The American edition (Dodd Mead, 1973) was read by Roger M. Wheeler of Tulsa, Oklahoma, who wrote suggesting that he accompany me to Nova Scotia to solve the mysteries of the Money Pit. I was forced to reply that, until the Triton Syndicate finished their work, there was no chance of securing a licence to search on the island. Recalling Wheeler's interest in solving mysteries, I told him about my search for Captain Kidd's treasure. He replied enthusiastically and I sent him copies of my charts, maps and photographs and the story of my first expedition. He telephoned his confirmation and sent information about himself.

He sounded the ideal partner. He had gained an engineering degree at the Massachusetts Institute of Technology, was US Navy Reserve and currently is Chairman and Executive Director of the American Telex Corporation. He possessed his own jet aircraft and would bring his two pilots and possibly one of his sons. We arranged to meet at Miami airport on 31 January 1976.

There were many details to discuss and settle, accommodation on the island, hire of a car and possibly shallow-draft skiffs by which to navigate the waterways, and the use of a bulldozer to cut a permanent track through the scrub to reach the areas of the two sites daily without the heavy labour of cutting and forcing our way through the matted undergrowth. We dismissed the possibility of hiring a helicopter to carry us in daily from the air strip because the nearest suitable model was located at Florida, 500 miles distant, too great a hop for its fuel capacity. I left it to Wheeler with his specialised knowledge to investigate the acquisition of suitable metal detectors.

Meanwhile I informed Mike Jennings, the government's Legal Adviser, of my return and he arranged with the new Governor, Mr Arthur C. Watson, for the extension of my licence to search on Crown Lands. I felt confident that my second expedition would be more successful than the first. Difficult enterprises of this nature, as I learned in Nova Scotia, require more than one visit. On my first I had experienced the difficulties, learned the lay of the land, discovered whom to contact about what, and made friends. I believed that I could now reach and identify the sites, whether or not they still contained 'treasure'.

I looked forward to my return to Providenciales, exhausting as the work would be. A new discovery spurred me on. I learned of the tradition (Ben Lucien Burman *The Mysterious Bahamas*, 1960) that Captain Kidd had moored his ships in a secluded harbour near Georgetown on the island of Grand Exuma, one of the Bahamas. He thus knew the islands where I had placed his charts.

Retracing Kidd's Footsteps

The day prior to my flight to Miami, Wheeler telephoned to say that he could not join me on 31 January as had been arranged but would send his pilot Tom Hecklin to accompany me to the island. He would stay for several days before returning to Tulsa to bring Wheeler. Meanwhile he had booked one of the large beach houses at the Leeward Development and had hired a car. Hecklin brought a copy of the Agreement, the draft of which I had sent to Wheeler, and I signed my copy as he had done his. This provided that, after any third party had been satisfied, meaning the government of the Turks and Caicos Islands, Wheeler and I would share equally the proceeds of any treasure that might be found. By my licence to search for concealed treasure on Crown Land, I would receive 75% of the value of treasure trove up to $50,000 and 50% thereafter. The term 'treasure trove' denotes articles of gold and silver of which no known owner can be traced. Both my areas of search were on Crown Land. This was a very satisfactory arrangement, far better than can be negotiated in some other territories where the governments are more rapacious, for the position can be one of exasperating uncertainty.

Hecklin and I took the scheduled Mackey Airways three days a week flight to Providenciales which takes three hours. As the four-engined Convair flew low over the island I pointed out the areas of search prior to landing at the air-strip. There we and the other passengers were greeted by the island's calypso band and we found the hired car awaiting us. It was a comparatively new Plymouth two-door sedan but a near-wreck after two years of travel over the island's rough roads. These roads, gouged out of the limestone and coral by bulldozer, extend over most of the island which until nine years ago had only tracks through the dense scrub. There has been considerable development and there are now two hotels and a number of houses catering both for the developers and for tourists, and an American owned store run by my friends Ron and Kay Simmons. The indigenous people, who number about 700, live in two settlements at Blue Hills on the north coast and Five Cays Bay on the southern shore. So far they have withstood remarkably well the shock of being projected suddenly into the twentieth century.

This may be due to their inherent good mature. They are well educated at the government school and know enough of the world to appreciate how fortunate they are to live in a society lacking in newspapers, radios and television and free from strife and stress. They like their British nationality and the stability brought by English Law, and accept the benefits they derive from the island's development which provides many jobs. A hundred or so men and women are employed at the island's two fish-factories which process the conch and other fish for sale abroad. All other foods and all articles are imported and are very expensive.

How long this idyllic state of affairs will last is uncertain. Many of the young islanders complain that there are no job opportunities other than casual labour and there have been cases recently within the island group of arson, possibly an expression of frustration. But I received only the utmost courtesy and expressions of great interest in my quest for pirate treasure. The people are aware of the island's disreputable past and tell stories of treasures and articles abandoned by the pirates of long ago. But they tend to dissolve into wishful thinking under examination. I heard two cases of men who had dreamed they had found treasure. One seemed so realistic that the dreamer was attacked when he refused to disclose its hiding place. Undoubtedly, coins, knives and swords have been found. One of the best authenticated stories relates the discovery of an ornamental dagger and sheath in the caves in the cliff where the Third Turtle Inn was built about seven years ago. An ancient cannon recovered from the reef reposes at the hotel's entrance. But the four hundred wrecks which are reputed to line the reef have not all been 'fished'. This may be due to the tradition that they were the victims of deliberate wrecking. Ships were decoyed by the simple expedient of hanging red and green lights on donkeys and leading them up and down the beach to give the impression of an open seaway. But these are things of the past. The island is now adequately policed and controlled by a District Commissioner, Nathaniel Robinson.

Following our landing I made my first call upon him. I had met him in 1975 and he knew of my return. I explained the progress I had made and my hope to find at least one of the two sites indicated in the charts. Should I find either I would need to report to Robinson as the government's representative. I called next upon my old friends Algernon and James Deane, our guides in 1975. Alas, Algernon had suffered a heart attack and would be unable to accompany me into the scrub. His younger brother James became my chief guide and without him I would have achieved little. The Deanes may be the only remaining islanders who know all the ancient tracks and the areas which were once cultivated by the American Loyalists and by their own ancestors.

I arranged with James to employ one of Algernon's ten sons, another James, and we scheduled our first journey for Monday at 6.00 a.m. My experience of the heat in the previous year convinced me of the need for an early start which, although we kept to it, was not required for the temperature was far lower than in 1975 as it was throughout Florida and the Bahamas. The strong breeze made walking through the scrub bearable.

The state of the tide was another factor requiring an early start for we proposed to navigate the shallow inland waterways on the island's southern shore.

On the Sunday I went over my charts, air photographs and maps with Tom Hecklin. I had acquired in England enlarged squares of the air photograph which enabled me to view the island stereoscopically which brought its contours into sharp relief. This enabled me to plan routes to avoid the steep hills but in practice we found it easier to climb them than to make wide detours through the dense scrub. It was best, I found, to show James where I wanted to go and leave the path to him. He had a wonderful feel for 'country' and seemed to know, even when deep in the scrub, where the inclines lay.

My previous partners had thought it unwise to take our guides into our confidence. I revealed my charts to Algernon and James and my confidences were not betrayed for neither in my absence had sought out my sites. I showed them my charts again and benefited from their advice. By this means I gained enthusiastic helpers, just what I needed on an expedition on which my new partner failed to show up.

I decided to concentrate first on Site 1, the place shown on the chart which appeared to indicate by the three tiny circles three 'caves' within a valley, and which provided a set of directions beginning '360 yards V. R. North'. The key to these directions lay, I believed, in determining the starting place from where to measure that distance. That required reconstruction of Kidd's actions. The same chart placed an 'ANCHORAGE' off-shore.

Kidd, I guessed, had drawn the chart to remind himself of the route to his place of concealment. He had reached the island in a small vessel which he had anchored off-shore. In the previous year I had misinterpreted the term 'ANCHORAGE' to mean a landing place. My yachtsman son-in-law, Hilary Watson, put me right. An 'anchorage' meant exactly what is said, a firm sandy sea-bed where an anchor would hold, in fact the place where the modern maps also show an anchor.

Kidd probably had only a small sum of money to hide. If, as I assume, he had joined the Buccaneers' expeditions against Spanish towns, his share of the loot would have been small. He was a young man in 1669 and could have been no more than an ordinary seaman in Morgan's crew. His share, when the spoils were divided amongst a thousand men, would have amounted only to a few hundred pieces of eight, each worth the equivalent of the modern dollar. The loot of Panama for example amounted to 750,000 pieces of eight. First the claims for loss of life and limb were satisfied. From the balance, Morgan took his 1/100 share, the King 1/15, the Duke of York as Admiral of the Navy 1/15 and each ship's captain the share of eight men. The 1,800 seamen were awarded 200 pieces of eight each. This was an exceptionally rich haul made two years after Kidd had drawn his charts. In his two or three years of possible buccaneering Kidd may have saved 1,000 pieces of eight, a large sum in those days.

More careful, for he was a Scotsman, than others and aware of the hazards and decline of buccaneering, he decided to conceal a small nest-egg for the future. When the buccaneers were forced to abandon their haunts and strongholds Kidd set his course for the nearest uninhabited island, which he may have known and certainly came to know well for he drew amazingly accurate charts of Providenciales. Reaching its southern shore and thereby avoiding the dangerous reefs to the north where he located three 'wrecks', he anchored his vessel and set out by canoe to navigate the numerous shallow waterways which gave easy access to the interior. The low ridge of hills offered privacy and easily identifiable land-marks. The scrub, as I have suggested, did not then exist in its present form. Kidd paddled up Well Creek and came to Pigeon Pond, possibly then an inland lake. Its toe would have caught his attention. It is a salient feature, jutting into the scrub-clad hills.

Ahead he would have seen a low 25 ft. ridge and beyond it another rising to 50 ft. and crowned by a 75 ft. elevation. Carrying his bag of coins, he ascended the nearby and then the further ridge noting its 'V' shaped form and walking approximately the distance of 360 yards. Reaching its summit he saw a shallow valley. His chart depicts such a valley and within it he marked three tiny circles, possibly three small caves. Kidd indicated the course to be followed by the letters 'VR' meaning a 'V' shaped 'Ridge', and by the direction 'North'. One strange feature on his chart seemed to confirm my interpretation. On the northern shore he had placed an inverted 'V', possibly to remind himself to seek a ridge so shaped.

I was eager to test my interpretation of the chart and its directions on the ground by retracing Kidd's footsteps. Nothing could be done until the Monday for the Deanes are unavailable on a Sunday being Deacons of the Baptist Church, one of the four Christian denominations on the island.

Hecklin and I spent a quiet Sunday afternoon in the luxurious leeward beach house and I attempted a bathe the sea, far more chilly than I had experienced in 1975. We retired early, setting our clocks for 6.00 a.m.

The Deanes were ready when we arrived. After they had loaded the outboard motor and tank of gasoline into the car we set off for Sapodilla cove on the southern shore where James moored his aluminium boat. There we were greeted by the conch fishermen who were preparing to sail to their fishing ground. The outboard motor belonged to nephew James who had brought it, rather than his uncle's, because of its greater power but, as we were to learn, it was less reliable. Within a few minutes it started spluttering to Tom Hecklins' consternation for, as he pointed out, we could be stranded or even shipwrecked and, lacking lifesaving gear, drowned. I took a less gruesome view, relying on the Deanes' seamanship. We were not far from the shore but to reach the entrance to Well Creek five miles by sea we would have to round West Harbor Bluff, a point jutting out to sea. Balked of this easy route up Well Creek we turned into Chalk Sound. That would leave a longer but safer land route to Pigeon Pond.

Skirting the shoals and twisting around islands, James brought the boat to the north-eastern corner of the Sound where he moored it to a shelf of jagged coral over which we were forced to scramble in order to reach the dry mud flats. Although walking then became easier, it took an hour to reach the Pond's prominent 'toe', my immediate objective. The delay caused by the faulty engine, the prospect of the long walk back and the falling tide limited our time. We scaled the two ridges ahead which enabled me to confirm the 'V' shaped form of the second ridge and gazed into the valley below. It was cloaked by scrub. To find anything within it we would need several additional helpers, each man armed with a machete.

We could not get them all there in one small boat. To my suggestion that the extra men could walk overland from the settlement James replied that without him they would lose their way through the scrub. There seemed to be no alternative. We would all have to use the overland route, two miles of rugged horror. Blissfully unaware of its difficulties, Hecklin welcomed it as an alternative to the potential dangers of the sea-passage. With the next morning's route decided we returned by the way we had come, a journey which destroyed completely one of my pairs of rubber-soled shoes.

We set off at 6.30 next morning led by the two James and followed by six extra men, their relatives and friends, each man carrying a machete and provided with a bag of oranges and apples, the best thirst quenchers on these expeditions. Tom Hecklin brought his Gemini metal detector and I carried my fisherman's stool and haversack.

We plunged into the scrub behind the Deanes' house and followed the track which was less arduous than the one I had previously walked twice over Conamurry Mountain. It avoided the worst hills and deposited us, after two hours walking, at Pigeon Pond. We made our way to its jutting toe where we stopped for a rest and refreshment.

We reascended the first and the second ridge, the men hacking a path to its summit. There, first James and then Hacklin climbed a tree to look around. James led the way into the valley below and we assembled at its bottom. The area of search covered several acres of ground completely obscured by scrub. It was impossible to see even the summit of the ridge which we had descended, and which jutted into the valley in the form of a 'V'.

I ordered the men to spread out and ascend the slope and to look out for anything that seemed unnatural, such as a pile of rocks, Kidd's next step in the set of directions, and for caves. The three circles seemed to form the 'Triangle' from where I was instructed to measure '55 ft'. The 'Three Stumps' may once have been the remains of trees which had, as they still do, grown from the sparse soil within these caves.

I heard rather than saw the cutters groping upwards through the scrub. I followed, bringing up the rear in the hope of spotting anything they might have missed. Within a few minutes there came an excited cry, from Tom Lightbourne I think. I hurried up to find him and James pointing to a pile of rocks. No natural agency could have arranged them overlapping and criss-crossing each other. Only the head of man could have piled them into the form of a rough pyramid. Peering through the scrub I saw ahead a wide, shallow cave and further away two smaller caves. They, I later learned, radiated approximately 55 feet from the centre of the triangle they formed.

The pile of rocks and the underside of the base rock showing the 'K'.

The cave some 20 ft. ahead of the pile of rocks was unusual. These caves are invariably circular with a continuous rocky rim. But the front of this cave was open, leaving a smooth path into its interior. Someone had cut away the rim to provide easy access. Twenty small steps carried me to its centre. Before I had time to turn I heard yet another excited cry, this time from James Deane. I found him pointing to the cave's eastern wall, to a large cavity. It was partly filled by debris and obstructed by the roots of an ancient tree, the age of which James assessed at two hundred years.

I sat on my stool while James attempted to clear the obstruction with his machete. But the knotted roots which ran beneath the wall were far too tough for such an instrument. To reveal the cavity's interior we would need picks, spades and an axe, tools we had not thought to bring for in my wildest imagination it seemed improbable that we would find Kidd's cache so quickly. I had expected to spend several days clearing the ground.

We returned by the way we came by an exhausting overland journey. Poor Tom complained of sore feet and aching limbs. By the time we reached the settlement my trousers were badly torn and my face bloody. I went at once to report my discovery to Nathaniel Robinson who was duly impressed.

We arranged to borrow the tools we required and collected them next morning before commencing our journey by boat. To overcome Tom's fear and to accommodate the extra helpers we used two boats, James's aluminium craft and his nephew's larger wooden vessel. His outboard motor still played up but we managed to enter the Chalk Sound and twist our way past the worst sand banks and shoals. An hour's walk brought us back to the site of my discovery.

While James Deane worked on the cavity, I set the others excavating the floor of the cave. It proved to contain a welter of broken stones intermingled with tree roots. Hecklin ran his metal detector over the surface obtaining no reaction until he reached a spade where it set up a buzz at a distance of two feet. It took James nearly an hour to clear the cavity but the knotted roots proved to be impervious to his axe. This did not matter for they obscured only a small part of the base of the cavity. I sifted the loose soil he threw out. He said he could hear a hollow sound. Bending my head I heard it too as he prodded with his spade. Discarding the tool and working with his hands he levered out the round, flat and

Clearing the site and showing the entrance to the 'cave'. Furneaux (sitting) with James Dean and helpers.

thin rock which filled the base of the cavity. Peering in I saw that the earth beneath the rock had recessed, leaving a deep 'V'-shaped gap beneath. That accounted for the hollow sound we had heard.

The rock had been inserted to form a platform across this area possibly where Kidd had dug a little too deeply. No such thin rock could have survived in that geological stratum in which the stones above and below are not less than 9″ thick. It would have been crushed to pieces thousands of years ago. The cavity had been man-made or enlarged. Kidd had placed his bag of coins on the platform and had probably filled the cavity with soil and loose rocks, throwing them out when he recovered his deposit. It is difficult otherwise to account for the presence of broken rocks in the floor of the cave. Hecklin obtained no reaction when he inserted his metal detector within the cavity.

Looking into the cavity I saw that it was some 3 ft. deep and 2½ ft. wide. Withdrawing my head I heard James speak a word which sounded like 'shelter'. He explained that the islanders called such cavities by that name because they could be used for the safe keeping of objects. His description reminded me of the word in the legend following the directions '20 ft.' from the Rocks which I had interpreted as 'Skeleton' for, according to piratical mythology, a man was sacrificed to provide a silent guardian for a treasure cache. Examining the faded word again I saw that it may have been 'SHELE(T)R' a mis-spelt form of SHELTER. The letter 'E' which followed indicated the cave's eastern wall in which lay the cavity. Then came a blank and words which seemed to read 'OF LEB'. I could not fathom what they meant. That no longer mattered for, without doubt, I had found Kidd's place of concealment.

He had returned to recover his money. Small as the sum may have been it provided the capital which launched him on a career as a prosperous merchant, operating from New York and trading with his one-time buccaneering friends in the West Indies and smuggling prohibited goods into the American colonies, a most respectable trade. By 1690 he had become a wealthy man, the owner of at least one vessel, a house in New York and a pew in Trinity Church, a person of acknowledged position rating the term 'Gentleman'.

Kidd had come and gone and now I stood by his place of concealment, his private bank where he had deposited what had become the world's most famous and long-sought treasure. Had he sailed away never to return, drowned at sea, or killed in some piratical fight, his sea-chests and charts would have gone too, and neither I nor anyone else would have sought his treasure on Providenciales Island. He kept his charts for the rest of his life as reminders of his youthful ingenuity.

Finally I dismantled the pile of rocks, the guide post to cave and cavity. The base rock was large and flat and had been placed on artificially levelled ground. Turning it over and examining its rough surface I noticed what appeared to be scratches green with age. Clearing them with my knife, the clear cut letter 'K' emerged. Like a dog marking his territory, Kidd had scratched his initial on the rock.

Hecklin was due back in Tulsa to bring Wheeler to the island. He took the scheduled flight to Miami and that was the last I saw of him. Having seen him off at the airstrip I visited the Deanes to discuss my search for site 2, that indicated in the other chart, the one marking a cross by the fourth black dot. I assumed that the four dots drawn in this chart represented four elevations in the ridge. Studying the chart and the map at home I had been struck by the relative position of these dots. The distance they were spaced apart conformed remarkably well with the relative spacing of the summits of the ridge, the elevations 125 ft., 100 ft., 75 ft. and 75 ft.

Kidd had picked these summits as guide posts and he had delineated the island's ridge far more accurately than he had done on the other chart. That would be difficult to do even now for its contours are not easily discernible from ground level. In 1975 I had climbed the 100 ft. hill which rises close to Johnny Caperon Bight within Chalk Sound. Looking northwards I had seen a series of elevations stretching away to Conamurry Mountain, the high elevation we had ascended to reach Pigeon Pond.

James Deane and I climbed again to the summit of the 100 ft. elevation. He easily recognised Conamurry Mountain and we counted several elevations along the ridge. But they were difficult to discern accurately for the high scrub hid their summits. James pointed out also the hill suggested by Söderqvist which we had climbed in 1975. It was far too much to the north-east to be the fourth dot on the chart. But which hill was represented by the fourth dot? We took compass bearings and descended to the boat.

James steered across the Sound and landed on its northern shore about half a mile from the Bight. We climbed the low cliff and viewed the ridge from a new angle. From there the four summits were more prominent. The fourth elevation seemed to be represented by the low ridge directly ahead and separated from the shore by a mile of dense scrub. An old track ran through the scrub, James remarked, but he had not trodden it since he was a boy. It crossed the ridge and linked the island's southern and northern shores. I thought it strange that anyone had sought to make such a track until James pointed to an old building nearby. The American Loyalists had 'farmed' the area and had built a stone house. The path had, said James, been used by the old islanders who also tried to cultivate the area by planting corn between the rocks.

While James's knowledge of an old track through the scrub was encouraging, his stories of ancient cultivation were discouraging. Unlike the virgin ground where I had found Site 1 this part of the island had been trodden since 1669. There were other disconcerting features. Reaching the ridge would be only a beginning. I would need to find the 'X' which was marked on the chart by the fourth black dot and then follow the directions written on the chart. They seemed incomprehensible and could not have provided any sure guide in 1669 or now. The British Museum experts had reported that several of the words and numerals were uncertain, far too faded to be recognised. The opening figures '515' were pure guesswork. Did they represent yards or feet? Either way they indicated that a long course needed to be followed presumably from the 'X', possibly a sign scratched on a rock or a cross made by rocks. Having walked the so many yards or feet to the south-east, I was directed to turn '50 N'. And why had Kidd repeated the direction '36 NE'?

Two statements only seemed helpful. He referred to 'ROCKS', possibly a cairn of rocks, and to a cave, for the dimensions '3 feet BY 3 feet BY 4' seemed to represent such a shaft. Neither would be easy to find in a square mile of scrub. What hopes I had of finding a cave of these dimensions were dashed by James who remarked that there were few 'caves' in this part of the island. They are a salient feature of the higher ground.

I embarked on my quest to Site 2 next day, with the two James and three extra machete-wielders. James had difficulty in tracing the old track which had grown over in several places. After an hour's walk we found ourselves on a low hill about 200 yards to the east of the ridge which seemed to be represented by the fourth dot. We affixed a white flag to a tree to identify the hill and hacked our way to the ridge we had seen from the shore. James pointed to a blackened mass of stones where his ancestors had burned lime and to scrubby bushes bearing the faded marks of knives and axes. The old farmers might have inadvertently obliterated the marks for which I was searching.

Spreading out we scoured the western slopes of the ridge and climbed to the top of the next summit, the third conspicuous feature of the central ridge. We repeated the process for two more days searching hopefully for anything that looked like a cross or a pile of rocks. It is impossible to exaggerate the difficulties. To survey the area completely it would have been necessary to cut down every bush or tree for while they remained we were forced to grope our way and were unable to see further than a few yards in any direction. Even had Wheeler been present I would have been loath to recommend the hire of a bulldozer which would have cost at least $1,000. And having successfully overcome these obstructions we would certainly find the place of concealment empty. Kidd had reclaimed one of his caches – he must have recovered the other. It shows his caution that he placed his eggs in two baskets.

I felt that I should be satisfied with 'what I already had' to employ and paraphrase Hewetson's advice to Kidd. I had solved the mystery, my purpose in travelling to Providenciales, and Wheeler had failed to appear. I had expected him on the Saturday following Hecklin's departure. On Friday evening Hecklin telephoned to say that he was flying Wheeler and several other people to St Thomas in the Virgin Islands for a yachting holiday. Five days later he telephoned again to report that the whole party would arrive on Friday 13 February. He would fly them to Grand Turk Island which possessed a paved runway where Wheeler would charter a flight for the 80 mile journey to Providenciales. The unpaved runway there was unsuitable for a jet aircraft.

I flew to Grand Turk by the inter-island plane which makes the round trip twice each weekday, had lunch with Mike Jennings, called upon the new governor and made enquiries about a charter flight for Wheeler and his party of eight. I learned that the 'Islander' aircraft which seats nine would be available between 11.00 a.m. and 1.00 p.m. I returned to Providenciales where I waited Hecklin's confirmatory call. It never came and no one arrived on the 13th.

I have yet to learn why Wheeler did not come to the island. He may have been disturbed by the prospect of a flight other than in his own jet aircraft, or he may have been put off by Hecklin's horror stories of our travels by sea and through the scrub. I was disappointed for I had been spurred on by Wheeler's earlier enthusiasm and unquestionable abilities. His presence on the island could have been stimulating and rewarding but it was not vital to my search.

I had achieved my purpose and learned how Kidd had saved the loot of his youth to make himself a prosperous merchant. But he was not content. He embarked late in life on, or was bullied into, a foolish venture which cost his life. He lacked even the satisfaction of knowing that his return to illegality had made him the world's most notorious pirate, the hero of countless stories beloved by his youthful admirers.

Several questions remain unanswered. Kidd's bluff that he could lead an expedition to recover the immense treasure he had lodged in the Indies failed because the authorities knew the fate that had befallen the *Quedah Merchant* and her cargo. Why did not Kidd display the treasure charts he had secreted in his sea-chests? They might have convinced the sceptics that he had once concealed a great treasure. He died silent about his youthful adventures which had provided the sinews of respectability, the quality of life for which he craved.

Unlike Kidd I left Providenciales Island empty-handed but happy that I had solved another mystery. I had made many friends and heard the intriguing theory that it was in these Caicos islands that Columbus had made his first landfall. Two facts seemed to support it. Its protagonists claim that Columbus could not have reached Hispaniola so quickly from Watling Island in the Bahamas, the island he named 'San Salvador', and when the replica of the *Santa Maria* made the voyage in 1970, by following Columbus's course, it ended up off the Caicos islands rather than in the Bahamas.

Providenciales Island may thus have two claims to fame, as the site of Kidd's treasure cache and as the second transatlantic land reached by a European. The Norsemen preceded Columbus by four hundred years, just as Kidd had preceded me.

Furneaux – Assessing his Claim

So Furneaux had no doubt whatsoever that he had found Kidd's island and solved the mystery of the charts. It is all very plausible and of course he could be right, who's to prove otherwise? But until someone actually turns up with the chests and publicises the solution to the charts that enabled him to find the island and said treasure, I will remain unconvinced.

Personally I do not believe Furneaux has found the right island. There are several things wrong with his solution to the problem. In the first place of course he looked for an island to fit the charts, casually dismissing the China Sea reference and totally ignoring the latitude and longitude. He admits the value of 9° 16′ is way out, suggesting that the '9' may have been preceded by a '1' to bring it somewhere near the 21° 40′ required. A glance at the chart shows that there is no room for, and never was, a figure before the nine. There is no doubt that '9 16″' are the original penned figures. This latitude as we know does cross the South China Sea.

Longitude is treated likewise: he tries to make '313' out of '?31° 30″'. There is no doubt about the last '0' in the group, that also was as originally penned.

I found it very strange that he should dismiss the obvious evidence of the latitude and longitude in such a way, and create evidence or theories to make them fit Providenciales, especially when looking at the problem of declination of magnetic north. On this subject he did the job properly by checking with the Geomagnetism Unit of the Institute of Geological Sciences. I checked Furneaux's figures with the help of the Geomagnetism Research Group and they tie in. In 1669 magnetic north was 2.5°E whereas today it is 7.6°W. Nothing like enough to make up the 40°+ difference we are looking for to bring it into line with Kidd's chart. Furneaux admits there is a large difference (25°) and leaves it at that!

Providenciales Island is only similar to the island depicted on the charts by the shape of its north coastline – a flattened out 'U'; the western part of the island is nothing like that on the charts. Also, as one can see, Providenciales is riddled with inlets and lakes, a few quite large – they cannot be ignored. So, even allowing for changes that may have taken place in three hundred years, I cannot find any convincing similarities.

From the observation of shape comparison alone, surely Providenciales cannot be the island.

There are also small islands immediately off the eastern end of the island, the nearest only a quarter of a mile offshore. Why didn't Kidd show these? He has shown an island or rock in the lagoon, so one would expect any others to be shown.

There is also the question of size, Providenciales is approximately 15 miles long. It is a lot easier to draw an island outline if the island is small, very difficult if the island is 15 miles long – unless it has a very high mountain giving one a birds-eye view. Whilst Kidd gives no clue to the island's size, I do not believe it to be as large as Providenciales, less than half that size I would think. The only possible clue to the island's size is in the margin on the 'key' chart: '360 yards V. R. NORTH'. With reference to the chart I would interpret that to mean: From the ANCHOR-AGE measure 360 yards and you will come to a valley running north. By scaling that would make the island approximately 1,000 yards wide through the valley and maybe 3 miles long. After all, it would be a lot easier to retrace your steps to a treasure on a small island; why trudge miles? As long as it is well hidden, there is no need to go far.

Besides the island's size, the 'lie' of the island is also wrong – by something like 40°. I do not accept that even three hundred years ago one would be that much out, and as seen, declination is only 9°.

On Providenciales, reefs stretch the whole length of the north coast. Kidd of course shows them (on all three charts) only around a central lagoon.

Kidd's charts show woods and trees; there are none on Providenciales. Furneaux is right in that during Kidd's time there were trees there. In fact, all the indigenous forest and bush on the island was uprooted and the whole island planted to cotton, and again later to sisal. Certainly any signs of caves or piles of stones could not have remained unexamined during the period of occupation by the American Loyalists in the eighteenth and nineteenth centuries.

A final question to be asked is: would Kidd have gone to the trouble of creating four or five documents – including the highly detailed charts – for just one bag of coins?

After all is said and done, Furneaux made two trips to Providenciales, firmly believing it was Kidd's island. Sadly, he passed away a few years later. Although no treasure was found on Providenciales he was quite happy with the outcome. He was a prolific writer of real life mysteries, enjoyed writing about them and solving them and we owe it to the memory of the man that he really believed his convictions, stood up and said so, and carried them out.

The Marshall Expedition

Thursday 10 July 1980 saw a full two page centre spread in the *Daily Star* with the headline: 'Treasure Island – How Captain Kidd's secret maps helped unlock a £70M riddle.' Further sub-titles said: 'Solved – the code that guards huge gold hoard' and 'Mystery of charts missing at museum'. Photographs showed Alan Marshall holding a large map with the caption: 'Alan's map, a complete picture of the secret island which he has built up from aerial photographs. Now all he needs is an adventurous backer.'

Another photograph showed the 'key' Kidd Palmer chart made to look 'olde worlde'.

The story described how Marshall – a part time maths lecturer – had broken the secret code and identified the island. It also told of how the British Museum has no record of the charts and gave a brief resumé of Kidd's life. Marshall's final quote in the article was: 'All I need is someone with a little money to be as convinced as I am.'

Some two years later, after a lot of money had been parted from the public, Marshall was the subject of a BBC TV Nationwide 'Watchdog' programme. Subsequently the Sheffield Fraud Squad became involved.

It was coincidental that I was starting serious research on this book at the same time. I had read two articles by Marshall in the magazine *Treasure Hunting*, and had noted various things that I was suspicious of and did not agree with; because of my interest I wanted to talk to him anyway. I might add that at that time the 'Watchdog' programme was yet to be seen and I was not aware of any 'con' – for want of a better word – at that time.

A letter to him went unanswered as did a letter to another member of one of his expeditions. I also tried to contact his main benefactor (£5,000) but all to no avail. At this moment (1986), Marshall, and anyone connected with his expeditions, seem to have vanished off the face of the earth.

Marshall's story was as follows. He deduced that as Kidd's father had been a Presbyterian minister, he (the father) would have had a knowledge of the Greek language; this would have been taught to the young Kidd. When Marshall realised this – 'Now I looked again at the charts, and what I saw shook me with excitement! Those strange signs and symbols all over the maps were not mysterious at all! They were Greek letters rho's, sigma's, omicron's and so forth.' He carries on to say that he then

Centre page of the *Daily Star*, Thursday 10 July 1980.

discovered an elaborate geometrical construction which focused on a single point on the island and also gave the true longitude and latitude of the island.

Now, having been at one time a design engineer and draughtsman, I do consider myself qualified in the area of geometry. To give an answer for latitude, an equation or geometrical construction is going to have to give us at least three figures (e.g. 9 16) and at the most four (say 36 45). Marshall's construction is also going to tell us N, S, E or W. It is going to have to be a very complicated geometric construction indeed to supply all of these answers. Besides, Greek letters are exactly that – letters – how are they transposed into figures? Another Marshall construction is also required for longitude. A point to mention here is that if Kidd had hidden the latitude and longitude within the chart, why show anything at all as he has done; there would be no need to. He showed the true position because only he was going to see the charts anyway. They were hidden in articles of his furniture for Kidd himself to recover.

If a single point (i.e. where the cache is) is identified on the island, two more straight line constructions are required for the transits: either that or something laid out on the ground indicating where the spot marked 'X' is. I would agree that this could be the significance of the three stumps and a triangle. However, elaborate geometrical constructions – no, there are none. Greek letters – there are none of those either. There are a lot of squiggles and funny shapes, some possibly resembling Greek letters I agree but they are merely the drawer's interpretation of how to depict reefs and rocks.

If symbols were employed to hide a code, they would more than likely have been astrological from the study of astronomy where, for example Υ represents 1 and Aries, and Ω represents 5 and Leo. But again the chart gives no symbols of astrology – except one or two that by accident are similar.

But those who do not know any better, and not in a position to argue, could be persuaded to go along with Marshall on his interpretation of the strange squiggles.

With reference to his article, Marshall comes unstuck before we get to the geometry. He implies that Palmer was particularly looking for Kidd relics because of the letter (see p. 155) Kidd wrote whilst in Newgate where he mentions 'treasure lodged in the Indies'. Palmer (wrote

Marshall) spent many an hour pouring over the dusty manuscripts and parchments in search of a clue to the whereabouts of the gold. That he certainly did, but *after* he found the first chart, not before. Palmer was a collector of pirate relics but he did not become particularly interested in Kidd until by accident he found the first chart.

Marshall also states that the four charts found depict two mystery islands, and that the map with the date 1669 was thirty years older than the other three, suggesting that the 1669 map was of a different island. Not true: in fact all the maps depict without question the same island. That the 'key' chart might be thirty years younger is pure supposition on Marshall's part to fit in with his idea that it was drawn at the time of the *Quedah Merchant* plundering. We have already seen that the 1669 chart found in the bureau was the same as the Hardy Chest chart; one only has to compare them all to see they are obviously of the same island.

Marshall had not done his homework on Nagashima either, as we have seen; what Nagashima did was to recover a Second World War deposit of Japanese bank gold, hidden by the Japanese and recovered in conjunction with the US Navy (see p. 189).

Having solved and plotted his geometrical construction which gave the true latitude and longitude of the island, Marshall goes on to say: 'Turning to a World Atlas, I saw at precisely that position a tiny dimensionless "dot".' 'Precisely', he says: we have already seen it was impossible to fix one's position with any sort of accuracy in the seventeenth century.

Subsequent to the initial publicity, Marshall found a backer to the tune of £5,000, enough – as he says – for a basic initial exploration. He, his wife, brother and backer left Heathrow in September 1980. During their visit – which terminated when the backer's money ran out – they went to the spot marked 'X' or focal point: nothing there. They looked down the hill and 'We suddenly stood rigid with astonishment at what lay before us. There, halfway down the hillside lay three tree stumps.' I think I would be rigid with astonishment to find three tree stumps still there after three hundred years!

Not only that but a large boulder was, yes, 55 ft. from the centre of these stumps! I wondered at this point why he should think that there should be anything 'from' the centre of the triangle. With reference to the key chart, how can anyone interpret what looks more like the word 'four' as 'from'? We can see how Kidd writes his r's: look at them in the word 'triangle' or 'under' on the Yunnan parchment. Whatever the word 'fou' is part of, it certainly is not the word 'from'.

Marshall's interpretation of part of the remaining instructions around the key chart were: 'from centre of triangle in L rocks'. The word 'from' has to be incorrect, even the word 'triangle' is suspicious the way Marshall interprets it; 'tri', yes, the rest of it is too spread out and disjointed. The word 'in' is also highly unlikely. I cannot see any resemblance to that word as it would have been written by Kidd in the faded marks that appear before 'L' – if 'L' is in fact what it is.

The Second Expedition

Marshall and his team returned home having plotted the stumps and an elaborate arrangement of stones around them. He could not finance another trip himself so he launched a fund-raising campaign. This included an invitation to readers of the article in the *Treasure Hunting* magazine to sponsor him.

He had decided to print an official maximum of 30,000 Agreements of entitlement at £5 a title. The publicity and subsequent funds brought in enough money for Marshall to return to the island in November 1981.

Two weeks were spent surveying the stumps and boulder site, no sense being made of any of it. Detectors were used and it was decided to excavate at a point some 120 ft. from the centre of the triangle, a spot on which a lot of the boulders apparently lined up. A large magnetometer signal had also previously been recorded here (magnetometers measure anomalies in the earth's magnetic field due to the presence of iron). After a few feet they hit solid bedrock but with the magnetometer signal as loud as ever.

Now, I dive with a group who are very knowledgeable about magnetometers; one of our group designs and builds them; we use them for underwater wreck searching. Magnetometers detect the presence of ferrous objects, i.e. iron, not silver, gold or copper. One would assume that any iron in a treasure cache would only be the reinforcing straps around the chests. The learned opinion of one who manufacturers magnetometers is that to give a large response on what is relatively a small mass of iron, the magnetometer would have to be as close as 4-5 feet. This point is important as we shall see.

Talking to local people, Marshall discovered the island had numerous caves and tunnels, with legends and folklore going back many generations about glowing lights emerging from the sea and slowly flickering out as they passed down into the caves. He deduced that the 'spirits' the natives had seen were really Kidd and his crew burying a treasure in one of the tunnels, the hiding place being where the large magnetometer signal was.

All the directions then lead to a place underground, not in the ground!

I would have thought that if treasure were buried at the end of a tunnel, then any directions for its recovery would be to the entrance of the tunnel. Distance to the cache would be given together with any appropriate directions and compass bearing should there be more than one passage.

Different passages there apparently were. Marshall narrowed the caves down to two groups in the northern part of the island, settling with a single network of five interlinked caves. A hundred yards in from the entrance they found a 3 ft. wide hole, this being the only way into the interior. They followed this due west for 210 yards to another cavern. Four passages led out. Following one of those going south, they travelled almost half a mile without encountering another branch off. They then came to another smaller cavern, apparently a dead-end because they made their way back to the previous cavern and took one of the other tunnels. They followed this passage for its entire length of almost a mile until, coming to two caverns, there, to their utter astonishment (and mine) they discovered writing on the wall in old blue dye. Those words that could be deciphered read: 'Alle Fletchers mene I sworn be done theire gold ive hid wythe skeletons.'

I would have expected to read something more like: 'Alle yea bl——y chests I be dragged alle this waye and be rightly nakered.'

Perhaps you have asked yourself the same question – 'Would I have dragged chests a mile or more underground?' You would need one hell of a ball of string! Who is really going to go to that sort of trouble – and then retrace it all above the ground to mark the spot where below lies the cache? With today's advanced surveying equipment it would be possible, but not three hundred years ago.

So Marshall had finally reached the spot marked 'X'! Alas no: pushing aside the skulls and bones littering the floor they found another small tunnel filled with rocks. Above it were the letters 'WK' and '1698'. He deduced that the gold lay in this tunnel and so set about clearing the rocks away. Five hours later they had penetrated about 12 ft. into the passage. At this point they had to give up through sheer exhaustion. That evening they plotted their progress on a chart and discovered that the cave lay 37 ft. from the excavation point above the ground, or 37 ft. from the treasure.

I mention now the earlier point regarding the range of a magnetometer. The *minimum* distance from the surface to the floor of a cavern underground, allowing for a reasonable thickness of overhead rock, would have to be 12 ft. In other words, it would be highly unlikely that a magnetometer could detect the presence of iron around a chest or even chests on the floor of a cavern at that depth.

However, having got this close, the team decided that to do the job properly they would need breathing equipment, pulley blocks and so on. So, amazingly, they abandoned the tunnel and came back home!

I am damned sure that if I had been that close I would not have come home. Five hours to clear the first third of the tunnel, so only ten to twelve hours to clear the rest to a fortune! I know what I would have done.

Coughing up for the Coffers

Having arrived home, Marshall embarked on another fund-raising campaign, seeking more sponsors for the final expedition. A sponsors' meeting at Sheffield City Hall on 23 January was a great success and raised £1,850 on the night; £1,400 of this from just two sponsors alone. Another article in the April 1982 issue of *Treasure Hunting* told the story to date and invited more subscribers to the scheme. (See pages 107 and 108 for Marshall's Sponsors/Subscribers offer and Agreement.) At that time, 1,150 people had sent in money.

In October that year the BBC TV 'Watchdog' (Nationwide) programme told the story and interviewed distressed couples who had lost their savings. Marshall it seems had done a 'runner' with the investors' and subscribers' money. All efforts to track him down since have proved unsuccessful.

To be fair, to those not knowing the true story of the charts, I suppose it sound like a good yarn, and who would not want to get a piece of the action and own a piece of pirate gold? To accumulate one had to speculate

Dear Sponsor

Thank you very much for your investment towards our imminent treasure expedition working from the British Museums famous 'Kidd-Palmer' Charts which I have been fortunate enough to be firest to solve.

Please find enclosed a copy of the expedition's Agreement which sets out the amount which you have invested, and guarantees you a share of all treasure found on the expedition.

The amount which you have invested is shown in the large brackets on the first page of the agreement.

Your small investment is very welcome. It will help us ever nearer to the £30,000 or so we need for the expedition.

However, if we fail to raise enough for the expedition by 31st December 1981, then we must cancel the expedition and return your investment to you.

You will be pleased to know however, that thanks to all our sponsors the total maount we have received is now well on the way towards our £30,000 target.

Every bit helps – thank you again for your small investment.

Please sign the agreement where I have signed, initial where I have initialled and return to us in the enclosed envelope as soon as possible.

Your Agreement could become very valuable. So not forget to sign the <u>COPY</u> and keep it for yourself.

If for any reason you have changed your mind and no longer wish to sponsor us, then wirte to us for a refund. Your money will then be returned within seven days.

<u>SPONSORS MEETING</u>

We also undertake of course, to keep you fully informed of developments by means of periodic bulletins. Sponsors will also be allowed access to confidential photographic material shot at the treasure site itself, and immediately prior to departure a meeting will be held at the City Hall Sheffield, where an audience of 2,200 sponsors at a time will be able to see exclusive movie film and slides, not only from the island but also the treasure-site itself. Also, for the very first time since I solved the charts and the first time in history, I shall discuss and reveal the actual *decipher*, which I have agreed to for the benefit of authors and historians, – though the island's location must remain the strictest most rigid secret. The actual treasure-site is already well protected through an agreement I have with the owners of the land.

The meetings will be covered by radio networks only, as cameras will not be allowed.

Alan Marshall

Treasure Hunter/Researcher.

Alan Marshall's subscribers'/sponsorship letter.

THIS AGREEMENT is made the   Day of   One thousand nine hundred and eighty two BETWEEN ALAN MARSHALL of 38 Linden Avenue Sheffield: ('the researcher') and the undersigned whose address is set out below ('the subscriber')

WHEREAS:

(1) The Reseracher has undertaken the necessary search to ascertain the approximate whereabouts of some gold bullion reputed to have been buried by Captain Kidd in 1699 ('the treasure')

(2) The Researcher has visited the site of the Treasure and has made the necessary arrangements with the site owner to enable the search for the Treasure to be made

(3) The sum of Thirty thousand pounds or such lesser amount as the Researcher considers enough to mount the Expedition ('the Contract Sum') is required to prepare the site and provide the necessary equipment, labour and administration costs to search for the Treasure ('the Expedition')

(4) The Subscriber will pay the Researcher the sum of (   ) Pounds ('the Fee') Towards the Contract Sum on the terms set out below

NOW IT IS HEREBY AGREED as follows:

1. THE Researcher will use the fee as part of the Contract Sum as long as the total fees paid to the Researcher amount to at least thirty thousand pounds of such lesser sum as the Researcher considers enough to mount the Expedition. If less than thirty thousand pounds or such lesser sum aforesaid is paid to the Researcher by the Subscriber and other Subscribers (who will all enter into a similar contract to this one) by the thirty first day of July One thousand nine hundred and eighty two then the Fee will be returned to the subscriber without interest.

2. If the Treasure is discovered and the Researcher personally realises more than the Contract Sum as a result twenty five per cent of the sum realised by the Researcher in excess of the Contract Sum will be paid to the subscribers in the proportion that the Fee bears to the total Fee received by the Researcher for the Expedition.

Marshall's 'agreement' sent to subscribers.

and it seems that the British are awfully gullible when it comes to parting with money.

Perhaps Marshall is on Kidd's island now, enjoying his ill-gotten gains of treasure. I myself would very much doubt it for the various reasons given so far. Marshall never found Kidd's treasure or seriously knew where it was. If he did, why has he not come forward to explain and reveal his geometrical constructions, Greek symbol theory and decipher as promised in the Agreement, so that someone with at least equal knowledge on the subject can give an opinion. I did not lose any money on his venture, so have no axe to grind; my interest lies in the charts themselves and the stories they have created. If you are reading this, Mr Marshall, I shall be pleased to give an unbiased opinion on your decipher and research.

Marshall's Island Identified

Marshall's island outline is I must admit very interesting, and except for the dog-bone shape to the north is a very good likeness to Kidd's chart. Examining the reproductions of Marshall's island I thought it had the appearance of a large island, too large to me to be the right one for reasons already explained in the Furneaux chapter, but I could be wrong.

I believe Marshall did the same as Furneaux: he looked for an island to fit the bill. In order to raise money from speculators he had to show evidence and convince people that he knew what he was talking about. Investing in a treasure island is no good unless one can 'see' the island, so Marshall had to find an island that closely resembled that on the Palmer charts. Having found one, he of course kept its identity and location a secret, not only to stop other treasure hunters following in his footsteps but also so that he could not be challenged on its location.

Being confident that Marshall had looked for an island to fit the charts I carried out a search myself to find his island. Having already studied the South China Sea area very thoroughly, I knew the island was not there. The most likely and acceptable area had to be the Caribbean Sea with the West Indies and the Bahama Islands to the north, an area some 2,000 miles wide and 1,300 miles deep, containing a couple of hundred likely islands. Using *The Times Concise Atlas of the World*, the search took me precisely one hour.

Marshall's island is Bonaire, one of the islands in the Lesser Antilles Group, which is in the south-eastern Caribbean Sea. Latitude 12° 10'N, longitude 60° 20'W; it is 24 miles long and 3-7 miles wide.

To accept Bonaire, as with Furneaux's Providenciales, we have to ignore the chart latitude, longitude and reference to the China Sea. Even if these are a 'blind', then with reference to the Bonaire map (p. 110) there are certain obvious features both on Bonaire and the 'key' chart

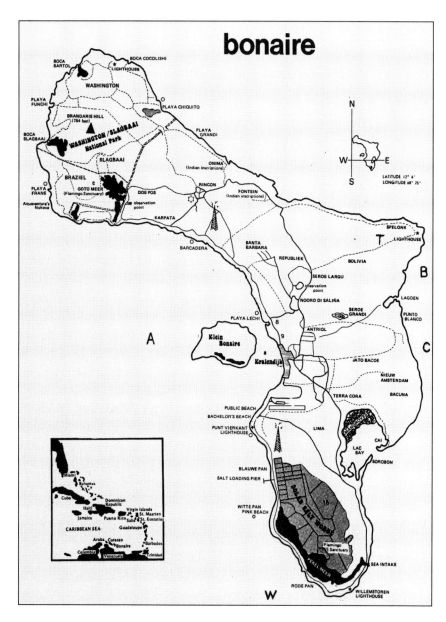

MAP M3: The island where Alan Marshall convinced many people that Kidd buried his treasure.

that must check out and coincide with each other for Bonaire to be Kidd's island. So that we can firmly prove or disprove this island, we must check them.

I needed to talk to someone of authority on the geology and geological history of Bonaire and I found that person in Dr David R. Kobluk, Associated Professor of Geology at Canada's University of Toronto. He is the acknowledged authority on Bonaire's reefs.

I put various questions to him regarding the geography and reefs of the island. In conjunction with the map, his reply to my letter was as follows:

Excuse my delay in answering your letter of May 22, but I had been in Bonaire until just a few days ago.

There is little known about Bonaire in any detail for the seventeenth century, but I will try to help answer your questions as well as I can.

The reef you ask about on the seaward side of Klein Bonaire (your 'A' on the map) has never existed (or at least not for millions of years); Klein Bonaire has in modern times always been fringed by reefs that encircle it only a few hundred feet from shore at the maximum.

There is a reef on the windward (eastern) side of Bonaire ('B' on your map), but it is a fringing reef and is very close to shore; it has, however, been there since the last ice age.

Lac Bay has been where it is, and was a bay, for at least 5,000 years. It has not been dry land since the last ice age.

There has not been a small island or rock at 'C' on your map since the last ice age. The sea floor on the east side of the island drops very rapidly from shore to 3,000 ft. depth. There is no possibility that in the past few thousand years there has been anything above water at the spot you indicate.

The shape of the Pekelmeer has changed, but this is due to the modifications made by the Antilles Salt Company. Certainly in the past few centuries it has had more or less the same configuration and size it has today.

The lakes (all salt lakes, by the way) at the northern end of the island almost certainly had been there 300 years ago, and probably in more or less the same configuration as today. This would be especially true of the Goto Meer. However, some of them, such as Boca Bartol and Funchi, and others on the north-east, north and east coasts are very close to the coast and are separated from the ocean by massive boulder (coral) ramparts deposited by hurricanes in the past. There is no doubt that some of them were connected directly to the sea as narrow, long bays in the past, but when is uncertain. Some of them *may* have been open to the sea in the seventeenth century, but we cannot be sure.

There are ballast stones cemented into the beachrock along the south-west coast (near the southernmost 'W' on your map), in loose rubble on beaches, and occasionally on the reef. Some of these may be from wrecks, but most are probably ballast dumped from salt ships while loading salt from the slave plantation in the nineteenth and eighteenth centuries. If there are any seventeenth century wrecks there, I am not aware of them.

There is no possibility that the area marked 'T' on your map was inhabited by turtles at any time in the past few thousand years. The sea cliffs all along that coast are 20-30 ft. high and vertical.

The entrance to the Lac Bay would have been a dangerous anchorage at any time. The seas there are very rough, and any attempt at anchoring there would have meant certain destruction. There is, however, a very narrow entrance into the quiet waters of the Lac Lagoon at its northern end that ships of the seventeenth century could probably have navigated. Everywhere else the Lac is cut off from the sea by a very rough water barrier reef. There is evidence, by the way, that seventeenth and eighteenth century sailors may have visited the area of the Lac – glass bottles from the period have been found well preserved in sand dunes at Sorobon, which is at the south-eastern tip of the shore of the Lac.

As an aside, the best all-weather anchorage for sailing ships around Bonaire has always been the area between Klein Bonaire and Bonaire, where modern Kralendijk is located, at Boca Slagbaai on the north-west coast, and along the south-west coast of Klein Bonaire. The very northern end of the island is a generally poor anchorage, although larger ships could probably have lain offshore reefed and under minimum sails, maintaining a headway, and had smaller boats navigate to shore to land at places like Bartol. On the north-eastern coast there are no safe anchorages, but again ships could have lain offshore, and had boats land on the rough water sand beaches in Boca Chiquitu and a few other spots like it. I cannot imagine, however, why they would want to do it, as there is no fresh water in the area, and no game, and the waves are chancy for even a small launch.

I hope that I have been of some help.

Sincerely yours,
David R. Kobluk
Associated Professor
Geology

From Dr Kobluk's letter, one can see that the major points of difference between Bonaire and the 'key' chart are:

1. The key chart shows a reef extending across the middle bay of the island; such a reef has never existed.

2. Where the anchorage is shown on the key chart, there is a large bay (Lac Bay) – 'a dangerous anchorage at any time'.

3. No possibility of turtles where indicated.

These, the other differences, the size of the island, the fact that even allowing for magnetic variation, north is approximately 40° East to that on Kidd's chart, all add up to convincing me that Bonaire is *not* Kidd's island.

End of the Trail?

The *Sunday Mirror* carried an article on 14 November 1982 titled 'Trail end for "Treasure" man'. The story described how the fantasy trail had come to a dead end for Marshall with no sign of a hoard of booty buried by Kidd, that Marshall had said he was close to finding on a *'tiny desert island'* (my italics). It was unlikely that the people who sponsored him to the tune of £30,000 would get their money back. Marshall, the article said, had told sponsors that his search had drawn a blank and that although the agreement entitled him to use any cash left over, he had not spent it on himself: if treasure is found, the sponsors would still get a share. One of his expedition members, cameraman Leo Kretscher, described Marshall's 'treasure island' as 'full of American holidaymakers, hotels, bars and restaurants'.

This newspaper article also mentioned that Bonaire was 'the' island but I came across the article after I had done my own research and written this chapter.

Richard Knight

I do not quite know what to make of Richard Knight. His is a very convincing story. After all, why would he tell me (eighteen months *before* his book came out) where *the* treasure island was? I would only do that if I had been there and removed the treasure which is exactly what Mr Knight says he has done. So he must be telling the truth – or is indeed a very good actor and story teller.

I first heard of Richard Knight and his exploits early in 1984, when newspaper reports told of his arrest on a Vietnamese island whilst searching for Kidd's treasure, and subsequent imprisonment in a Vietnamese jail.

He was released in August 1984 after fourteen months in jail, having been accused of spying. Because of my interest I obviously wanted to talk to him and through one of his benefactors who helped get together some of the £7,700 fine required to release him, I was able to contact Mr Knight and explain what I was doing.

It was during a telephone conversation that he told me that the treasure was buried on the island of Hon Tre Lon and that I would find the island on an old French chart number 3686, appropriately called 'Iles de Pirates'.

As mentioned earlier, the fact that he gave me this information suggests that he knew what he was talking about – knew the treasure was there and did not mind anybody else knowing now because he had removed it. This was a very strong point in his favour and I was much impressed with what he told me.

My first contact with him was early in 1985 when I received a letter, part of which reads as follows:

At the present moment I am not doing much on the next expedition though I hope in the next few weeks to be making a move and will certainly keep you informed on any definite developments and of course if there is a possibility of anything that may be 'up your street' I will certainly contact you. I will possibly be able to give you some further information *re* Kidd and my recent experience.

Very best wishes
Keep in touch
Sincerely
Richard Knight.

I have tried to keep in touch, but, Mr Knight is very elusive and I have not spoken with him since.[*] Fortunately, his book came out in the middle of my research and I was able to fill in the gaps in his story which is as follows:

Richard Knight and I obviously have a lot in common: he is also interested in mysteries, intrigued by the unusual and fascinated by stories of buried treasure, in particular Oak Island and Cocos Island, and of course we both have the same fascination for Kidd's charts. I can only write about them, expound my own theories and tell their story. Richard went one step further: he, like Furneaux, was in the enviable position of being able – after many disappointments – to pursue his own convictions. He put his (backer's) money where his mouth was, went after the treasure and found it – we are led to believe.

The story really starts in Hollywood in 1978. Knight was there as an unemployed actor, doing odd jobs and spending a lot of time in the LA library. It was here that he picked up Rupert Furneaux's book *Money Pit: The Mystery of Oak Island*. As mentioned before, many people believed Oak Island was the hiding place of Kidd's treasure and Knight came to the same conclusion as Furneaux: Kidd did not bury a treasure there.

Knight was intrigued with Anthony Howlett's story of the charts as re-told by Furneaux and formed an opinion that people were trying to find an island to fit the charts. Knight decided to accept Kidd's charts

---

* See p. 129

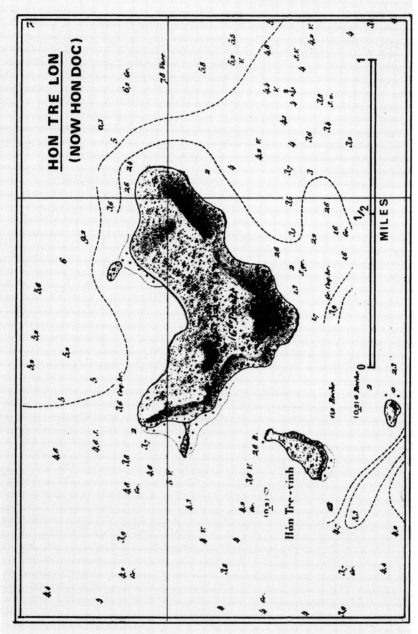

C7. The island in the gulf of Thailand where Richard Knight says he found Kidd's treasure. From the French (Service Hydrographique et Océanographique de la Marine) Chart no 3686 drawn 1887.

at their face value: in other words, if Kidd had written 'China Sea', he meant China Sea.

Knight spent some time pondering on the legend around the key chart and eventually deciphered it as follows:

360 yards Veer Right North 3 Stumps =
55 feet from centre of triangle in Left Rocks
20 feet East of Skeleton of hieb (? or lieb?)

He could not really make any sense of the last word.

Knight looked at the latitude and longitude, deciding longitude had to be 131° and then discovering – as we have in the 'Where?' chapter – that there are no islands there. It then appears that he did what he said he was not going to do – to ignore longitude and look for an island shape to fit the chart, as had Marshall and Furneaux. He thought the Spratley Islands likely (8° 39′N, 111° 55′E) but nothing there was the right shape.

He then realised that the accuracy by which sailors positioned themselves on the globe was likely to be a lot less in Kidd's time than today and he wondered if latitude and longitude had changed since then.

Knight then discovered the problems already related in the 'Where?' chapter. He mentions just one meridian in his book – Ferro – leaving the unsuspecting reader to believe this was *the* meridian. We know it could have been one of several.

He then decided that Kidd's island must lie in a strip between 5° and 15°N deep and 1,000 miles wide, between Burma and the Philippines. Again, if he had done his homework right he could have narrowed his search area down considerably to at the most ± 1° on 9° 16′, say between 8° and 10°N.

Many weeks followed with Knight pouring over charts at the University of Southern California.

In the meanwhile he decided to try and make some money out of the Kidd chart and advertised in the *New York Times*, offering authentic copies of Kidd's treasure map. He had no replies.

Finally, on the point of giving up, he came across the French Admiralty Chart No. 3686 and there he found it – Grand Pirate Island, in Vietnamese Hon Tre Lon (now Hon Doc). It was the right shape – true; it was in the right orientation – not true; it had the same north-south axis – not true; it had the latitude and longitude to an incredible degree – that is open to question. In fact Hon Tre Lon is at 10° 19′N, 104° 20′E, off the west coast of south Vietnam. (see p. 116)

The next problem was to find a backer. Tentative enquiries in his locality drew him to the conclusion that to the Americans that area (Vietnam) was still too political and the war was still very real in their minds.

He decided to go back to Brazil, an old haunt with friends that might be able to back him (one of his friends was Ronnie Biggs, the great train robber). He got no joy there so went on to Australia which he knew from his days as entertainments officer on a cruise ship. It was now September 1980. He took odd jobs including dishwashing and as a waiter. Here he met his backer Duncan Parrish and a deal was done whereby Knight's expenses would be paid, 8% would go to each crew member and the rest would be divided equally between Parrish and Knight.

Knight had in the meanwhile obtained NASA satellite pictures of the island, confirming its location.

They decided to try and get permission to visit the islands legally by posing as geologists prospecting for mineral rights and even invented a company, but they had no reply.

They next tried through a tour operator – to visit the beautiful islands off the coast of Vietnam; this time they received a reply – 'Regret . . . not permissible' etc.

The First Trip

Time flew to the middle of 1981 and they took the decision to mount an illegal expedition. Consultation and advice was sought with the Navy, Vietnamese refugees, ex-commandos and veterans of the Vietnam war.

A crew was found, also a suitable metal detector costing $700; they practised using that on the beach.

In September 1981 Knight arrived in Singapore to look for a suitable boat and to buy equipment. A week later he flew to Thailand where arms were easy enough to come by, but still no boat. So back he went to Singapore, and summoned the crew over from Australia but still could not find a boat, most owners being frightened off by the activities of modern pirates in the area of interest.

A couple of months went by and most of the crew dropped out one by one. Knight crossed into Malaysia to Kuala Trengganu on the east coast and found three boats in turn but was eventually let down with each one.

December came and his luck changed. He moved down the coast and managed to hire a typical fishing vessel for $750 a month, also a light 12 ft. dinghy with 4 h.p. outboard, a dinghy being essential for the shallow waters around Hon Tre Lon. He stocked up with fuel, equipment and food and phoned for the surviving crew member. Unfortunately his backer had disappeared, leaving the crew member without any funds to fly from Australia.

Parrish reappeared shortly after, but too late. Knight decided to look locally for a crew amongst the backpackers – single men tourists – with no responsibilities, but when they discovered they were required to go to a dangerous area off Vietnam, they too backed down.

Knight realised at this stage he would have to go it alone. He told Parrish, who decided he would come, but in the event, he didn't turn up either.

Going alone, Knight took about three days of uneventful chugging along before he came to his home base and anchored off the small island of Poulo Cici, about 8 miles south-west of Hon Tre Lon.

He rested all day and transferred all necessary equipment into the dinghy. Early in the morning, when any islanders would be sound asleep he cast off. About an hour and a half later he landed on the north coast of Hon Tre Lon. It was Thursday 21 January 1982.

Kidd's Treasure Island

Knight pulled the dinghy up the sandy beach to a thick line of vegetation and hid it under some bushes. He waited until dawn and with his camera and metal detector walked 200 yards along the beach. He then turned right and made his way inland through woods and vegetation, climbed up a hill for a better view and noticed a few native dwellings further along the coast.

He then set off in the direction indicated by the chart. There were no houses or people. He saw the little island in the bay – further north than on the chart – but no lagoons or reefs. There was also a stone-built jetty.

Knight reckoned that he needed to be about 200 yards from the north shore to be 360 yards from the 'ANCHORAGE', assuming his deductions of the chart were correct. He turned into a valley and walked 150 yards, reckoning he was now in the area of the three stumps. It was partly wooded with patches of thick undergrowth. There were obviously no signs of any stumps or grave. The area was enclosed, about 50 yards square sloping up on the west side to a hill. He climbed this and checked that the coast was clear.

Having assembled the three parts of the metal detector together he tuned out the 'ground effect' (electrical noise generated by the ground) and started methodically to scan the area. It was two hours before he received a large bleep registering over a large area about 4×3 yards.

Before going back the 400 yards or so to the beach to get his digging equipment, he went back up the hill to check that no one was around. Although he was obviously madly excited, the sobering thought struck him at this stage that buried here was nothing more than ammunition, buried by the French during their eighty-year occupation of Indo-China. However, nothing ventured nothing gained: Knight assembled the auger (corkscrew drill) and drove it down. Nothing. He went down 7 ft. Still nothing. He tried another spot 18 inches over and went down 4 ft. He pulled it out - there were chips of wood in the blade.

He started to dig and 4 ft. down hit something dark and solid. It was an old oak chest 3 ft. 6 ins by 2 ft. with metal bands. There was no inscription writing or identification, and a single lock was in the centre of the lid. He crowbarred the lock off and opened the lid. There before him were coins of every description, gold, silver and copper including pieces of eight: mainly European coins but also oriental, Chinese and Korean with dates mainly between 1650 and 1660. The chest was three-quarters full.

Whilst uncovering this chest he had noticed another about six inches to the left. Quickly he uncovered this which turned out to be the same size but with two locks; this chest was also three-quarters full but with works of art: vases, figurines, little buddhas and statuettes in jade and porcelain. Underneath were more gold and silver coins as before and beneath these about three dozen gold bars each about $5'' \times 1\frac{1}{2}'' \times \frac{1}{2}''$. These were lying on top of folded lengths of painted oriental fabric.

A run up the hill to the lookout revealed a couple of fishing boats and a few occupants of the huts further along the coast. Back at the hole

Knight wondered if there were any more chests. He opened out the hole either side and found another one, a lot smaller measuring only 18″ × 15″, but its contents the most valuable so far. It was full of jewellery: amulets, gold and silver rings and another small box containing cut diamonds and emeralds. Knight spent the next hour in a state of wonderful exhilaration just gazing at and examining his finds.

A check around the hole with the metal detector revealed no more signals so he carefully photographed the contents of each chest. Everything in the chests was put into sacks and taken to the boat, which took six trips. He returned and refilled the hole, leaving the empty chests in it.

A Second Cache?

Whilst waiting for darkness Knight decided to look for other caches. According to his calculations there should be one about 150 yards from the first. He paced it out and started searching with the metal detector. Soon he got a reading, this time over a larger area about six yards by four. The auger was once again put down in the centre and again wood chips were struck to the retrieved blade; this time bits of porcelain were also attached. 'I was in agony of temptation,' he says, but he knew it would take a couple of hours to dig. It would then be dark and he could not work by torchlight in case the local inhabitants spotted him. So he decided to play safe and get away with what he had so far.

When dark, he loaded up the dinghy, threw away the auger and tools and made his way back to the boat at Poulo Cici. There he hid the sacks in the hold and covered them with fishing gear, rope and old nets.

His return journey was much more eventful than the outward one. On the second morning a large Thai vessel with six men closed in and stopped him. They helped themselves to cartons of cigarettes, the cameras and a cash box containing the four rolls of film, but they did not search the hold.

He was stopped again later in the day. This time two men came aboard. Knight was ready and immediately handed over $200; they left without a word – or the treasure.

It was all getting too much for Knight, what with the added possible problem of patrol boats, more pirates and the problem of getting it all out of the country. He decided the only answer was to re-bury the treasure and come back for it when he was better organised. He sought out a wild area on the east Malayan coast where there were no villages, chose a place 40 yards from the waterline and buried the treasure 4 ft. down in a thickly wooded area. He decided not to write the exact location down in case anyone found his map.

Some days later he was back in Chennering, went to Kuala Lumpur and phoned Parrish in Australia. He was terribly excited and promised to work on plans to dispose of the treasure.

Back in Singapore, Knight wanted to get it all off his chest and contacted David Watts, the *Sunday Times* correspondent. He told him everything and was flown back to London to sign a contract with the newspaper. In the event the contract was never signed, Knight deciding he wanted to write his own story.

During September his backer phoned to say the problem of disposal of the treasure was solved and so at his expense Knight flew back to the Far East in October to renew the business deal. He was to get things going again in Bangkok whilst Parrish obtained a yacht and crew in Australia. They had decided to concentrate on what he had reburied – the ten sacks of treasure somewhere on the east coast of Malaya in the Gulf of Thailand.

It was now New Year 1983 and the yacht sailed for Singapore with a crew of three, but Knight's luck ran out again. One of the crew left and then disaster! Duncan Parrish, his backer for two years, simply disappeared. Knight had to start again; he found another backer in the Singapore Yacht Club, and told him that he had the Kidd maps and knew where to look. Knight had made his mind up at this stage to go back for the second cache.

Back to Bangkok again to look for a suitable boat – it was obvious he could not go back to Trengannu. More disappointments were to follow and it was May 1983 before he was finally in a position to sail, this time in a fishing vessel hired for $1,000 and with a crew of two Thai fishermen who were on 10% each.

During this time Knight was introduced to Fred Graham, a young American photo-journalist, who, interested in getting a good story, agreed to go along for a 40% cut. Knight still kept a secret the fact that he had already recovered one cache.

To go with the boat they hired a dinghy with a 35 h.p. motor and finally got going. Five days later they were anchored twenty miles south of Poulu Dama. The equipment was loaded into the dinghy and in the late afternoon they started on the forty mile (not sixty as in Knight's book) trip to Hon Tre Lon, leaving the two fishermen with the main boat to go and find more fuel.

After dodging various fishing boats they finally made Hon Tre Lon at about three in the afternoon and landed on the north-west tip. They dragged the boat up the beach and hid it under some bushes. They were elated but apprehensive, as they had been seen by some fishing boats as they neared the island. Knight hoped they had been mistaken for a Vietnamese patrol boat.

They unloaded the equipment and provisions and made a base camp, deciding – as it would soon be dark – to go for the treasure first thing in the morning. It was when it was dark and they were bedding down for the night that a torch was suddenly flashed on them and rifle fire let off. They found themselves surrounded by Vietnamese guards who rapidly tied their hands behind their backs.

'What are you doing here on this island?'

'Looking for buried treasure,' Knight answered. Of course they didn't believe him.

They were taken to the local guard house and from there by boat to Hatien on the mainland, then to Rach Gia. After a few months they were transferred to Saigon in July 1983, where Knight was kept for nine months, his total imprisonment being for fourteen months. Graham's fine was paid by his family and he was released before Knight. The two Thai fishermen were arrested a week after Knight's capture but eventually freed.

During his imprisonment and about a month after he was captured, Knight was taken back to the island. The Vietnamese wanted to know where the treasure was and told Knight to search for it. This he did but avoiding the obvious areas, but after a week they got fed up and took him back to prison. In the end he got so depressed that he asked to be taken back again to 'accidentally' find the second cache. This would prove he was not a spy and he should then be released straight away.But, they didn't take him up on his offer.

Could he really have found it?

Well, what has Richard Knight got going for him regarding his story?

First of all it is very readable, told in a simple honest way. One cannot help but believe it – one wants to believe it. There is no doubt he was imprisoned in Vietnam; I would like to think it was worth it. I was initially so convinced that I offered to accompany him on his return to recover his reburied treasure. He did not take me up on my offer, and now, having sat down and thought very hard over it all over a long period during my research, I am glad he didn't.

There are many questions that need to be answered and pondered over; there are mistakes in his book too. Let us look at them:

On the very first page of his book is a most suspicious and glaring error. The island of Hon Tre Lon is *not* in the middle of the South China Sea, or even in it. It is in the Gulf of Thailand. Kidd's chart of course refers to the China Sea.

Further on there is more evidence that Knight did not do his homework thoroughly – Palmer did not leave the charts to a solicitor friend who locked them in his safe, as we have seen in the 'Charts' chapter.

Possibly this is a typing error but 9° 18′ repeats itself several times. It should of course be 9° 16′.

Obvious questions I asked myself when reading his book are these:

Why hasn't he reprinted or redrawn the island of Hon Tre Lon as shown on the French chart 3686? Readers would want to see just how similar the island is to that on Kidd's chart.

As we know, Hon Tre Lon is in the Gulf of Thailand. In the seventeenth century it was known as the Gulf of Siam and Kidd would have known that. If Hon Tre Lon is *the* island, why should Kidd put China Sea?

Why hasn't Knight mentioned anything about Marshall, or Rupert Furneaux's expedition to Providenciales? Furneaux was convinced he had found the hiding place, surely of interest in any book about the search.

When he returned to Hon Tre Lon with his Vietnamese captors why didn't he take them to the site of the first cache and pretend to have found it for the first time? That would have convinced them he was telling the truth. The fact that the chests were empty – well, unfortunately someone had beaten him to it!

His interpretation of part of Kidd's writing around the margin of the chart cannot be right, as we have seen in the 'Charts' chapter. 'From' it cannot be; the rest of his interpretation is also questionable. He admits himself that he was in a valley whilst at the site of the cache. The chart shows what must be a valley, so surely 'V. R. NORTH' means Valley runs North, and not 'Veer Right North'. The compass north is pointing directly through the valley.

It is common sense to assume that where 'ANCHORAGE' is shown on the chart, that is where Kidd anchored: in other words it was deep enough there for his ship to anchor. If it was shallow, as the waters around Hon Tre Lon obviously are, then he would not have been able to get that close inshore.

On his second trip, why didn't he go at night to avoid detection as before? It was a bit tactless to go in broad daylight and that was his downfall.

The area in which the first cache was found was about fifty square yards, not very big when you consider it is only perhaps five yards by ten. Being a metal detectorist myself I know that an area of that size is easily covered in at the most half an hour, yet he says he took two hours. On top of that he says he received signals over an area 4 yds. $\times$ 3 yds., i.e. 12 sq. yds.: in other words, a quarter of the whole area. He should have found that very quickly.

I also do not understand why he did not publish the other Kidd/Palmer charts. Furneaux published two of the three in *Money Pit – The Mystery of Oak Island*. Unless he did not want the reader to see other evidence or clues on the charts that did not tie in with his theories. After all, the 'bureau' chart shows just one 'X', indicating just one cache and the Yunnan Parchment as we know – assuming it is genuine – refers to a cave.

He reports the island as having the right latitude and longitude to an incredible degree, with reference to what meridian? He doesn't say. From our own previous observations we know it could be one of several. He does mention Ferro, but this was the most western part of the Canary Island *not* the Azores as stated by Knight. Referring to our previous work in the 'Where' chapter, the nearest calculated longitude to Hon Tre Lon is position 3 at 105° 30'E. This is using one of the islands in the Azores as the meridian. If Kidd used this meridian then Hon Tre Lon is (just) within the allowed tolerance of error, but we also have to accept that the latitude of 10° 19' is within the allowed tolerance of error for latitude, i.e. more than a degree out, and I doubt that we should. Knight also says that the island has the same north-south axis which of course is wrong, it does not. As we can see from chart C7 (p. 116) Hon Tre Lon is lying exactly on a east-west axis, but Kidd's island is at an angle of 45° to this. Magnetic declination certainly has not varied that much in three hundred years, I know because I checked; Knight obviously did not. With thanks to British Geological Survey, Edinburgh: in 1700, at 10°N, 104°E, declination was – .72°. In 1986, at 10°N, 104°E, declination is – .33°: a difference of less than ½°. So we are looking for an island that still lies (within ½°) as Kidd drew it, if in this area.

Why didn't Knight look a bit further north? Just five miles away is Hon Dung, roughly the right shape and lying the right way. On older charts this island was known as Pirate du Nord.

One small point in his favour is his observation of the small island in the lagoon which he says is further north than the island shown on the 'key' chart. In fact the island *is* shown further north on the 'skull' chest chart. He also admits there was no reef, and it would have been easy to say there was – as shown on the chart. Of course, he may be being just very clever.

Finally we come to the evidence – there is none. Conveniently – or inconveniently, depending on your point of view – the box containing the films was stolen. Conveniently Duncan Parrish vanished – we cannot check anything with him. It is no good asking Fred Graham either; he did not see any treasure. He apparently said later of the ill conceived adventure: 'It was pretty stupid.'

When Knight was stopped by the Thai pirates, why didn't they search his boat, particularly as he was a westerner? I would have been curious. If they had, and found the treasure, they most certainly would have killed him. Knight would not have had a story (or book) to tell then, would he?

The thing that really bothers me though is how on earth does he hope to retrieve the re-buried treasure or return to Hon Tre Lon now that he has told his story and the whole world knows? He is going to be watched like a hawk. Apparently a writ is out for his arrest in Bangkok and anyway, the treasure – if it does exist – legally belongs to the Vietnamese Government.

At risk of boring the reader, I must repeat some previous observations: Why has Knight ignored the 'skull' chest chart? It gets a brief one-line mention in his book, yet is surely as important as the 'key' chart. It is not discussed or reprinted. Perhaps this particular chart was too much of a problem and therefore easier to ignore. If I had found the treasure the way he did, I would try and 'work back' through the instructions by relating them to actual observations and measurements on the island. This would be added proof to my claim by showing how the instructions on the charts were to be interpreted.

The island of Hon Tre Lon would to my way of thinking have been the priority chart drawing to show. I eagerly looked through the section of 'plates' in his book but it was not there. A reprint of a nineteenth century chart of the Gulf of Siam, yes, but the islands are shown as miniscule dots. Why has he not supplied the reader with the only chart diagram that he would really be interested in? I am able to do it, as my readers can see. It wasn't easy, but I managed to obtain a copy of the old French chart. Why didn't you, Richard, or your publishers? Was it because that chart perhaps reveals too much detail and might spoil a good story? I don't know: it is a good story and I must admit, the island outline is remarkably similar to that shown on the Kidd charts. I would have plumped for it myself except that the island is lying 45° out of position. Another dissimilarity is the small islet to the west of the island not shown on the 'key' chart; one would expect it to be as the one to the north of the island is shown. The Kidd charts also all show a definite indentation at the north-east end of the island marked 'NORTH SA E' on the 'key' chart. This end of Hon Tre Lon is smooth and well rounded, certainly no cliffs or jagged coastline here. There is no (smugglers) cove where indicated on the 'key' chart; the hill here appears to slope right down to the water's edge. There are no reefs guarding the south of the island as shown on the 'key' and 'skull' charts, no lagoon on the north side either with rocks. There are five small hills shown on the French chart of the island. Three are shown on the 'key' chart, two on the 'skull' chart.

The shape of the southern coastline of Hon Tre Lon is remarkably similar to the charts and except for Smugglers Cove almost exact, too exact really to be true. As previously discussed, it would have been impossible three hundred years ago to obtain such a close likeness without modern surveying equipment and/or satellite photography. If Hon Tre Lon is the right island, it mystifies me that Kidd's chart ('key' chart) almost exactly depicts the right shape. Having said that, the small islet off the north coast of Hon Tre Lon has facing it an obvious promontory not shown on the Kidd charts. Hon Tre Vinh, the island less than a quarter of a mile south-west, is not shown on the Kidd charts. This is adjacent to the area where 'ANCHORAGE' is shown. It is obvious from the French chart that it is very shallow here, between 1 and 2 fathoms. There is certainly no room or water deep enough here today for a sailing ship to have a safe anchorage; perhaps there was three hundred years ago.

Yet Hon Tre Lon was known as Grand Pirate Island; there has to be a good reason for that. Knight could be right and, as said before, I hope he was. Most of the similarities are there, and the size is right – about a quarter of a mile across – but I keep coming back to the main stumbling block: all the Kidd/Palmer charts show north to be 45° East to that of Hon Tre Lon, which is lying on almost an exact east-west axis. Perhaps also, more importance should be placed on the fact that the Kidd/Palmer charts show a lagoon and reefs, even mentioning coral. Knight's island has none of these important qualifying features.

Coded Messages

REGRET DELAY. CONFECTIONERY NOW MOVED TO NEW STORE. MANUFACTURERS REPS. MOVED IN. PHONING TUESDAY PM OR WED AM REQUEST G R ADDRESS OR PHONE NO, SILENCE STILL ESSENTIAL. HAVING A HEAT WAVE. PLEASE ACKNOWLEDGE WITHIN THE HOUR. CAPTAIN WILLIAM KIDD. TKS.

The above is a copy of a telex sent by Richard Knight to the publishers of his book. It appeared in the January 1987 issue of *Treasure Hunting* magazine. Richard, by his conspicuous absence, we assume returned to Thailand to retrieve his reburied cache. His publishers have apparently received a number of coded progress reports from him. The one above seems to signify the successful retrieval of the cache.

Knight obviously cannot bring all the treasure back to this country and will have to dispose of it somehow from wherever he is. But to convince the doubters, why has he not taken colour photographs of the complete hoard and sent copies back here for everyone to see? After all, because of his book it is not a secret; he would have nothing to lose, would gain a lot more publicity and would add some credibility to his claim.

Sadly, Richard seems to have got himself in something of a mess again. On 4 April 1987, I received a collect call from him in the middle of China of all places. He had turned to me as a last resort to see if I would help get him out of some financial difficulties. In return he promised me the *true* story. I thought about it and decided I would help him. Why? you may ask, if I do not believe his story. For a start, he promised to repay me, and, even if I do not see him or my money in the future, I look on it as payment for a good story.

It took several attempts by phone to reach him, and before I told him I would help, I asked him a few questions. The first was, 'Have you really found it?' He hesitated for a couple of seconds before saying 'Yes, I have,' For obvious reasons, on the phone he couldn't say too much in answer to some of my other rather pointed questions. He did promise me though that when he organised another expedition to retrieve the cache, I would be invited along.

I subsequently cabled some money out to him and now await developments. It will be interesting to see what – if anything – does develop.

Why is he in the middle of China and why is he out of cash? If his story is true, he should of course be a very rich man by now. I think that maybe my earlier conclusions may be correct.

At the time of going to press (1995) I have yet to receive a thank you from Richard for sending him the cash he required (he promised to write to me), nor have I had the promised invitation to help retrieve the treasure.

The Edmunds Expedition

So everyone looks for an island to fit the charts; it does not matter where it is as long as the shape is right. I may as well have my two-pennyworth, so to speak, and I reckon my island fits the charts better than anything seen so far. I didn't even have to look for it, but came across it quite by chance.

Whilst researching this book I happened to open a book called *Cast-away*. I nearly fell off my chair, as staring at me from the inside cover was Kidd's island. I couldn't believe it; it was almost identical to the island depicted on Kidd's charts. The reefs north and south were there, the island or rock in the lagoon and even the rock off the south coast shown on the 'skull' chest chart. Small hills are also shown in their right

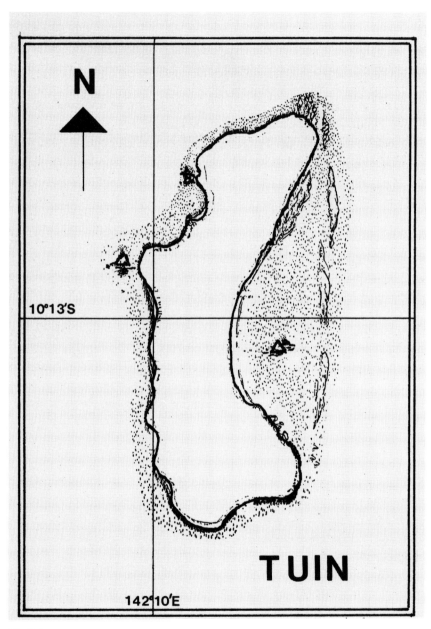

C8. Tuin.

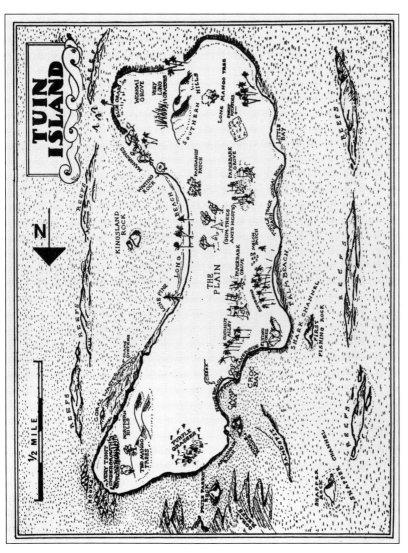

C8a. Tuin Island.

place at each end of the island, even Turtle Beach where turtles are mentioned on the Kidd chart. The size is about right as well, two miles long. The similarity is amazing.

My island is Tuin Island, in the Torres Strait between the north coast of Australia and New Guinea, at Latitude 10° 13'S and Longitude 142° 10'E. *Castaway* by Lucy Irvine (Victor Gollancz Ltd.) tells the story of how she and a companion spent a year (voluntarily) on a desert island; it has now been made into a film.

To get sponsorship and backers I of course have to convince them that Tuin is 'the' island, so how do we make the chart information fit Tuin? Well, it is quite easy and we do it like this:

Tuin lies at 10° 13'S, 142° 10'E, as shown in the diagram, the opposite way round to Kidd's island, but Kidd of course drew his island the wrong way around to throw everybody off the scent. 'TURTLES' means 'turn turtle' or upside down; do this to Kidd's chart and it's lying the same way as Tuin. We have to do the same to the compass rose of course, south now becomes north and LAT 9.16 N becomes 9.16 S. It is only 1° out but acceptable for three hundred years ago. Longitude of course will not change; the fact that it is 11° out we know was easily possible for that time. Would Kidd have sailed these seas? Of course. The Torres Strait separates the Coral Sea to the east and the Arafura Sea to the west, so separating the West Pacific Ocean and the Indian Ocean. It has been a principal waterway for over three hundred years for ships entering and leaving the Pacific. The Spanish regularly plied the area. Kidd would have been no stranger to this part of the world.

So there we have it. Tuin *must* be Kidd's Island. Mustn't it??

All monies for an expedition will be gratefully accepted. I do not guarantee to find the treasure of course – Kidd may have collected it – but I do guarantee you that I will have a good time.

Perhaps I am being a little over sarcastic, but I think I have demonstrated how easy it is for anyone to find Kidd's island – and convince others he is right.

Chapter 4

Kidd's Life, Travels and End

The Early Years

The details of parentage, birth and greater part of the life of William Kidd are lost in obscurity. Until 1688 when Kidd was about forty-three years of age, nothing really definite or reliable is known about him. The last ten years of his life, the years which brought him everlasting infamy and erroneously established him in popular regard as the most celebrated pirate of all time, are very fully documented and known in considerable detail. Unfortunately, it is the earlier period of his life we would like to know a lot more about.

Anthony Howlett accounts the early years of Kidd's life as follows:

He was born in Scotland, probably in 1645 at Greenock, then a mere fishing village on the River Clyde. His father is said to have been a Minister of Religion, but this seems doubtful. He appears to have received a good education, for he could read well and write a good letter in a clear legible hand – no small accomplishment in those days. When he was still very young he moved to Leith, the port of Edinburgh. (Anthony Howlett has an oak chest given him by Mrs Dick which has an engraved plate on it which reads: Willm Kidd, Leith Scotland.) He was clearly bred to the sea and it seems that at about the age of fourteen, he sailed before the mast to the West Indies. During the following ten years he appears to have gained wide experience on the seas in various parts of the globe, making several voyages to North America and India. It is also probable that he sailed to the East Indies and perhaps even ventured into the South China Seas. Some time during this period he rose to command his own ship, the *Adventure Galley* – not to be confused with the ship of the same name he commanded over thirty years later.

A tradition, recorded in 1825 and not made known during his trial in 1701, relates that as a young man Kidd traded with the Buccaneers, the notorious pirates who acted between about 1630 and 1670 as England's unofficial Navy in the Caribbean in the long undeclared war with the Spaniards. A document preserved at the Public Records Office in London implies that Kidd knew and 'resented' Henry Morgan, the Buccaneers' Admiral. It is possible that Kidd was a member of the famous Brotherhood taking part in Morgan's expeditions and gaining a share of the loot. Kidd was credited in 1695 with knowing most of the pirates and being acquainted with their haunts.

Another author says: 'He was pressed into the Navy in 1673 and subsequently served in the Dutch Wars on the flagship *Prince Royal*. His creditable naval record stood Kidd in good stead and by 1680 he had left the Navy and purchased his own brigantine.' I would be interested to know where that information came from, but that same author says that out of Kidd's marriage two children were born. The first, a daughter, died in infancy, while the second, a son, died in 1715. So perhaps the earlier information is also incorrect.

We first hear of Kidd officially in 1688. It is on record in New York that he was purchasing 56 Wall St. from Sarah Bradley Cox, who became his wife three years later.

At this time Kidd was probably engaged in legitimate trading between New York and the West Indies, possibly also doing some privateering against the enemies of England. Indeed, he placed his vessel, the *Blessed William* (which he had captured from the French and renamed) at the disposal of the Governor of the Leeward Islands and saw action against the French on at least two occasions. He suffered the first of one of his many misfortunes here: after the French had been driven off, he was ashore at St Martins when his crew turned pirate and made off with his vessel. One of the members of that crew was Robert Culliford, about whom we will hear more later. In appreciation of the gallant services rendered by Kidd, the Governor (General Christopher Codrington) presented him with another ship which he named *Antigua*.

1691 sees Kidd in favour again. He was voted the sum of £150 by the local Council Assembly for valuable services. He had opposed Jacob Leisler, who had tried to seize Fort James and set himself up as governor. Kidd helped Major Ingoldsby to land his troops to put down the Leisler rebellion.

In May of that same year he married the widow Sarah Oort, and for the next few years little is known of his movements. It would appear he was a stout citizen, well liked in the neighbourhood. When he left New York for London in the summer of 1695 to trade, the governor of New York declared him to be 'on the whole a gentleman and neither in his domestic relations nor his personal history previous could be said aught against him.'

During this time, England was at war with France; piracy was also taking a huge toll on unprotected merchant ships. The Navy was sorely stretched and obviously could not be everywhere. Merchant fleets sometimes had to wait five months for escort vessels before they could sail. Any pirate who knew his job knew that the best loot was in the lucrative trade going from India to the Red Sea. Earlier the pirate Avery had taken a ship belonging to the Great Moghul, the Ruler of Delhi. This ship – the *Gang-i-Sawai*, was a formidable vessel carrying over a thousand passengers, crew and soldiers. Amongst them were high-ranking officials of the Great Mogul's court and a number of Turkish girls. The people on board were treated with terrible barbarity. It was considered normal in those times to brutalise the dark skinned 'heathens'. Men and women alike were tortured to reveal the whereabouts of their valuables. The men were then butchered and the women raped, some of them dying of their resulting injuries. Even the aged wife of a high-ranking official suffered the same fate. Rather than submit to the pirates some of the women threw themselves overboard, whilst some killed themselves. A huge treasure was also taken.

This one action put the entire business of the East India Company in jeopardy. The Moghul threatened vengeance and declared he would come with an army and drive the East India Company from India. Fearful for their trading rights, this huge and powerful monopoly put pressure on the government to send a man-of-war. The London merchants were also complaining as it was affecting their trade.

Something had to be done about the piracies in the Indian Ocean but what? The Admiralty had no ships of war to spare. It was whilst discussing the complaints of the London merchantmen with his council of Advisors that we are told that the King suggested, 'Why not make it a private undertaking?'

This of course was an age of privateering, a well recognised and respectable profession for the adventurous which had existed for many centuries. The privateer was simply a private ship whose owners or master held commissions of reprisals, called letters of marque, issued from one government to capture and plunder the ships of another. The privateer was the King's left hand at sea legally commissioned as a naval auxiliary. The King usually took one tenth of the prize value. The crew were not paid; they signed on 'No purchase, no pay' without set wages, but each had a share of the booty. Letters of marque were often granted freely, in peace or war, either by the Sovereign or by his representative abroad and their terms were liberally interpreted. In fact privateering was actively encouraged, for it was profitable to all concerned and also provided a valuable reserve of ships and trained seamen to supplement the official navies.

The relationship between privateering and piracy was therefore very close and was often well nigh indistinguishable. In fact, whether a particular person was a privateer or a pirate frequently depended upon which side he was on and even in one's own country much depended upon the attitude of the authorities and political considerations at the time. If one was lucky and the loot extensive one might be knighted, if unlucky one was hanged.

In the Wrong Place at the Wrong Time.

This then was the background to the beginning of Kidd's end. The King's idea languished for a while until one Robert Livingston, a prominent New Yorker (and friend of Kidd's), called on Lord Bellomont at his London home. Bellomont was the recently appointed Governor of New York and New England with express command to clear out that 'nest of pirates': those who used the American colonies as a base for their depredations in the Indian Ocean.

One of the outcomes of their meeting was that they should back the King's idea. Livingston was asked by Bellomont if he could suggest a suitable commander for the venture, and said he knew of just the man who was in London at that very moment – Captain William Kidd. Bellomont agreed to make all the arrangements and find backers. Livingston was to enlist Kidd and make the practical arrangements. Bellomont enlisted as financial backers for the venture four of England's most powerful men: The Duke of Shrewsbury, Secretary of State; Sir John

Somers, Lord Keeper of the Great Seal; Sir Edward Russell, First Lord of the Admiralty; and the Earl of Romney, Master General of Ordnance. These gentlemen were pleased to put money into the venture, provided their names were not mentioned. They saw it not so much as an international act to placate the East India Company but as a means of making an awful lot of money.

When first approached Kidd was reluctant, but Livingston and Bellomont put great pressure on him, suggesting it would be disloyal to refuse the King's commission, also suggesting that he might have trouble getting his ship (the *Antigua*) free of Customs to return to America.

In October 1695, Bellomont, Livingston and Kidd signed the Articles of Agreement. With such powerful backers and armed with a King's commission Kidd may have thought himself safe. He and Livingston were forced to put up one-fifth of the cost of the venture, to enter into bonds £10,000 and £20,000 respectively, and to pay its entire cost if Kidd failed to gain sufficient booty to recoup the backers. On the other hand, Kidd was to receive the ship as a bonus if the 'take' of the cruise was more than £100,000. Kidd was permitted to offer his crew a share of the booty not exceeding one-quarter of the total, on the usual basis: 'No purchase, no pay'. That was an invitation to turn pirate for they could earn nothing unless Kidd took prizes. Livingston and Kidd were promised one-tenth of the distributable booty. Kidd was forced to sell the *Antigua* to raise his share of the cost.

In December 1695, the *Adventure Galley*, as he named his ship, was launched at Deptford. She was of 287 tons, carried 34 guns and was flush-decked, frigate rigged with a bank of 23 oars each side on the lower deck (hence the term 'galley').

Kidd sailed with two commissions: one known as the Great Seal Commission was dated 26 January 1696. It is from King William III and has the Great Seal of England affixed to it. It is addressed to ' . . . our trusty and well beloved Captain William Kidd, Commander of the *Adventure Galley* . . . ' The commission charges him to apprehend pirates, specifically mentioning four: Captains Tew, John Ireland, Thomas Wake and William Mace (or Maze). The privateering commission or Letter of Marque, dated 11 December 1695, charges that Captain Kidd 'set fourth in a war like manner and therewith by force of arms to apprehend, seize and take ships, vessels and goods belonging to the French King and his subjects within the domain of the French King . . . '

The Voyage

This account of Kidd's voyage until he returned in chains in April 1700 is obviously not a full detailed account; it would take a very large volume to do that, and besides, it is already well documented elsewhere. One of the best books I can recommend is *The fateful voyage of Captain Kidd* by Dunbar Maury Hinricks (1955). I do not claim that mine is an exact and true account because even the best reference works on Kidd's voyage differ on some points, dates and places, and besides, this book is about the charts and the searches resulting from their discovery. However, to make this book as complete as possible one has to give all the facts appertaining to the subject including what is known about his travels. A condensed version is therefore presented which includes all that is of particular interest to us.

Kidd sailed on 1 March 1696. Going down the Thames he failed to salute a Navy yacht at Greenwich. The yacht fired a shot to make him show respect. Kidd, with his King's commission, obviously thought himself above that and his crew responded by slapping their backsides in derision. Shortly after, they did the same thing to another Royal ship. The respective captains were furious and complained bitterly to the Admiralty. Their Lordships were none too pleased at this slur and gave orders to board the offending vessel. Shortly after, at the Nore, where HMS *Duchess of Queensborough* was at anchor, a press gang from that ship boarded them and forcibly carried off about seventy of Kidd's men, replacing them only after an intervention by Admiral Russell. Most of the replacements were a rag-tag collection of Navy rejects.

They called at Plymouth on the way west and he put ashore the worst of the crew that had been forced on him. He left there on 23 April, arriving in New York in July where he sold a French fishing boat he had taken as a prize on the way.

At New York Kidd produced his commission under the Great Seal of England and recruited eighty-five seamen to bring his crew once again up to 150 men. Many of the new men were pirates whom he had been commissioned to seize. Fletcher, who was still Governor, described them as men of desperate fortune. He told the Lords of Trade: 'It is generally believed here that they will get money one way or another, and that if he [Kidd] misses the design named in his commission he will not be able to govern such a herd of men under no pay.' If anyone was qualified to predict the behaviour of such a crew it was governor Fletcher of New York. Livingston, who was back in New York, wrote that many of Kidd's men were mutinous but he still hoped for a good voyage.

Kidd recruited his crew under the same articles as previously, i.e. 'No purchase, no pay' with awards of the accepted number of pieces of eight for loss of life and limb.

One of these new men was the former pirate Darby Mullins. He had served with Culliford, who had sailed off with Kidd's ship the *Blessed William* some seven or eight years before. Mullins, who was condemned and hanged with Kidd, claimed in extenuation for his crimes that 'he had not known but it was very lawful to plunder ships and goods belonging to the enemies of Christianity', meaning the Moslem merchants who traded in the Indian Ocean. With Kidd sailed also his young brother-in-law, Samuel Bradley.

Kidd dallied in New York through the summer, loath to embark on an enterprise which promised little reward and certain peril. After two months he again set sail on 6 September, and arrived off the Cape of Good Hope on 12 December, having come by the Madeira, Canary and Cape Verde Islands. Off the Cape, he fell in with a Navy squadron under Commadore Thomas Warren who had apparently lost a lot of his men and asked Kidd if he could spare him some of his. Kidd said he would but slipped away under oars in the night. At the Cape he ordered Captain Giffard of HMS *Sydney* to lower his pennant which he flew as senior Captain and threatened to board him if he did not. When Giffard threatened in return to board the *Adventure Galley* Kidd pretended to have been only joking. To prove that his intentions were absolutely honest he invited the Captain to dinner. This created further suspicion for it was a common trick of pirates to render their prey defenceless by enticing away their officers.

In March 1697 he landed at Mohela Island in the Comoros and had the ship careened (i.e. hull cleaned). About fifty of his men died here of disease caught from the crew of a sloop they had taken earlier.

It was now a year since starting the voyage and they had not earned a penny; provisions were low and the new recruits were beginning openly to advocate piracy. A month later they again set sail for the Red Sea and in July lay in wait amongst its islands. They were waiting for the big convoys of Arab merchant ships that passed this way from Mocha, chief port of the Yemen coffee trade. Moorish ships were regarded as fair prey to captains of Christian privateers.

On 14 August, a fleet sailed out of Mocha and Kidd went after it. The fleet was neither pirate nor French; some ships flew English or Dutch colours. Edward Barlow, Master of the *Sceptre*, one of the well-armed escorts, reported Kidd showed no colours, only a red broad pennant which Barlow took to mean surrender or no quarter given. Kidd appeared to have singled out a large Moorish merchant ship. Barlow let Kidd come on and was nearly abreast before he hoisted up his English colours and fired a few shots. Kidd came alongside the Moor and fired a broadside, hitting her in the hull and sails. The *Sceptre* immediately gave chase. Kidd retreated under sail and oars. By next morning the *Adventure Galley* was out of sight.

By the end of August he was off the Malabar coast of India. He met with a small Moorish barque manned by Moors under an English captain named Parker and a Portuguese mate. Kidd's crew boarded her, took some stores and the two Europeans prisoner, the Portuguese mate to act as an interpreter. It appears that Kidd then uncharacteristically abused these two – or it may have been two of the Moors. However, to tell the whereabouts of any gold or silver on board they were hoisted up by the arms and drubbed with a naked cutlass. There was apparently no treasure aboard.

In September Kidd put in for water and wood at Karawa, a port on the Malabar coast. By now word had spread of his activities and two English officers of the East India Company boarded and demanded the release of Parker and the Portuguese mate (who were both locked in the hold). Kidd denied their existence and the two officers left. Two of Kidd's crew, not liking the turn of events, jumped ship here and later made depositions to the East India Company saying that Kidd was 'going on an ill design of piracy'. Two Portuguese ships of 44 and 20 guns were sent after Kidd who fought off the smaller vessel, losing ten of his men. His ship suffered damage before he was chased off by the larger vessel.

Edward Barlow of the Mocha convoy reached here about a month later and soon the whole coast was talking about the pirate chaser who had turned pirate.

At Calient, Kidd was refused wood and water by the local East India Company. He continued his cruise, wandering on across the empty ocean. In the Maldives they stopped to water and take on wood. One of the crew was murdered by the natives whilst ashore and Kidd sent more men ashore to take revenge. They plundered boats and burnt houses; they tied one of the natives they had captured to a tree and shot him.

Early in November they overhauled a cargo ship sailing northwards along the coast. There was great excitement on board the *Adventure Galley* at the prospect of a big prize at last. But when they came close to the merchantman Kidd saw she was the *Loyal Captain* flying English colours, outward bound from Madras to Surat, Captain Howe commander. His papers were in order and Kidd let her go. William Moore, the gunner on the *Adventure Galley,* proposed they attack the vessel anyway. Kidd refused to consider it. 'I dare not do such a thing,' he said. This infuriated the crew who brought out their small arms and prepared to go over in the longboat. Kidd said, 'If you desert my ship you shall never come aboard again.' The mutiny fizzled out and they remained on board.

About two weeks later Moore and Kidd clashed again. Possibly Moore was still sore at being denied a big prize. Angry words were exchanged, Moore claiming Kidd had ruined them when they could easily have taken Howe's ship and never been the worse for it. Kidd called Moore 'a lousy dog' and Moore answered, 'If I am a lousy dog, you have brought me to it, you have ruined me.'

'Have I brought you ruin, you dog?' replied Kidd, 'You are a saucy fellow to give me these words.'

With that, Kidd seized an iron bound bucket and struck Moore on the side of the head with it. Moore died the next day.

At the end of November they sighted a sail. They bore down on the vessel and Kidd ordered French colours run up – an often used ruse to make the stranger do the same: this she did. The ship was the *Rouparelle* (sometimes referred to as the *Maiden*) bound for Surat with a cargo of cotton, quilts and sugar. The captain was Mohammedan, two officers Dutch and the crew Moors. The captain produced a French pass indicating that she sailed under French auspices. Kidd believed this made the *Rouparelle* a legitimate prize. He turned the crew loose and sold the cargo ashore for cash and gold, which he shared with his crew – a contravention of his contract, which said that spoils were to be divided at the end of the voyage. He renamed the captured ship *November* and took her along with a prize crew aboard.

Kidd had, unknowingly perhaps, committed piracy. The French pass was meaningless; shipowners routinely obtained a pass from every nation operating in the area. The Captain of the *Rouparelle* would have had others in his possession and his ship was actually Indian owned.

Three days after Christmas 1697 they seized another Moorish ketch and took some of her cargo of candy and coffee. Early in January 1698 they plundered a Portuguese ship, making off with gunpowder, opium, rice, iron, beeswax and butter.

It was 1 February when they found the *Quedah Merchant* making heavy weather off the Indian coast. Kidd pursued her for four hours, fired shot across her bows and hoisted the French flag. She was found to be a 500-ton merchantman outward bound from Benegal to Surat with a rich cargo of silks, muslins, sugar, iron, saltpetre, guns and gold coin. She was commanded by an Englishman named Wright.

Kidd ordered the captain aboard, but it was not Wright who arrived but an old French gunner posing as the captain. On boarding, to the Frenchman's great surprise Kidd ran up the English flag and claimed the merchantman as a prize. The old gunner handed over a French pass (as with the *Rouparelle*, a French pass did not make her a French ship). The Armenian owners were on board and offered to ransom the ship for 20,000 rupees, nearly £3,000, an offer Kidd scorned as insufficient. Instead he sold some of the cargo ashore for between £10,000 and £12,000 and divided the proceeds amongst the crew. He then sailed for Madagascar with both the *November* and the *Quedah Merchant* as prizes. It was not until some days later that the true identity of the *Quedah Merchant*'s master was revealed. Wright was brought before Kidd who was upset to discover that he had unwittingly broken his own rules and captured an Englishman's command. Realising the extent to which he had now compromised himself, Kidd summoned the crew and addressed them: 'The taking of this ship would make a great noise in England.' He proposed that they hand the ship back to Wright, but his crew would not hear of it.

They reached Madagascar on 1 April and entered the pirates' haven of St Mary's Island. Also at anchor there was the *Mocha* frigate, a captured East Indiaman commanded by Robert Culliford who had deserted Kidd ten years before. Kidd urged his men to seize the *Mocha*. They refused, threatened Kidd and began to share out the spoils of the *Quedah Merchant*. Kidd got his share but after that ninety-seven of his men deserted to Culliford. The deserters sacked and burned the *November* and started to strip both the *Adventure Galley* and the *Quedah Merchant*. They burned Kidd's log and threatened to kill him. This they most certainly would have done had he not barricaded himself in his cabin with a brace of pistols. Kidd had eventually to surrender and his life was spared. The *Quedah Merchant* was allowed to stay afloat with a fair share of booty still in her hold. A couple of months later Culliford in the *Mocha* sailed out into the Indian Ocean, his crew swollen to 130 and her guns up to 40 at Kidd's expense.

Kidd decided to prepare for England. The *Adventure Galley* was by this time in no fit state to sail; she was half full of water and resting on a sand bar. Kidd had her stripped and her hull burned for its iron. He then refitted the *Quedah Merchant* (now also known as the *Adventure Prize*) and recruited a local crew. He had to wait another five months before the north-east monsoons could blow him around the Cape and he finally left St Mary's on 15 November 1698.

Declared a Pirate

About this time the East India Company wrote from its Headquarters in Surat to the Lord Justices in London. The letter contained a number of extreme accusations of piracy levelled against Kidd. The response of the Government was vigorous and immediate. They ordered a Naval Squadron, on the point of sailing to the Indian Ocean, to capture Kidd. At the same time the Admiralty despatched a circular letter to the Governors of the American Colonies, ordering them to apprehend Kidd so that 'he and his associates be prosecuted with the utmost Rigour of the Law'. Finally, with the object of isolating Kidd, a free pardon was offered to every pirate east of the Cape except Kidd and two other Captains, one of whom was Henry Avery.

In April 1699 Kidd made landfall in Anguilla in the Leeward Islands and sent his boat ashore. It returned with the devastating news that Kidd and his crew had been declared pirates and were to be arrested on sight.

Kidd wanted to see it through; he had powerful friends in both London and New York. He had the two French passes from the vessels he had plundered, so he was not a pirate – so he believed. He decided to make for New York where he reckoned he could count on the protection of the new Governor – the Lord Bellomont, who was one of the instigators of the cruise. *En route* he stopped off at St Thomas Island and his brother-in-law Samuel Bradley was put ashore at his own request with four others. Bradley had been ill for two years and had had enough.

Kidd sailed north and decided that the *Quedah Merchant* had to be replaced – she just wasn't fast enough. They met with the sloop *St Anthony* (or *Antonio*), Samuel Wood master, with the owner Henry Bolton, a merchant aboard. Kidd tried to buy the sloop off Bolton who initially refused but agreed to try and procure one for Kidd, also buyers for his cargo. He returned with a Dutch sloop that traded and eventually negotiated a deal to sell the *St Anthony* for 3,000 pieces of eight.

The two vessels then sailed up the River Higuey, in the Mona Passage area of Hispaniola, and moored the *Quedah Merchant* to the bank and rocks on shore. Kidd sold goods worth another 8,200 pieces of eight mainly to Bolton but also to other merchants who came aboard. Kidd then transferred most of the *Quedah Merchant* booty to the *St Anthony* including his own personal treasure – gold bars, gold dust, silver plate, precious and semi-precious stones and fine silks. He hired Bolton to guard the *Quedah Merchant* and sell the remaining goods on his behalf and also showed him the two French passes to prove that what he had was a legitimate prize. Kidd promised he would be back in two to three months time and with a crew of twelve – the rest remaining behind, wanting nothing more to do with the business – he set sail for New York. A lot of valuable plunder was still left in the hold of the *Quedah Merchant*.

As soon as Kidd had gone and over the next five weeks, the men left to guard the *Quedah Merchant* themselves plundered what they could of her cargo, selling it to passing ships. Most of the crew made 'three or four hundred pounds a man' and told Bolton to 'stay in the ship and be damned if they would stay no longer'. Bolton was powerless to stop them, and fearing Kidd's return the men made off. Bolton stayed on another week but then he too made off when he heard that a Spanish ship was looking for them. Bolton was later arrested and he also ended up in Newgate.

What happened to the *Quedah Merchant* next has never been made clear. It appears she was burnt to the water-line but by whom is not known. Obviously Bolton, before making off, would have taken off anything of real value left, and he didn't have time to burn her. Dunbar Hinrichs in his book also makes the point here that Kidd had little or no opportunity to go off and bury treasure in the vicinity of the Higuey river. He was under the constant surveillance of others and anyway, as we know, he took the bulk of the treasure (the good stuff anyway) with him in the sloop *St Anthony*.

Kidd in the meanwhile was slowly making for New York. He stopped at Delaware on the way for wood and water. On 10 June he rounded Long Island and anchored in Oyster Bay. From here he sent a letter to an old friend, James Emmott, asking him to come out to the ship. Emmott arrived a couple of days later, then hastened to Boston with Kidd's letter to meet with Bellomont. Emmott handed over the two French passes to show that Kidd was innocent of piracy and proposed that Bellomont should grant Kidd a pardon. Handing over the only evidence that could prove him innocent was another fatal move on Kidd's part. These French passes were not made available to Kidd during his trial.

Bellomont wrote back to the effect that if Kidd was as innocent as he made out, then he would do all that he could for him. Kidd, over-confident now perhaps, sent a 'gift' to Bellomont's young and pretty wife, including a magnificent enamelled box with four diamonds set in gold. He handed out gifts to many people besides friends, hoping to ingratiate himself. He sold merchandise, and friends took away treasure and merchandise for safe keeping. On 25 or 26 June he buried the bulk of his gold and gems in the orchard of Gardiner's island at the eastern tip of Long Island. John Gardiner's statement, or 'Narrative' as it was called, of 17 July 1699 is obviously of interest to us and is as follows:

That about twenty dayes agoe, Mr. Emot of New Yorke came to the Narrators House, and desires a boat to go for New Yorke telling the Narrator he came from my Lord at Boston. Whereupon the Narrator furnished the said Emot with a boat, and he went for New Yorke, and that Evening the Narrator saw a sloop with Six Guns rideing at an Anchore off Gardiners Island. and two days afterwards in the Evening the Narrator went aboard said Sloop to enquire what she was, and so soon as he came an board Captain Kidd (then unknown to the Narrator) asked him how himselfe and Family did, telling him that he the said Kidd was going to my Lord at Boston, and desired the Narrator to carry three Negroes, two boys and a girle, ashore, to keep till he the said Kidd or his Order should call for them, which the Narrator accordingly did. That about two hours after the Narrator had got the said Negroes ashore Captain Kidd sent his boat ashore with two bailfs of Goods and a Negro Boy, and the morning after, said Kidd desired the Narrator to come immediately on board and bring Six Sheep with him for his the said Kidds Voyage to Boston, which the Narrator did, when Kidd asked him to spare a barrel of Cyder, which the Narrator with great importunity consented to, and sent two of his men for it, who brought the Cyder on board said Sloop, but whilst the men were gone for the Cyder, Captain Kidd offered the Narrator several Pieces of damnified Muslin and Bengalls as a Present to his wife which the said Kidd put in a bagg, and gave the Narrator, and about a Quarter of an Hour afterwards the said Kidd tooke up two or three pieces of damnified Muslin and gave the Narrator for his proper use. And the Narrators men then coming on board with the said Barrel of Cyder as aforesaid, the said Kidd gave them four pieces of Arabian Gold for their trouble and also for bringing him wood. Then the said Kidd, ready to saile, told this Narrator he would pay him for the Cyder, to which the Narrator answered That he was already satisfied for it by the Present made to his Wife. And this Narrator observed that some of Kidds men gave to the Narrators men some inconsiderable things of small value, which this Narrator believes were Muslins for Neckclothes. And then the Narrator took leave of the said Kidd and went ashore, and at parting the said Kidd fired four Guns and stood for Block Island.

About three Dayes afterwards the said Kidd sent the Master of the Sloop and one Clarke in his boat for the Narrator, who went on board with them, And the said Kidd desired this Narrator to take on shore with him and keep for him, the said Kidd, and Order, a Chest, and a box of gold and a bundle of Quilts and four Bayles of Goods, which box of gold the said Kidd told the Narrator was intended for my Lord; and the Narrator complied with the said Kidds request and took on shore the said Chest, box of gold, Quilts and bayels of Goods.

And the Narrator further saith That two of Kidds Crew, who went by the Names of Cooke and Parrat, delivered to him, the Narrator, two baggs of Silver, which they told the Narrator weighed thirty pound weight, for which he gave receipt. And That another of Kidds men delivered to the Narrator a small bundle of gold, and gold dust of about a pound weight, to keep for him, and did also present the Narrator with a Sash and a pair of worsted Stockins. And just before the Sloop sayled Captain Kidd presented the Narrator with a bagg of Sugar, and then tooke leave and sayled for Boston.

And the Narrator further saith, he knew nothing of Kidd being proclaimed a Pyrate, and if he had, he durst not have acted otherwise than he has done, having no force to oppose them, and for that he hath formerly been threatned to be killed by Privateers, if he should carry unkindly to them.

The within named Narrator further saith That whilst Captain Kidd lay with the Sloop at Gardiners Island, there was a New Yorke Sloop, whereof one Coster is Master, and his Mate was a little black man, unknown to the Narrator by name, who, as it was said, had been formerly Captain Kidds Quarter Master, and another Sloop belonging to New Yorke, Jacob Fenick Master, both which lay near to Kidds Sloop three dayes together, and whilst the Narrator was on board with Captain Kidd, there was several Bayles of Goods and other things put out of the said Kidds Sloop and put on board the other two Sloops aforesaid, and the said two Sloops sayled up the Sound. After which Kidd sayled with his Sloop for Block Island, and being absent by the Space of three dayes returned to Gardiners Island again in company of another Sloop belonging to New Yorke, Cornelius Quick Master, on board of which was one Thomas Clarke of Setauket, commonly called Whisking Clarke, and one Harrison of Jamaica, Father to a boy that was with Captain Kidd, and Captain Kids Wife was then on board his own Sloop. And Quick remained with his Sloop there from noon to the evening of the same day, and tooke on board two chests that came out of the said Kidds Sloop, under the observance of this Narrator, and he believes several Goods more, and then sayled up the Sound. Kidd remained there with his Sloop until next morning, and then set saile intending, as he said, for Boston. Further the Narrator saith That the next day after Quick sayled with his sloop from Gardiners Island, he saw him turning out of a Bay called Oyster-Pan Bay, although the wind was all the time fair to carry him up the Sound; the Narrator supposes he went in thither to land some Goods.

It is interesting to note that nowhere in that statement does it say that Kidd's treasure was *buried*. Gardiner was asked to 'keep' them for him, they were 'took on shore'. Bellomont in his statement to London on 26 July mentions parcels of treasure and jewels 'delivered up' by Mr Gardiner but also that '. . . Kidd having owned he had buried some gold on that island'.

Gardiner's statement also tells us that at least two chests (we don't know what was in them) were moved out of Kidd's ship. Bellomont had the aforementioned Thomas Clarke arrested and charged him with having privately deposited £10,000 worth of Kidd's treasure. Clarke promised to restore it but whether or not all of it was restored is of course another question. We are also told that Kidd was away for three days when he went to Block Island. Who's to know that he didn't deposit something somewhere on that little trip?

Kidd's wife and daughter had by now joined him on his ship and stayed with him for the journey to Boston. Here they arrived on 28 June. Kidd unwisely sent another 'gift' to Lady Bellomont, this time £1,000 of small gold bars sewn up in a green silk bag. She immediately sent them back. The next day Kidd was interviewed by Bellomont who asked for a detailed account of his movements. Kidd told him his log had been destroyed by his mutinous crew and it would take some time to write a new account of his voyage. Bellomont ordered it done but Kidd failed to deliver it at the appointed time. Bellomont, his patience at an end, showed his Council his orders to seize Kidd and they voted he should be arrested. Kidd was apprehended outside Bellomont's house. He tried to draw his sword, broke away and rushed into the house. He was caught and his arms pinned down in the presence of one of the chief instigators of the enterprise for which he was now being accused. He was clapped into prison and confined in irons weighing 16 pounds. He was subsequently treated more like an animal than as one who had held the King's commission.

An Inventory of Loot

Bellomont being party to and with a financial interest in Kidd's expedition had to save himself from disgrace. He probably realised that his only salvation lay in complete cooperation with the Government and a complete persecution of Kidd. To this end he put a great deal of enthusiasm into rounding up Kidd's crew and gathering evidence. A frantic search was made to uncover Kidd's treasure. His lodgings were ransacked. His gifts to various friends were collected and his treasure on Gardiner's Island recovered. Three weeks after his arrest, an inventory of recovered booty was drawn up:

1,111	ounces of gold
2,353	ounces of silver
17&3/8	ounces of precious stones
57	bags of sugar
41	bales of merchandise
17	pieces of canvas

The gold, silver and precious stones were made up as follows:

In Kidd's Box:

One bag	Fifty-three Silver Barrs
One bag	Seventy-nine Barrs and pieces of silver
One bag	Seventy-four Barrs Silver
	One Enamel'd Silver box in which are four diamonds set in gold Lockets, one diamond loose, one large diamond set in a gold ring.

Found in Mr. Duncan Campbell's House:

Seven bags of gold

One Handkerchief Gold

Twenty Dollars

One halfe and one quart. pes. of eight

Nine English Crowns

One small Barr of Silver

One small lump Silver

A small chain and small bottle

A Corral Necklace

One pc. white and one pc. of Checquer'd Silk

In Kidd's Chest:

Two Silver Boxons

Two Silver Candlesticks
One Silver Porringer
Some small things of Silver
Sixty-seven Rubies small and great
Two Green Stones
One large Load Stone
Received from Mr. John Gardiner:
Two bags dust gold
One p'cl dust gold
One Bag Coyned Gold and in it silver
Two Bags gold Barrs
Two Bags Silver Bars
One Bag three Silver Rings and Sundry precious stones
One bag of unpolished Stones
One ps. of Cristol and Bazer Stone
Two Cornelion Rings
Two small Agats
Two Amathests
One Bag Silver Buttons and a Lamp
One Bag broken Silver

Everything was eventually shipped to the Treasury in England.

Duncan Campbell made a statement to Bellomont on 12 July regarding Kidd's treasure and presents given as follows:

Kidd gave me 100 pieces of eight when I was on board his sloop at Rhode Island. He lately admitted that a box of gold was buried on Gardiners Island, and that in the same box was 40lb weight of gold, about 300 or 400 pieces of eight, some pieces of eight belonging to his boy Barlycorn and his negro man which he had got by washing for the men. I know of no other treasure concealed by Kidd. Off Block Island, Kidd gave me two speckled handkerchiefs, and ¼lb. of tea, and bought of me a wigg for which he paid four pistolls of gold. The second time of his going, Kidd handed over to me 90–100 pieces of eight in New York money, which he said was his wife's, for charges and things I bought for him. He gave me 3–4 pieces of muslin and a gold chain for my wife, and sent by me a present to the Countess of Bellomont of an enamelled gilt box, with four sparkes or stones therein set in gold, one loose and a stone ring, which, at my arrival in Boston, I showed to Mr. Legarre, a French goldsmith, who said they were in value about £55. He gave Mr. Menzies, who went on board the sloop with me, 8 or 9 pieces of Arabian gold. On the morning of the fourth of July, Kidd delivered me a green silk bag, sewed up, of about 4 to 5 lb. weight, of bar gold to be presd. to the Countess of Bellomont, in his name which my Lady, refusing to accept, I returned to Kidd. When I was on board his sloop off Block Island, Kidd gave me 2–3 pieces of Arabian gold to drink with some Gentlemen in Boston, and two of the sloops company gave me each a pistoll of gold. Captain Kidd's company promised me £500 vallue for my trouble and pains if they had their liberties.

Robert Livingston (the instigator of Kidd's venture) had in the meanwhile rushed to Boston and met with Bellomont on 12 July. He had this to say:

I came directly from Albany ye nearest way through the woods to meet Kidd and wait on his lordp. Capt. Kidd, in Boston, on my arrival, said he had about 80 pds. weight in Plate, but whether on board the sloop or not, I cannot remember. He also said he had forty pounds weight in gold, which he had hid and secured in some place in the Sound, betwixt this and New Yorke, withal saying nobody could find it but himself, and that all the goods, gold plate and sloop was for the accompt of the owners of the 'Adventure Galley', of which I am one. Kidd said he had been forced to let his men remove their chests and bundles from the sloop. He said he gave Mr. Duncan Campbell 100 pieces of eight when he was on board his sloop at Rhode Island. I know of no other concealement of goods or treasure made by Captain Kidd, his company and accomplices. Yesterday, Kidd acknowledged to me that the gold before mentioned was hid upon Gardiner's Island, and was about 50 lb. weight, and in the same box with it was 300 to 400 pieces of eight, and some pieces of plate belonging to his boy Barlycorn, and his negro man, gotten by washing for the men. Kidd gave me a boy and another to Mr. Duncan Campbell.

Pieces of Eight

It might be opportune to explain at this point, to readers who are none the wiser, what a 'piece of eight' was.

The 'piastre', or 'peso', or piece of eight was an old Spanish coin of eight reales value. Sometimes referred to as a 'rial' or 'ryall', it was dollar-size (about the size of an English crown) and made of silver. In Spanish it was called the 'peso de plata', *plata* being the Spanish word for silver. Coins were also stuck in denominations of 4, 2, 1, ½ and ¼ reales. The coins were mostly struck in the Spanish Colonial mints of Peru or Mexico during the period 1536 to 1734. The early coins were called 'cobs' and were of irregular shape owing to their method of manufacture – cut from a rough bar of silver, hammer struck and then trimmed with shears.

Gold doubloons were 8 escudos, or 4 pistoles. The pistole was 2 escudos of Spain, equal to 4 pieces of eight. A doubloon therefore was equal to 16 pieces of eight and known in Spanish as the 'peso do oro' (golden peso).

In Kidd's time, the value of a piece of eight was roughly the same as the English crown, i.e. 5 to 6 shillings. Today, depending on condition, you can pay anything between £50 and £100 for one.

It is commonly believed that the dollar sign ($) is derived from the piece of eight, the two vertical lines through an 8 being said to represent the two Pillars of Hercules which were formerly stamped on some of the later dollars.

Sent Back in Chains

On 6 February 1700, seven months after his arrest, Kidd and his crew were escorted on board HMS *Advice*. Kidd was locked up in a steerage cabin and his crew chained up in the gun room. All the treasure, goods and merchandise collected when Kidd was captured was sent back, including his own personal effects – which would include, we assume, his sea chests.

They arrived in the Thames Estuary on 11 April. Kidd was transferred to the Royal Yacht *Katherine* and rushed to Greenwich where he was kept for a while in the custody of the Admiralty Marshal. After a brief meeting with the Admiralty Board in the middle of April, where he again pleaded his case and innocence, he was committed to Newgate rather than the Admiralty's own jail, the Marshalsea. He was kept in Newgate until the next session of the House of Commons, so here he was to stay for more than a year in close confinement.

Today, it is difficult to imagine what a hell-hole and disgusting place Newgate was. It was already very old then, having been rebuilt once in 1672. Lice were so numerous they crunched under foot, as one inmate put it 'like shells on a garden path'. Prisoners slept two or three to a bed and were washed in vinegar before appearing in court. The prison was run as a private business, prisoners being made to pay rent and extortionate fees for anything they wanted.

Kidd was allowed no exercise and no visitors – except an elderly uncle and a relative of his wife.

The Trial

At the end of March 1701, Kidd was suddenly called before the House of Commons. He pleaded his own innocence but did not implicate the Whig statesmen who had sponsored his voyage. If he had involved them he might have yet won a pardon. It appears that when Kidd made this first appearance before the Bar he was intoxicated and made a contempt-ible appearance. One of the members remarked, 'This fellow, I thought, had been only a knave, but, unfortunately, he happens to be a fool likewise.'

The next day the House recommended that he should ' . . . be pro-ceeded against according to law.' The trial was fixed for 8 May. Kidd's trial was an injustice from the start. The French passes, two vital pieces of evidence, were withheld from him. He was without any legal council until virtually the last hour before the trial which was held before six justices and consisted of four separate trials on six indictments.

For those students who want a detailed account of Kidd's trial I recommend *Trial of Captain Kidd* in the Notable British Trials Series ed-ited by Graham Brooks, published 1930 by William Hodge & Co. Ltd.

The first indictment at his trial (8 and 9 May 1701) was not for piracy at all but for the murder of his gunner William Moore on board the *Adventure Galley*.

It may seem unusual for those times that a Captain – given absolute authority on the high seas – be tried for murder. Commanders in those days thought nothing of lashing sailors, keelhauling them or 'dunking' them in the sea for a lot less than the mutinous behaviour of Moore. But even Captains did not have the right to commit murder, and there are at least two other instances of Captains being tried for this crime. Kidd pleaded 'not guilty' to the charge and when the proceedings were over (during which Kidd had to conduct his own cross-examination) he said, 'I had no design to kill him, it was not designedly done but in my passion, for which I am heartely sorry.'

The Chief Justice Sir Edward Ward summarised the case for the jury who then left the courtroom. The court proceedings did not stop there. They straight away went on to consider the charges of piracy, this time against all the prisoners involved.

Kidd and eight members of his crew were charged with five acts of piracy against the *Quedah Merchant*, the *Maiden (Rouparelle)* and three other unnamed ships, two Moorish and one Portuguese.

The two main prosecution witnesses, Palmer and Bradinham, who had deserted Kidd at Madagascar, stuck to their well rehearsed biased evidence against him. Kidd conducted his own defence in an inept and clumsy way and could make no impression. He had no material witnesses to call (he was only allowed to question the prosecution witnesses) and no French passes to produce as evidence.

It didn't help that when Dr Newton, the Admiralty's Advocate, was halfway through reading the charge to the new jury, he was interrupted by the first jury returning to declare their verdict. It was guilty. So Kidd was already condemned to death in the middle of a trial for his life on the charge of piracy and with no appeal except to the King.

In the end Kidd must have realised the hopelessness of his situation. These extracts from his cross-examination show how:

Kidd: 'This man [Bradinham] contradicts himself in a hundred places.' and further on, 'He tells a thousand lies.'

Solicitor General: 'Captain Kidd, will you ask him any more questions?'

Kidd: 'No, no, it signifies nothing.'

Clerk; 'Now, if you will ask this witness [Palmer] any questions you may.'

Kidd: 'What signifies it to ask him any questions? We have no witnesses, and what we say signifies nothing.'

As the trial come to a close, Kidd broke in: 'Mr Bradinham, are you not promised your life to take away mine?'

The jury was out for less than half an hour and found Kidd and his codefendants guilty.

After reading the indictments, the Clerk said to Kidd, 'William Kidd, hold up thy hand. What canst thou say for thyself? Thou hast been indicted for several piracies, and robberies, and murder, and hereupon hast been convicted. What hast thou to say for thyself why thou shouldst not die according to law?'

Kidd: 'I have nothing to say, but that I have been sworn against by perjured and wicked people.'

The Clerk read out the sentence to Kidd and those convicted with him. The last part of the sentence read: 'You shall be taken from the place where you are, and be carried to the place from whence you came, and from thence to the place of execution, and there be severally hanged by your necks until you be dead. And the Lord have mercy on your souls.'

Kidd in reply said: 'My Lord, it is a very hard sentence. For my part, I am the innocentest person of them all, only I have been sworn against by perjured persons.'

Treasure in the Indies

After being sentenced, Kidd wrote a letter (12 May) to Robert Harley, Speaker of the House of Commons. It was a last desperate plea and attempt to buy himself out, but the Lords took no notice.

S'r

The Sence of my present Condition (being under Condemnation) and the thoughts of haveing bene imposed on by such as seek't my destruction thereby to fulfill their ambitious desires makes me uncapable of Expressing my selfe in those terms as I aught, therefore doe most humbly pray that you will be pleased to represent to the Hon'bl. house of Comons, that in my late proceedings in the Indies. I have lodged goods and Treasure to the value of one hundred thousand pounds, which I desire the Government may have the benefitt of, in order thereto I shall desire no manner of liberty but to be kept prisonner on board such shipp as may be appointed for that purpose, and only give the necessary directions and in case I faile therein I desire no favour but to be forthwith Executed acording to my Sentence. if y'r honbl. house will please to order a Comittee to come to me I doubt not but to give such satisfaction as may obtaine mercy, most Humbly submitting to the wisdom of your great assembly I am

S'r Y'r Unfortunate humble servant
Wm Kidd

Just one line in that letter: ' . . . I have lodged goods and Tresure to the value of one hundred thousand pounds . . . ' is responsible for sending so many treasure hunters off on a wild goose chase.

Kidd, it will be noted, does say ' . . . In my *late* proceedings.' So he is obviously referring to treasure taken during his fateful cruise and not anything before that. Perhaps he is referring to the *Quedah Merchant* loot he left *lodged* with Bolton and was not aware that those goods had themselves been plundered. He may of course also be referring to plunder he had deposited elsewhere. In a letter to Bellomont whilst in jail in Boston, Kidd asked if he would let him go to the place where he left the *Quedah Merchant and* to St Thomas *and* Curacao. He would undertake to bring off 50 or threescore thousand pounds, 'that otherwise would be lost.' This suggests that Kidd may have buried treasure in these two latter places and even elsewhere. Bellomont did not take him up on his offer because of the costs involved in fitting out a ship and subsequently being told that the *Quedah Merchant* had been burned out anyway. Kidd must have known that his Gardiner's Island treasure was recovered, so he must have been referring to some other cache or caches.

A lot of people believe that all the treasure taken during this the last of Kidd's cruises was recovered. I do not, for reasons made obvious above. However, I do not believe either that our Kidd/Palmer charts point the way to any of this treasure.

Did Kidd have a fair trial? It has been said he did according to the standards of the age, although being denied witnesses and evidence can hardly be said to be fair. He was allowed £50 for Counsel but the fee was withheld until the night before he was due to appear at the Old

Bailey. His Counsel refused to act until he had been paid; even so, they were only allowed to raise matters of law: unfair today maybe, but that was how the law demanded it then.

Was Kidd guilty of piracy? If one recognises pirates by their acts of murder, terror, torture and rape, then he was not a pirate. Under the definition 'Robbery with violence at sea,' then yes, he was.

His modern defenders claim that he was convicted on flimsy evidence and was 'no pirate at all'. Deeper understanding suggests that the French passes possessed by the *Roupelle* and the *Quedah Merchant*, though technically placing them under French protection, did not change the fact that these vessels belonged to friendly nations. Kidd also captured English, Portuguese and Moorish vessels for which there was no excuse other than his claim to have been coerced by his crew. He could satisfy his backers only by making a rich haul. He fraternised with the pirates he had been ordered to destroy, and he failed, as the law provided, to bring prizes for condemnation by an Admiralty Court. But such courts were not authorised in the American Colonies and West Indies until 1699. To fulfil this condition he would have needed to sail them to London. Kidd fell victim of his own weakness. He had allowed himself to be prevailed upon to command an impossible enterprise. Deprived of the majority of his original crew, he was unable to control men who stood to gain their living only if he took prizes, irrespective of their nationality.

Hung, Tarred and 'Framed'

During the afternoon of 23 May 1701, before he was put to death, Kidd was visited by the Chaplain, Paul Lorrain. He found Kidd very unwilling to confess to the crimes he was convicted of, which of course is not surprising, since the 56-year-old Kidd did not believe he had committed any crime at all.

By the time he emerged from the great arch of Newgate he was in a sorry state. Someone had slipped him a considerable amount of alcohol and he was therefore oblivious to the howls of the mob outside. He was taken in an open carriage, preceded by the Admiralty's Deputy Marshal bearing over his shoulder the silver oar that symbolised the authority of the Admiralty. Behind came the Marshal himself; finally, flanked by an escort, came the cart carrying Kidd. Darby Mullins followed in a second cart with two condemned French pirates. (All those who had been tried and convicted with Kidd were, with the exception of Mullins, reprieved.)

Execution day was fête day in London and the procession was followed by a huge crowd. It was two hours before they reached Execution Dock at Wapping on the edge of the Thames. The gallows, water covering its base at high tide, stuck out of the mud.

Bad luck was not to desert Kidd, even at this late hour. Having been pushed off the cart into space, he dangled only briefly before the rope snapped and he tumbled down into the mud. Confused and stunned, he was manhandled up again and the ladder pulled away; this time the rope held. When he had stopped twitching, the executioner cut him down and chained his body to a post and left it there until the tide had ebbed and flowed over it three times, as Admiralty Law then prescribed. The body was then recovered, painted with tar and encased in a gibbet irons; this cage was specially constructed so that the skull and bone would stay in place after the corpse had rotted. It was hung on a gibbet specially built at Tilbury Point, where it could be seen plainly by everyone sailing in and out of the Thames so that it would serve 'as a great terrour to all Persons from Committing ye like crimes for the time to come.'

Kidd's bones apparently swung there for some years.

There was a curious sequel to the execution of Kidd. Two of his reprieved crew, Churchill and Howe, were released from gaol after each paid the Keeper of the Old Bailey 300 guineas. They no doubt sailed past Kidd's rotting corpse on their way to Pennsylvania, where they dug up £800 and £1,500 respectively in Arabian gold, buried in the woods before their arrest with Kidd. Churchill was apparently arrested in Barbados later because he couldn't produce his Certificate of Pardon. He was sent back to England in a British man-o-war to get the missing document.

How many more of Kidd's crew did the same as Churchill and Howe? Once Kidd knew he was outlawed, I would be very surprised if he didn't bury something somewhere on the way back.

The Crown witnesses, Palmer and Bradinham, were rewarded with a full pardon. Culliford, the pirate to whom most of Kidd's crew had deserted, was tried and convicted on the same day as Kidd. He was released after a year as he had surrendered under the Royal Pardon.

Kidd's family lived in seclusion in New York and his widow remarried

Kidd's body would have been encased in a Gibbet-cage the same as, or very similar to, this. This particular set of irons can be seen at Rye (Kent) and still contain part of the skull of a butcher named Breed who murdered the local Mayor in 1742.

(With thanks to Mr G. Bagley, Hon. Curator Rye museum.)

about eighteen months after his death. She lived another forty-three years. Her daughters grew up, married and had children of their own.

The Lord Bellomont died destitute three months before Kidd's execution.

The French passes – withheld at the trial, probably because it had already been decided that Kidd should be found guilty as a necessary scapegoat – did exist. Ralph D. Paine, whilst researching his *The Book of Buried Treasure*, found them amongst the state papers in the Public Record Office in 1911.

In 1932, a dredger working on the site of Execution Dock dredged up a chain harness and ancient padlock of eighteenth century make. The British Museum said they had probably been used on Kidd and they are now kept there.

The Siam Connection

The previous account of Kidd's *known* voyage shows that when on the King's business, he was nowhere near the South China Sea (or Gulf of Siam), yet he was familiar with people who had knowledge of those parts, even if he hadn't been there. His old enemy Robert Culliford, when in prison in Newgate gaol, said he sailed with Captain Kidd and was commander of the *Mocha* frigate. The ship had taken him aboard *off the coast of Siam*, where he had been imprisoned after running away with a ship belonging to the East India Company.

The coast of Siam was not of course restricted to the Gulf of Siam. Culliford was more than likely referring to the west coast facing the Andaman Sea. This does show however that western pirates were prepared to travel long distances from their traditional hunting grounds in search of new riches. Maybe Kidd did, at some time earlier in his career!

Ill gotten gain for the Ill

When happened to Kidd's sequestered goods? Section 14 of the Statute of 1705, reads in part as follows:

That it shall and may be lawful for her Majesty (Queen Anne) if she pleaseth, to dispose as a Charity, to and for the Use and Benefit of the Royal Hospital for Seamen at Greenwich the sum of

£6,472-1s . . . being money or the proceed of Goods and Merchandizes which were taken with William Kidd a notorious Pirate, who was taken and executed several Years since.

Sarah Kidd's possessions were not forfeited. She was put into jail after Kidd's arrest and all her property seized. Bellomont had no reason to keep her; she regained her freedom and her property.

It might be appropriate to end this chapter by quoting the 'Piracy Act 1837' which is still in force:

Item 2, Punishment of piracy when murder is attempted.

. . . Whosoever, with intent to commit or at the time or immediately before or immediately after committing the crime of piracy in respect of any ship or vessel, shall assault, with intent to murder, any person being on board of or belonging to such ship or vessel, or shall stab, cut or wound any such person, or unlawfully do any act by which the life of such person may be endangered, shall be guilty of felony, and being convicted thereof shall suffer death . . .

In other words, the death penalty still applies in Britain for those convicted of piracy.

Chapter 5

Kidd Connections

Good Reading, Bad Facts

There are many many books and publications about Kidd and his treasure. The majority are hopelessly inaccurate. Over the years stories of his life and treasure have become mixed up with those of other pirates, tales have become 'fact', mistakes and theories copied, re-written and enlarged upon. When reading about Kidd today, unless you are something of an authority on the subject, you have to accept that what is written is fact and that the author knows what he is talking about. Unfortunately, he may be writing what he believes the reader would *like* to read; facts are 'adjusted' or created to make a better story line. The unsuspecting reader is probably thoroughly enjoying what he is reading (and what more could an author want?) and is in no position to argue with the story line presented to him.

One of the best examples of the above is *Treasure Seekers* by Hans Roden. The story of the discovery of the charts is hopelessly wrong: the date on Ned Ward's chest is given as 1696 not 1699 and he says that around the edge of the first chart found were the words: 'The path that must be followed to find my treasure, Captain William Kidd 1691.' It is sheer imagination; he has even got the date wrong again. Another paragraph says: 'Admiral Sir Reginald Hall, head of British Naval Intelligence during the First World War, expressed a desire to see these fascinating treasure charts.' That he may have done, but he certainly did not advise Palmer to fit out a ship 'under the auspices of the Admiralty to look for the island' as Roden says. Further on he states that after the death sentence was passed on Kidd, his wife Sarah was given permission to spend time with him and that during their time together, those present noticed that he passed a scrap of parchment to her which was immediately confiscated. On it were four sets of numbers: 44–10–66–18, about which Kidd's wife would say nothing. At this point we of course recognise the Olmstead/Deer Island story, from which the above gem of a tale is taken.[*] Perhaps Roden did not know that story to be a hoax, and if he did, he decided to use it anyway. Another point of course is that the last time Kidd saw his wife before his death was when he was imprisoned by Bellomont in America.

Later on in the chapter Roden goes on to say that in 1932 a discovery of especial interest was made which confirmed that Kidd had landed in America. On an island in Fundy Bay (west of Nova Scotia) someone had found near to a lake a badly weatherworn marble slab on which the outline of the lake was carved, with pictures of parts of the coastline; on it were also the words 'W. Kidd, five fathoms eastward in two fathoms depth'. That particular story may be true, although nowhere have I seen confirmation of it, but it does bear resemblance to a story to follow later; and it does lead me on to the fact that stories linking Kidd with this particular part of Canada and North America abound, and suggest there is a strong connection with Nova Scotia somewhere or in several places here.

Oak Island

The connection which is most written about is of course Oak Island in Mahone Bay, east of Nova Scotia. I do not intend to tell the story of the 'Money Pit' here; it is already well known (see Bibliography). Suffice to say:

In the mid 1700s or before, Oak Island was the scene of a mysterious and ingenious engineering project, where a shaft was excavated to nearly 200 feet to conceal something of enormous wealth or importance (so it is believed). Access to the bottom of the shaft is prevented by a tidal flood system through two tunnels, one at 111 ft., one at 151 ft. It has been estimated that so great was the task involved, it must have taken an army of men at least two years to complete. It has taken more than an army of men since then and hundreds of thousands of pounds to recover – precisely nothing.

The search however carries on. A Montreal and Nova Scotia-based

---

[*] Roy Norvill's book *The Treasure Seeker's Treasury* repeats the same false information.

treasure seeking consortium intend spending $10 million in a drive to solve the mystery.

David Tobias, president of Triton Alliance, said (July 1987) that the group is committed to a large-scale digging operation to unravel the secret of the island 'once and for all'. He carried on to say that it would be the largest undertaking of its kind that side of the Atlantic and would be a very professional, very methodical determination of what the island's ancient workings were built to protect.

Triton Alliance have so far spent more than $1 million trying to uncover the secret of the pit. They plan to excavate a 60 ft. wide hole in the area of the original pit. The new shaft will be located to take in the areas examined by some thirty-eight exploration holes and drill sites which have caved in or been abandoned. No previous shaft has gone below 170 ft. and they intend this new shaft to go to the bedrock at 200 ft.

To avoid the flooding problem the group intends to construct coffer dams around the two areas on the shore which are believed to act as the pit's flood tunnels.

Artifacts so far recovered by Triton which have been carbon tested, point to the date of the original workings of the pit to be the late sixteenth century. Mr Tobias said that this would coincide with the second or third voyages of Drake in 1578 and 1582 (nearly 100 years before Kidd was on the scene) and although Drake was commissioned by Queen Elizabeth I to explore, he may have actually been plundering the Spanish.

Mr Tobias goes on to suggest that the pit could be Drake's depot on that side of the Atlantic. He points out that Oak Island is only 400 miles off a traditional sailing route to Europe.

It is an interesting theory but lacking in evidence and possibly research. A study of Drake's voyages during this latter part of the sixteenth century shows that on the first he arrived home in just one ship (*The Golden Hind*) by way of the Canaries in 1580. The second voyage in 1585-6 certainly brought him close to Canadian waters on his way home, but his last stop was on the west coast of Virginia. He sailed from there direct to England. His third and final voyage took him to Panama and he died at sea of fever in 1596.

Drake's voyages are documented well enough for us to know that he never called at Oak Island. I certainly do not believe it was he who constructed the 'money pit'.

One of the later theories is that it might hold the lost treasure of the Knights Templars – a trove touted as so fabulous that it could contain the Holy Grail or even Christ's bones. Fred Nolan, who owns the north-central part of the island, discovered five cone-shaped 10-tonne granite boulders on his land. On a map, lines connecting the boulders create a huge Christian Cross more than 250m long and 220m wide.

Nolan is keeping his options open. He still thinks there could be a link with Kidd. Copies of the Kidd/Palmer charts were published by Reginald Harris in his book *Oak Island Mystery* in the late fifties. Everyone discounted the charts at that time, Nolan said because they couldn't relate the figures and interpretations of measurements to Oak Island. Nolan said he believes the measurements weren't being taken correctly back then. The charts, he says, cite three stumps and a series of stakes by the edge of a lake. He has located at least sixty stakes as well as the three stumps in a muddy swamp on the exact co-ordinates mentioned in the charts. He believes the triangle is actually an arrow pointing to the stakes and stumps.

By 1992, Triton Alliance, who own the land around the pit area, had still not started the operation to dig a now massive 80 ft. diameter hole supported by caissons. They have now spent over $4 million on digging and drilling and have tried unsuccessfully to get government loan guarantees to fund the operation. Tobias hasn't yet cast aside the Drake theory. He said (in 1992), 'When the evidence is linked with new information on British Admiral Sir Francis Drake, there is a solid case for the pit's origin. Recent research by British historians indicates that Drake dispatched Welsh miners across the Atlantic for a secret mission at about the time the system of tunnels was built.'

In the meanwhile Nolan and his assistant John Wall carry on quietly. He and Triton have never co-operated. Animosity began in earnest when Tobias bought the island in 1977 for $125,000. A dispute quickly arose over the 600 ft. causeway and Nolan's ownership of seven lots strained relations. In 1985 after numerous confrontations the dispute ended up in court. The judge accepted Nolan's title on the island but rejected his claim to land at the foot of the causeway. Triton now prohibit Nolan from crossing it and he has to use a boat.

Nolan is reluctant to talk about details of his latest explorations. He doesn't want to give his fellow treasure hunters any clue to what he is doing. 'They have their theories, I have my own,' is his typical response when pressed for details. But he is mystified by the continuing animosity. 'Why don't they want me on the island? If they're confident they have the solution, what are they afraid of?'

Discord continues, but now apparently within the Triton camp. Dan Blankenship is, or was, a partner with David Tobias in Triton Alliance. As field manager he has spent the last twenty-seven years seeking the solution to the Oak Island mystery. He moved to the island in 1969, lured by the stories and tales of buried treasure. This sturdy seventy-three-year-old is persistent in his belief in buried treasure. 'There are chests down there,' he says, as he points to a series of photographs in his bungalow. The photographs, taken in 1971 by a remote underwater TV camera, show he says, chest shaped objects, mining tools and part of a preserved body believed to be a hand.

Mr Blankenship resigned from Triton's executive in 1994 when they disagreed about future operations on the island and Mr Tobias said there would be no more money spent in the field. Blankenship believes completion of his 'borehole 10X' (he has only 55 feet to go) will solve the mystery, but after investing $140,000 of his own money he does not have anything left to finance further exploration. Although he is a 17 per cent shareholder, Triton has declined to give him the $350,000 he says he needs to finish the work.

Instead, Triton have done a deal with Oak Island Discoveries to conduct extensive scientific research of the site. Under the agreement, Discoveries have exclusive media rights to the pit in perpetuity and 15 per cent of whatever is found there. This new company has put up $500,000 to cover the cost and has brought in the Woods Hole Oceanographic Institution from Massachusetts (the group famous for finding the *Titanic*) to conduct scientific tests employing camera probes and high-tech equipment. Depending on the test results, Discoveries has agreed to help shareholders raise $10 million for a final assault on the pit.

More and more money is being poured into this bottomless hole – or pit!

Perhaps this latest venture is *the* common sense approach rather than a drill-and-dig attitude. It will be interesting to see what a sophisticated scientific examination will reveal.

Is there anything there?

The constructors of the pit were obviously disciplined and skilled in engineering, and had plenty of time and labour to carry out the work. Pirates just did not have this amount of time and they were certainly not skilled in mining and hydraulic engineering techniques. Never in a thousand years would they use such methods to bury their illgotten gains!

I would guess that the work involved to construct the pit and tunnels would have taken at least a year, and disciplined organisation would be needed. Pirate crews – except on rare occasions – were far from disciplined and organised. They were never the same size or composition from one month to the next. They owned allegiance to no one, neither ship nor Captain. I cannot accept that the monumental effort involved was to bury a few pirate chests – or even a lot of pirate chests!

There must have been a very large work force, with not only strict discipline but tight security. To my knowledge, nothing was written down by these unknown engineers and it would seem that none of the participants even wrote about what they had done. It is strange that there is no record of anything by anyone. They were either under strict orders not to talk – suggesting strict regimentation (the military?) – or they were under fear of death – or both. If it was a military operation of some sort then there was purposely no record kept.

Such a vast undertaking would have been commissioned only to hide something of fabulous wealth. Nobody is going to go to that trouble to hide a couple of chests. At the time of the pit's construction, probably between 1650 and 1750, wealth was measured in terms of gold, silver and precious stones; so to warrant such an undertaking and engineering feat, there must have been an enormous amount of gold and silver etc. We are talking a large mass of bullion here. So why is it therefore that in two hundred years up to the present day, of digging and drilling hundreds, maybe thousands, of bore and test holes down to nearly two hundred feet, there has been *no* evidence of any large deposit of gold or silver – or anything?

Where in fact is the evidence to say that the pit was constructed to *hide* something? Assuming there is something at the bottom worth recovering, and that the recovery team knew how to shut off the two tidal tunnels, there is still the immense task of digging back down through at least 200 feet of earth and clay etc. Furthermore, at about 10-foot intervals there are – or were – ten strongly built platforms of oak, spruce and stones. Who is going to go to all that trouble, and why? The work involved to recover whatever it is down there is as much as the work involved in constructing the pit, probably more to ensure the pit does not flood.

It would seem to me that maybe the pit was meant to stay shut and I am suggesting that perhaps it was created for an entirely different reason than that commonly supposed. Maybe we should be thinking laterally!

The only treasure found?

The only evidence I could find of anything being found on Oak Island came from a statement made by a Carl Mosher, who lives in a Veterans' unit of the Fisherman's Memorial Hospital in Lunenburg. Mr Mosher who is in his eighties recalled the day his grandmother showed him an old chest:

'I was only thirteen or fourteen years of age,' he said. 'My grandmother Lucy Vaughan took me into her bedroom. She opened up a wooden trunk and in it was a bunch of bags – all kinds of white bags tied at the top with blue string. My grandfather George Vaughan told me he got that chest off Oak Island. He lived right across from it.'

Unfortunately the chest and its curious contents no longer exist. Apparently an uncle, Edward Vaugham, got hold of it and did a runner with it many years ago. He left his family, property and business. He must have thought the contents of the chest – whatever they were – worth it!

The Oak Island mystery is unique in that we know where the treasure is (if that is what is in the pit) but don't know how to get it out. I could put it another way. We know a pit was constructed here for some reason, and, as I suggested earlier, maybe *not* to hide something. The other unfortunate fact is that the hunters cannot be absolutely sure now of the original location of the pit. There have been too many excavations with no surveyor's record kept of the early ones. So the earlier sentence should read; The Oak Island mystery is unique, in that we know its whereabouts, we don't know why, where it was or if anything's there!

Kidd and Oak Island

It has always been the opinion that a pirate treasure is buried in the pit and, what with the legends that abound around here regarding Kidd, it was commonly assumed that it was he who constructed it and deposited his loot in it. His proposition to the Speaker of the House of Commons whilst awaiting execution helped this belief ' . . . I have lodged goods and tresure to the value of one hundred thousand pounds . . . '

In fact, there is no positive evidence at all to link Kidd with Oak Island. There is no way that the Kidd/Palmer charts could depict that island. People have, over the years, tried to make the information contained in the charts fit and relate. For example the spread-out letters spelling 'OAK' can of course be made out on the 'key' chart on the ridge at the western end of the island. What is mistaken for an 'O', by comparison, is obviously depicting something else. The T, A and K, could have been constructed by a coincidence of marks; on the other hand, as suggested in a previous chapter, they could be significant: 'Treasure At K' for example.

Another author has suggested that allowing for the change in Prime Meridian (since 1669, when the map was dated), and reversing the directions, one will arrive at Oak Island. Now Oak Island is at 44° 31'N, 64° 18'W, and in making that statement he is conveniently ignoring latitude because it does not matter how you manipulate 9° 16'N ('key' chart), you can never arrive at 44° 31'N. He is also assuming that the Prime Meridian at that time was Ferro (Hierro) and that the *single* system of navigation was used. Oak Island's position East of Ferro is therefore calculated as follows:

Oak Island is   64° 18'   West of Greenwich. Actual
                -18° 00'   Ferro, West of Greenwich
          = $\overline{46° 18'}$ Oak Island, West of Ferro
              360° 00'
          - 46° 18'   W
          = $\overline{313° 42'}$ East of Ferro

I believe it was Reginald V. Harris (Author of *The Oak Island Mystery*, 1958) who made the above observation. He didn't get it quite right as he arrives at a figure of 315° 43'E. Unfortunately it would appear that Rupert Furneaux in his book *Money Pit, The Mystery of Oak Island* copied Harris, for he quotes exactly the same figure. This was unusual for Furneaux: he usually checked things out for himself.

If the single system was used, we must assume that the 'key' chart actual figure was 331° 30'E and by working back, we will arrive at a position for prime meridian of 35° 80′ West of Greenwich. The nearest possible meridian to that is the Azores at 31°W.

The reader can make his own mind up but I think it is nonsense to suggest that the 'key' chart figures can in any way represent the position of Oak Island.

Wilkins' Maps

Gilbert Heddon was one of the searchers on Oak Island from 1934 to 1938. He had no more success than the others before or since, but he did have a mystifying experience. He was shown a copy of H. T. Wilkins book *Captain Kidd and his Skeleton Island*. The two drawings of Kidd's island in the book (See C1 & C2 p. 4) together with various features and similarities led Heddon to believe they might be of Oak Island. In particular he looked at the set of directions that called for the laying out of a course (see chart C.1). Carrying the book, he searched the area around the Money Pit. To the north he found a large boulder with holes drilled in it. His partner said there was another like it near the beach at Smiths Cove. They subsequently discovered that the distance between these boulders corresponded to the first line of figures on the chart and was measured in rods (1 rod = 16½ feet). They followed the second set of directions, which took them to a tangle of bushes. Upon clearing these away they discovered the triangle of stones that had been first noticed thirty-eight years before, but forgotten about. This arrow of stones 14 ft. long pointed directly to the Money Pit. The directions, concluded Heddon, led to the Pit. They could not however work out the meaning of the final line '7 By 8 By 4'. These discoveries, together with the other similarities, convinced Heddon that Kidd must have buried his treasure here. He travelled to England in 1938 and traced Wilkins who was dumbfounded when told of the similarities between his chart and Oak Island. He said there could be no possible connection between his charts and an island in Nova Scotia; he had never even seen Oak Island. Heddon left disappointed. The reasons for the similarities were as follows:

As we know, Wilkins was very familiar with Palmer's work and the Kidd charts. When Wilkins' book was published, Palmer had not allowed any of the charts to be reprinted. Wilkins' charts therefore were composite drawings, drawn from memory of the Kidd charts and embellished with symbols and marks shown on contemporary Admiralty charts. The legend of the directions were a figment of his imagination and indeed were different to those on the other frontispiece chart. The reason for this was that when a frontispiece was required Wilkins did not have the first drawing in his possession at that time so he reproduced it as well as his memory would allow him, which accounts for the difference between the two charts.

Those of you who are keen observationists will have also noted that the flag drawing on both charts at the bottom right hand corner, is a copy of the flag engraved on the top of the Hardy chest (between the date 1699).

Whilst in England, Heddon met Palmer who allowed him to examine his charts. Another example of incorrect information is in Harris's book (*The Oak Island Mystery*) where he states that Heddon learned from Palmer that the four charts were for many years in the family of a very old British seafaring family (i.e. Thomas Hardy). As we know, that family had only one of the charts, hidden in a chest.

It is interesting to relate what Heddon says of these charts, as there are some differences to what is accepted. The 'key' chart, he says, reads:

360 yards VD North three stumps 50 feet Depart centre of triangle,
4 rocks 20 feet S [or 5] Depart stakes E in edge of Lake Start til E.

The longitude he says was '130 80 E of W'. The 'skull' chart directions he gives are those that we know except for the first line. This reads, he says:

'50 S E and by 50 N Tree'

We have now, as you see, another different set of interpretations to confuse you. Personally I would ignore them. His recollections of the 'key' chart instructions I just cannot accept; my views are clear in the earlier chapter 'Analysing the Evidence'. I think Heddon's memory must have been playing tricks when he wrote down what he had seen; Palmer after all would not have allowed him to copy the charts directly. My reaction to 'E of W' is the same: that has caused a lot of confusion. Howlett does not recall this being on the chart and he very carefully examined them.

Furneaux in his book suggests that Wilkins did *not* tell Heddon the truth. He says that Wilkins, through his association with James Patrick

Nolan, about whom he later wrote a book (1948) called *A Modern Treasure Hunter*, was put in touch with one Herman Westhaver. Westhaver with a friend Joseph Smith (also known as Amos Smith) found in 1912 a box containing charts in a cairn of stones on Cochrane Island (sometimes called Plum Island) in Shad Bay which is in St Margaret's Bay, north of Mahone Bay. Westhaver showed one of the charts to Robert Gay – a man obsessed with the search for Kidd's treasure – and promised it would come to him after Westhaver's death (it did not when Westhaver died in 1967). Gay drew the map for Furneaux when Furneaux was in Halifax researching his book on Oak Island. Furneaux recognised the directions that Wilkins had used on his chart and noted also that the island was called 'Gloucester Isle'; he knew this was the name originally given to Oak Island by a British Admiralty Surveyor in 1773. Westhaver consulted Wilkins for help in learning the island's identity and Wilkins subsequently incorporated some of what he had learned into his own charts, not knowing the island's actual identity.

Heddon's opinion (1973) was that Kidd *knew* of Oak Island but had nothing to do with burying anything there. Kidd had, said Heddon, information on the mysterious underground workings there and had made notes about the island, so, instead of burying a treasure on Oak Island, Kidd may have been looking for it.

Ghosts, Plum Island and Captain Allen

The story of the discovery of the aforementioned charts on Plum Island (also called Clam or Redmond's Island) by Westhaver and Smith is in the best *Boys Own* tradition and is typical of the pirate treasure and ghost stories that abound in these parts. This particular story though is true; there are such things as ghosts and most certainly the story of the discovery of the charts is true.

The story starts in about 1874 when a Captain Allen arrived in Shad Bay. He called at one of the homes on the east side of the bay and asked the owner, a man named Sillex, if he could tell him where Plum Island was. 'No Sir,' said Sillex, 'I've never heard of it, and my folks have been settled here for many years past.' (It was known as Cochrane's Island then.) It transpired that Allen was a descendant of a pirate who in the early eighteenth century helped bury a treasure on Plum Island. Allen said the cache consisted of gold in kegs and barrels, wine and brandy – the pirates had hoped to return in a few years – all timbered around and shored with heavy props to support the roof. He searched the bays, creeks and coves between Halifax and Lunenburg for years, never showing anyone the papers he was working from, though he did say that he was looking for a well, which was one of the principal markers. However, there came a day when he had had enough; he handed his gear and certain information to one Captain Pickles of Mahone Bay, telling him:

'What you must look for is an island with three small piles of stones. This island is not large and lies at the head of a bay. A stream flows out of one end and east of the triangle of stones is a well which is near a wooded gully.'

Pickles had no more luck than Allen until one day, whilst having lunch on a beach with his mate, he idly traced the outline of the island in the sand. His mate recognised it straight away and took Pickles there – to Cochrane's Island. They landed and looked for the three stone mounds which Pickles found behind a grove of fir trees. Two were cairns of bee-hive shape, the third, the largest, in the shape of a pyramid. Locals soon arrived from the mainland, curious to see what the activity was about. 'Boys,' said Pickles, 'This is the Plum Island Captain Allen was looking for and somewhere near the eastern shore we must look for an old dry stone wall. Close by is a well, show me where it is and there lies the clue to the treasure.' He also promised $400 to the man who found the well, but they never found that or the wall. Eventually Pickles gave up; neither he nor Allen ever came back. The locals searched for years but never found anything.

Twenty years were to pass before another search was started by one of the locals who had searched earlier and his brother-in-law Thomas Ganter who had revived his interest. Ganter found the old well purely by chance. It was under a couple of feet of watery moss he was trying to cross in a ravine. Instead of contacting Pickles – who was still alive – to share their knowledge, they decided to try and find the treasure for themselves. This treasure hunt was to last, with intermissions, for forty-three years. They found the site of the old fireplace where the pirates cooked; it lay under two feet of earth. The treasure was supposed to be north of that, at the summit of the hillock in the eastern part of the island. Ganter concentrated on a site where he could hear sounds come from underground. Trenches criss-crossed the area and they finally dug a pit down to 36 feet. Alas, come 1936, Ganter, now aged seventy had had enough. For years he had made no effort to get in touch with Pickles, and now, when he did, it was too late, Mrs Pickles wrote back from Florida to say her husband had died five years earlier.

This was the situation when James P. Nolan, with a couple of friends, arrived. He had heard of the treasure hunt and wanted to see for himself. They made an agreement with Ganter and Nolan started work with his aluminium 'dowsing' rods – or gold finders as he called them. He walked up the gully with the pull of the rods getting stronger all the way and pointing straight down over the Ganter workings.

This was the beginning of many strange experiences that befell Nolan and his crew, experiences he refers to as 'spooky' or supernormal. The locals had long since regarded the place as haunted and were not surprised at the things that were to happen – good sound equipment failing, parts breaking, all their tools lying at the bottom of the pit next morning; another time they even found their pump engine down there, the sound of footsteps with no one around, eerie voices talking around the workings but no one there and so on.

They ran out of money and good weather. Nolan went off prospecting for gold (his real trade) but they were back in 1937 with an expert driller, air drills and compressors. Even so, they could make no real progress. 'Damn me,' swore the driller, 'This place is a mystery to me.'

Their cook had a mysterious and frightening experience at this time. They were all asleep when a voice said to him, 'Get up, come and see something.' Albert got up; the five other men in the cabin were fast asleep. He went out; it was very early in the morning with a full moon. He saw, at anchor in the cove, a large two-masted schooner, a long boat with six men on the beach and another just coming ashore. The men started to carry something up the beach; they were followed by men from the second boat holding up torches that shone brilliantly. One man was dressed like a monk, the others wore dark drooping hats and long cloaks such as were worn in the seventeenth century. The first party went up the gully in the direction of the workings, carrying a large chest or box. Presently the gang returned and stopped at the end of the gully; they drew swords and lunged at the monk, killing him. Albert, gazing on, was horrified; he let out a screech in terror and ran back to the cabin, apparently pursued by the apparitions flourishing their swords. Albert leaped into his bunk and pulled the blankets over his head but he still had the sensation of something trying to choke him. His companions were wide awake by now and asked him what the hell was the matter. 'Go outside and you'll see, they've already killed a monk.' They rushed outside but all was peaceful and as quiet as a tomb, no ship or men to be seen.

One of the other men had a similar unnerving experience later when alone one night on the island, but never said what it was.

In 1938 a diamond driller and digger arrived but the gremlins were still at work. The engine would stop, machinery break down, tools fall down the shaft with no one handling them, the diamond drill wore flat and so on, just as before. Finally the drill broke through the rock into a cavity 57 feet from the top of the shaft. They stopped now, having achieved their goal, and took a break. I stop at this point to wonder what on earth made them think that anyone would bury anything that deep down; to my knowledge, no treasure has ever been recovered deeper than 11 ft., 4-6 ft. is the usual. However, in Halifax they parked their car, engine switched off, whilst they went off. The car stood for about half an hour then decided to move. It suddenly moved off on its own down the street and went into another street knocking a sign down on the way before stopping on the pavement. The astonished passers-by, when told the car belonged to the Plum Island boys, were not surprised. They said the spooks were following them and they'd get no peace whilst digging for that blood-money on that island.

June 1938 came and Nolan was once again down to his last couple of pounds. He swore, 'I will sure get myself clear from this damned Plum Island and its devils.' His backers however decided to vote more money to the operation. They used dynamite but still could not get through to the cavity. Nolan wondered what the hell they were up against! Finances ran out again and he decided to look in more detail at the rest of the island with his gold finders. He found four gold veins running right across the island, and one six-foot vein ran right across their shaft!

Ghostly Ships and Shad Bay

An old local first told Nolan about Westhaver. He said that years ago, before the Great War, Joseph Smith, an old pilot, was out in his pilot boat waiting for a boat to come up from Cape Breton. She never come and it was dark when Smith started back. He then saw a strange-looking ship sailing on a course for Shad Bay. Thinking it might be his ship he got closer, but saw there was something strange about her rig and sails. He hailed her and got no answer, then suddenly the ship vanished. He realised he had seen the phantom ship spoken of by the old folk and seen only once a year in August, and it was August the 9th.

It was a couple of night before he admitted that he had seen the ghost ship. Westhaver, who was his assistant, didn't ridicule him as did their mates but questioned him on what he saw. Smith agreed that Westhaver could accompany him on the next anniversary.

Westhaver confirmed this story to Nolan and H. T. Wilkins when they met him and told them the rest of the story which went as follows:

9 August 1912 saw them out in the bay. They waited for hours and it was about 9.30 p.m. when Smith said, 'Good God, what is that?' A ship was approaching them under full sail – although there was no wind – and passed close by. The vessel was lit up but they couldn't see anyone aboard. She changed course into Shad Bay and they followed. In the lee of Cochrane's Island the strange ship anchored. Smith and Westhaver anchored off the north shore and watched. A long boat was lowered with thirteen men in it. They landed in a small cove, took something out of the boat, lashed it to the oars and carried it up into the island. They were armed with old flintlocks. A second boat left the ship with three men in it, each with a large basket-hilt sword and superior quality clothing to the other men. Their clothing was typical of English noblemen of the seventeenth century. The three officers – as Westhaver took them to be – went up a gully, followed quietly by Westhaver. They stopped by a large flat stone on the ground and after a few minutes came back. Westhaver walked on to see if he could see the other thirteen men but lost his way. When he found the beach again he called out loudly to Smith and saw the phantom ship promptly vanish.

When he found Smith, who was quaking in his shoes, he persuaded him to go up the gully with him to where he had seen the three men stop. They found the flat stone which they prised up. On the underside were inscriptions in Latin and English some of which he could read and copied down as follows:

'S. 25 steps to stone V E 89 steps N 10 steps down 10.'
'N 17 steps to shore . . .'

They excavated the pebbles from under where the slab had been and found a small iron box. They couldn't open it there so went back to Smith's house in St Margaret's Bay. There in the presence of some friends they managed to open it. In it was a ship's log and several charts, all in a foreign writing they could not understand. The papers were torn and rotten from the damp and like a jig-saw to put together. A date was recognised, believed to be 1768, also June 11, 1798; Plum Island was also mentioned. One particular name appeared several times – 'Keede' and 'William Edward Keede'. They had the charts translated by a Jew in Halifax and destroyed the originals which were too brittle to handle.

It would appear that the charts gave directions to treasure in at least three different locations. Westhaver said the charts showed that Keede must have buried a vast amount of gold somewhere on this coast, the deepest cache being 11 ft. down and containing £3,000,000 in gold in boxes, in a cave. There were other caches not so deep. One of the documents, chart number 7, reads in part:

Stored today June 11 1768 [?] 3 sea chests, one barrel burried bye the setting sun . . .
beheaded two to guard.

The charts direct the recoverers to other islands. In other words, Plum Island is where the directions are (were) buried. A treasure is buried on Plum Island though, the legend on the flat stone slab apparently gave the directions to it; we will remember also that Captain Allen was looking for a treasure here. The charts show also that a pirate by the name of Cult buried treasure in a 'queer island'. Wilkins gives it the fictitious name of 'Moose Island' and it consists of the proceeds of three years of robbery and murder on the high seas in the middle of the eighteenth century. Westhaver had men digging for it in 1923. The charts say the treasure is stored in a strong room made of wood in a cave 18 ft. × 18 ft. × 8 ft. deep, the top being 4 ft. down. This cache, according to the charts, contains:

One barrel of gold pieces, One sea chest of Spanish silver pesos, One small chest of gold bars and gold dust, One small chest of dyamuns and pearls and rubis, all valued at three millions.

Other merchandise was also stored in the cave including cannon and gunpowder.

Shortly after the discovery of the charts, Smith and Westhaver went to one of the islands depicted: it is not clear which one. They found the appropriate markers, measured off a distance and found a drain. Further tests and excavations indicated that what felt like wood was underneath. They left to get more gear and help. Next night, as soon as they commenced digging, something so frightening and uncanny happened that they dropped everything and ran. They wouldn't say what it was but vowed never to go back. They made an agreement that neither would go for the treasure without the other and after that scare Smith could never be persuaded to go for the treasure again.

One of the charts found in the box named another unknown island. It was written in the old style – 'Gloucefter Ifle'. The chart also bore the mysterious letters, 'H.S.O.H.E.' and a ship's name *BELMORE* or *BAL-MORE*. There was also a date, June 6 1638 or 1738.

Blake, Keede and Captain Cult

Another chart was to link Westhaver with Kidd and it wasn't one of those found in the box from Plum Island. In 1928 he was introduced to a Mr Blake who had arrived from England. Westhaver was sought out because, being a coastal pilot, he knew all the islands and coves. Blake had brought with him two charts relating to pirate caches buried by one Captain Cult. He showed one to Westhaver and asked him if he knew where the place depicted was. Westhaver did, and agreed to take Blake there. To cut a long story short, they went to Gaspé harbour which is on the east end of the Gaspé peninsula, hired a boat, and found the cove they were seeking and a large boulder with ancient marks on it that stood near the shore. Paces were measured out and a hole dug in which was found a skull. The skull was removed and reburied a certain distance away. They returned to the original hole, dug deeper and recovered an old iron box full of gold coins. Next day, back in Halifax, Blake showed Westhaver the second chart and asked him if he recognised the place. Westhave gazed at it and started in astonishment for the island on it was identical with an island on one of the charts that he and Smith had found on Cochrane's Island. Their chart was signed 'W. E. KEEDE'. Blake's chart however, although signed 'Capt Cult', was also signed 'Capt Kidd, Spain 9 March'. Another date also appeared: 'June 6, 1689.'

Blake's chart was larger than Westhaver's, gave the outline of the coast from Halifax and showed sailing courses to Shad Bay and Dover N. S. The chart bore the following inscription:
'CLOSE HARBOUR THREE BRITISH 3,000,000 IN GOLD MARKS SOUTH CLIFF EAST SIDE OF BIG BAY.'

With reference to chart C9 below, which is Wilkins' copy of Westhaver's copy, we can see the similarity in inscriptions; unfortunately we cannot compare island shapes. The chart is immediately recognised as typically Wilkins and should therefore not be taken too seriously – he does tend to add a bit of 'colour' and make a pirate's chart look like what he thinks it should look like. However, until (and if ever) Blake's or Westhaver's chart turns up we will never know.

What we have then are two charts from different sources, both apparently depicting the same island and it would appear the same treasure, one signed 'Capt Kidd, 1689', the other signed 'W.E.K 1742', i.e. 'William Edward Keede'. If true, the names are a remarkable coincidence. It also suggests that Cult and/or Kidd buried a treasure in 1689 and Keede

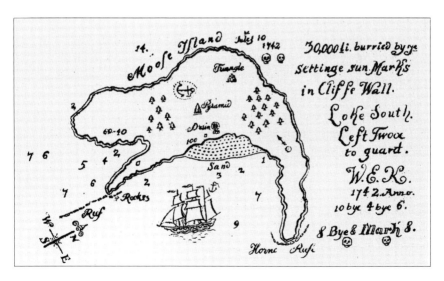

C9. Copy of a chart found with others by Smith and Westhaver in 1912 on Plum Island. A Mr Blake had a chart found in a haunted house in England of the same island, his chart being signed Kidd and Cult.

did the same thing in 1742. It all sounds a bit too strange to me. To add to the confusion, I known for a fact that Kidd's wife signed her name at least once 'Sarah Keede'.

W. E. Keede was obviously active in this area. A Wilkins copy of one of the other charts found by Westhaver and Smith (see chart C10) shows that he buried a cache here in 1768. Again, the copy is typical Wilkins, so one wonders how seriously one should take it.

We have digressed, so to come back to Westhaver and the second chart showed him by Blake: Westhaver had already searched for a cache on this island in 1923. Moose Island is not its real name and the Cochrane papers list the treasure there as quoted earlier.

Westhaver took Blake to the location where Blake studied another paper. They measured off 150 feet and with a steel bar punched down into the sand. At a depth of four feet it struck what seemed to be wood. As Westhaver was probing the sand they were suddenly and unaccountably surrounded by a cloud of black darkness and the earth beneath them trembled. He said it was frightful and indescribable; they were two of the most frightened men alive.

They threw down their tools and got out as fast as they could. Westhaver vowed never to return. Blake said it proved to him the truth of this instructions and was happy to leave it at that. He gave Westhaver the chart with certain bizarre instructions for its release. That however is another story, not really connected with our subject – Kidd.

It would appear here that someone is getting their stories mixed up, Wilkins, Westhaver or Nolan, and Wilkins' books *are* somewhat confusing. This latter tale is almost identical to the earlier one; time and probably age have confused the incident. We are left in no doubt that something uncanny did happen all those years ago and the charts certainly were found.

As related earlier, one of Westhaver's charts bore the name 'Gloucefter Ifle' and therefore must have been drawn *after* 1776 when the chart of that area was first printed by the Admiralty and the island was shown to have that name. Furneaux (Gay drew the island for him) said that two named ships and an anchor were shown off the coast beyond the island's south-west shore. The interior bore two 'marks' and the chart was dated 17_8. The directions which Wilkins had printed in his 'Skeleton Island' book were there, also a sailing course '40N × 63W, steer NW¼.' The chart also bore the mysterious letters 'H.S.O.H.E.', which would identify it as the chart mentioned earlier, one of the ships' names being *Balmore*. But here we have another puzzle: the earlier mentioned chart is dated *before* 1776. That date could of course refer to when the island was visited and not necessarily when drawn. What does seem clear is that the island depicted is Oak Island. 'Gloucefter Ifle' was the name given it by the British Admiralty Hydrographer Joseph F. W. Des Barres, when he surveyed Mahone Bay in 1773. As this chart was discovered with several others in the box found by Smith and Westhaver on Cochrane's Island, it is reasonable to assume there is a pirate treasure buried on Oak Island – not necessarily in the Money Pit – and by Cult or Keede, possibly even Kidd.

H.S.O.H.E. stands for Hydrographic Survey Office Halifax Establishment. It appears on Westhaver's chart probably because the original

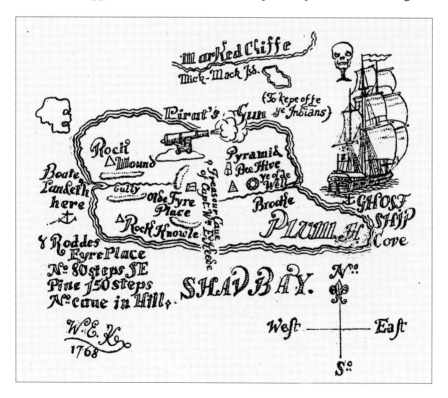

C10. Another one of the charts found by Smith and Westhaver on Plum Island, searched for by Captain Allen and supposed to contain a pirate treasure.

chart used was one of the Admiralty prints and therefore carried that abbreviation. *Belmore* or *Balmore* was most probably the name of the vessel used in the survey and whilst not listed in the list of Admiralty Survey vessels (I checked with the Hydrographic Department) they said it could have been a (local) vessel hired for the purpose.

These observations almost certainly identify the author of the charts as British. The Admiralty charts mentioned were only made available to British naval and military officers.

Ancient Boulder Marks

James Nolan found another connection with Kidd in 1937. He was walking the shore of a bay then known as Galleon or Spanish Ship Bay when he came across a large boulder previously hidden by a large and very old tree that had blown down. The large granite boulder has a flat top and contains a complex of inscribed lines and figures; one of the figures closely resembles a 'boot'. William S. Crooker, author of *The Oak Island Quest* made the sketch shown (See drawing D1) and feels that what we are looking at is a graphic message rather than a code, the 'boot' representing an island. The outline is similar to the Blake/Keede charts – also the Kidd/Palmer charts.

Wilkins in his *A Modern Treasure Hunter* refers to this rock and the 'sign of ye Old Boot in Galleon Bay'. This poses another mystery to us as the actual location of the boulder (according to Crooker) is about 120 miles east of Oak Island near the mouth of Gasperaux Brook in Liscomb, Colchester County, Nova Scotia: in other words nowhere near Galleon Bay which is about sixty miles further down the coast in Halifax County. The inscribed slab of stone found in this (Galleon) Bay is shown in drawing D2 and is from a sketch made by Westhaver. There are obvious similarities between the two inscriptions: both are referred to using the word 'boot'. My immediate reaction is that they both refer to the same stone or boulder, Westhaver's sketch being done from memory. Crooker's sketch shows the actual inscription because he went to the boulder and copied it. That though doesn't explain the two locations sixty miles apart. Perhaps there really are two rock inscriptions, I don't know. Hopefully my readers in Nova Scotia will enlighten me.

We have seen earlier how Wilkins and/or Nolan, possibly Westhaver

D1: Sketch made by William S. Crooker of marks to be found on a boulder at the mouth of Gasperaux Brook, Guysborough County, Nova Scotia.

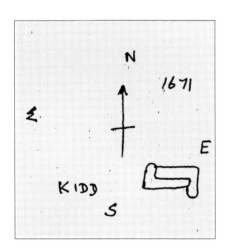

D2: Sketch made by Herman Westhaver of marks on a stone to be found in Galleon or Spanish Ship Bay, Halifax County, Nova Scotia.

also, could be getting their stories mixed up and I don't believe also that there can be two *large* boulders with graphic inscriptions, both making reference to Kidd. We will recall that one of the markers that Blake and Westhaver looked for when searching for the first cache, was a large boulder with 'ancient' marks on it. They went to Gaspé Harbour at the end of the Gaspé peninsula, which is over three hundred miles away due north-west in the Gulf of St Lawrence. I don't believe they did go there. The boulder from which William Crooker copied an inscription, as we have seen, is at Gasperaux Brook, Nova Scotia., 'Gaspé' being the important connection. It must surely be the same boulder found by Blake and Westhaver. Blake sought out Westhaver because he had expert knowledge of the local (Nova Scotia) waters. I doubt very much if his expertise carried as far north as the Gaspé Passage, nowhere near Nova Scotia.

To me, it seems like another case of information presented incorrectly to us.

For obvious reasons it would have been nice to talk to Herman Westhaver. He apparently passed away in 1967 in Englishtown, Cape Breton Island. Should any of his descendants be reading this, I would appreciate you contacting me through the publishers.

The Oak Island Stone

Back to Oak Island, still in Nova Scotia. During the 1804 excavations, they found, at about the 90 ft. level, a large inscribed flagstone – yes, another one! – it was about 3 feet long, 16 inches wide and 10 inches thick. The stone was unique in that it was not indigenous to that coast and was very hard. On the stone strange characters had been cut (See drawing D3). The inscription is a simple cryptogram in English and has been deciphered as follows:

FORTY FEET BELOW
TWO MILLION
POUNDS ARE BURIED

John Smith (one of the original discoverers of the pit) took the stone home and it was eventually built into the fireplace of his son's house. Many years later (1865 or 1866) it was removed and taken to Halifax to have the inscription deciphered. It was then put on display in a shop window of a bookbinder's firm. When taken in it was found to be ideal to beat leather on and eventually every trace of the inscription was worn out. Thorough searches since have failed to discover the stone.

Our interest in that stone lies in the theory of one Vic Marcellus of Milwaukee. He says (*Treasure Magazine*, December 1986) that the inscription is made up of old surveyor's coordinates, and according to his figures the treasure is approximately 40 rods (660 ft.) north-east of the main pit. William Kidd, says Marcellus, worked as a surveyor in his

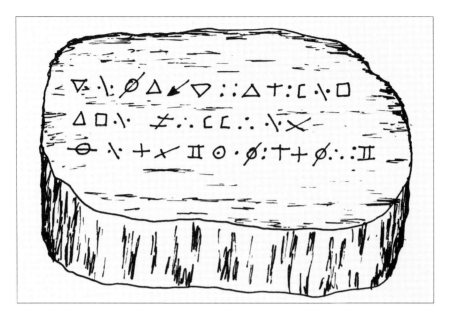

D3: Inscription found on a stone slab at about the 90 foot level in the 'money pit', Oak Island. N.S. (I do not vouch that the number of inscriptions shown per line are as originally scribed)

early days before turning privateer and it was he who made the inscriptions. He goes on to say that the deciphered inscriptions are also found on Kidd's chart.

Marcellus has apparently sent his findings to Triton Alliance who control most of the island but they don't bother to reply now to the many such letters they get every year. Marcellus does not elaborate on his theory so we cannot check it out. For my part, I can see nothing in the Kidd charts that bears any resemblance to the inscriptions on the stone.

Whilst on the subject of this stone, a correspondent of Furneaux's living in Gaysborough County, Nova Scotia, says:

> The inscription is a simple number code, to be read backwards and there is an over-lay that must go with it. For the top line of the stone, the two things that are on the over-lay are the words, South, and East by North. The top line gives the location for stopping the water from the East shore. It is simple addition and the answers are 151 ft South, 284 ft, 43 degrees East by North.

I do not see anything simple in it myself, but it is included for your perusal, should you be interested. He gives the break down of the number code as follows:

$0 =$ Ø
$1 =$ ᵒ\₀
$2 =$:
$3 =$ △▽⊏
$4 =$ ☐
$20 =$ T
$22 =$ ::
$45 =$ ✓

The starting point is the money pit.

Richard Barlicorn

Our final story relating to the shores of Nova Scotia is concerned with Richard Barlicorn, who was Kidd's cabin boy on the *Adventure Galley*. He was probably still a teenager at the time of Kidd's death when he was called to give evidence at Kidd's trail. After the execution, when it was thought wise by anyone connected with Kidd to be a long way away, Barlicorn was put on a ship bound for North America and was put ashore in the Bay of Fundy.

His story, it is said, has been handed down through the generations of a family whose ancestor took him in, and was unknown until fifty years ago. Barlicorn lived and died in Cape Sable Island near present day Wedgeport, Goose Bay, on the south-west end of Nova Scotia and when he knew he had not long to live, he told the sons of the friend who took him in that he saw Kidd bury a treasure on an island hereabouts. He said that he (Barlicorn) came to these parts by design and not by accident. He was with Kidd when he came here and although he wasn't allowed on the island at the time, he saw Kidd go ashore with iron-bound and wooden trunks and leather and canvas bags with much gold and other valuables in them. The island he said he could see every day as it was (sic) only about four or five miles off shore. The only marker to the treasure that he knew of was a very hard stick of lignum vitae driven into a split rock.

Having told the boys this story, they persuaded him to take them to the island which he shortly did. After much searching they found, in a wooded cove not far from the shore line, a queer shaped boulder with some old sticks stuck in it. They searched around for the cache and any other markers and clues but found nothing more. They searched for years after the old man's death but to no avail and eventually they didn't bother any more and it was left at that. The story was kept in the family for nearly two hundred years and is quite possibly little known in the area even now.

The above story, to be true, means that the treasure buried was taken during Kidd's last fateful voyage and therefore must have been buried before he arrived in Boston. The official accounts of Kidd's voyage obviously make no reference to any trip to Nova Scotia so we have to look at when he could have fitted one in. As his voyage is pretty well documented that should not be too difficult to check out. Cape Sable Island is about three hundred miles from Block Island or about three days sailing, say a week at least for a round trip. When would he have had that sort of time to go there with nobody knowing about it? His last known movements, leading up to his arrest, were as follows:

Early May: Left the *Quedagh Merchant* and Mona Passage.

6 June: After a journey of some 1,400 miles was sighted off the Delaware Capes and landed at Lewes to let some men off and take on wood and water.

10 June: Rounded Long Island, ran up the Sound and anchored in Oyster Bay; left message for Emmot to meet with him.

12 June: Sailed back up the Sound, landed Emmot at Stonington, Rhode Island, with letter for Bellomont.

24 June: Wrote to Bellomont from Block Island.

25/26 June: Deposited treasure at Gardiner's Island.

27/28 June: Rounded Cape Cod.

1/2 July: Landed in Boston.

3/6 July: At liberty in Boston and writing his Narrative.

6 July: Arrested.

I do not vouch that the dates quoted are precise; even the more respected books on Kidd differ quite often by a day or two. It would appear though that there is a period in the middle of June when there is nothing definite documented concerning his movements. We do know that for a few days

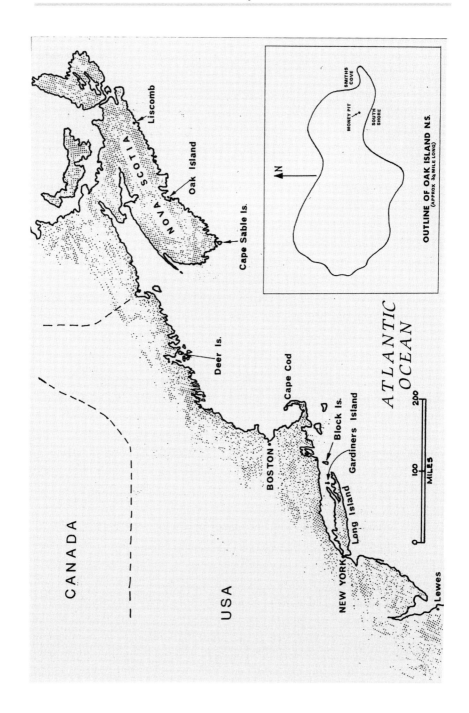

he was scurrying back and forth between Block Island and Gardiner's Island. Even so, there is still at least a week that seems to be unaccounted for.

If he did go to the waters of Nova Scotia it makes sense. It was far enough away not to be seen by anyone he knew and close enough to recover anything in a few days. If the earlier stories are true, Kidd obviously knew this area well and of course one would expect him to, having lived for many years only a few days' sailing away.

It would appear to me that we should not dismiss out of hand that Kidd did not have time to bury treasure anywhere other than at Gardiner's Island. I would also think it obvious that Block Island would be another good place to look for something.

It was reported that in March 1951, a fisherman trolling for turtles on the New Jersey shore hooked a brass plate inscribed 'William Kidd' and the word 'Quedah', believed to have been attached to a sea chest, but I don't know how reliable that story is.

The Nagashima-Kidd Treasure

I have mentioned earlier the problem of misleading information. A story repeated in at least two books, those already mentioned by Roden and Norvill, was that Kidd's treasure, or one of his treasures, was found in the early fifties by a Japanese called Masahiro Nagashima, on the island of Yokoate Shima (formerly Jokoata). This island lies at 28° 50′N, 129° 00′E and is one of the northernmost islands of the Ryuku Retto Group.

The popular story was that some Japanese fishermen, sheltering there during a storm, found carved on a rock some drawings of a horned animal. This find was subsequently reported and came to the attention of Nagashima, a scholar of Kidd. He had heard that Kidd had sometimes used a drawing of a goat (or kid) as a signature and thought that the rock drawing could be a guide to his treasure. An expedition was organised to the island and Nagashima easily found the spot described by the fishermen. After a thorough search he found the entrance to a concealed cave which contained a heap of iron boxes. When opened they were found to contain a fortune in gold and silver, afterwards estimated at £30 million. The treasure was transported to Tokyo where it vanished together with Nagashima.

That is the accepted story. What really happened was that when the fall of Japan was imminent at the end of the Second World War, the gold bullion in question was smuggled out of the country by the authorities and hidden on the island. It was later recovered by Nagashima in conjunction with the United States Navy. There was even a newsreel film about it.

This sort of treasure story of course leaves the unsuspecting reader deflated at the thought that Kidd's treasure has been found. I might add that nowhere in my research have I come across any reference to Kidd using the drawing of a goat as a signature.

Those not getting it right

Incorrect information on Kidd and the charts continues to be presented to us. On 25 March 1987, whilst I was still writing this manuscrupt, an article appeared in the *London Evening Standard*. It was titled 'OK, Kidd, where's it buried?' The author had phoned me up a few days prior to publication, and asked me a few questions and for some of my thoughts on the business of the charts. The article referred to myself and the work I had done (i.e. the research and manuscript for this book) and gave a very brief description of Kidd's life and this whole business. He also mentions Knight. I was amused to read: 'But silence has now fallen again and Mr Knight's whereabouts are unknown.' You will have already read that I knew exactly where Richard Knight was.

However, a most glaring error appeared in the article: 'The workbox had a secret bottom and in it, unbelievably, were *four* [my italics] yellow cloth maps.'

I wrote to the author pointing out his error, and made a few other comments at the same time. But of course the damage had already been done. Anyone reading in that article for the first time about these charts is almost bound to go along with the quoted statement, i.e. it is 'unbelievable', and straight away ridicule the fact that they are genuine. After all, who is going to believe that four genuine pirate treasure maps were found in one secret compartment?

Unfortunately, it is another case of an author not doing diligent research and possibly putting readers off what is undoubtedly a fascinating but true story.

Similar errors keep cropping up. In the book *Buried and Sunken Treasure* (Marshall Cavendish Publications Ltd. 1974), it states that the maps were all obtained from genuine old sea chests which bore Kidd's name. We know that one was found in a bureau and one in a workbox. Only two were found in chests.

In 1986, *Lost Treasures of the World* (Admiral Books) included a story titled 'The Quest for Kidd's Cache'. In it the author states that the seventeenth century oak chest bore the inscription 'Captain William Kidd – *Adventure Galley* 1699'. It should of course be 1669. The same error is repeated where the author states the map was dated 1699. Further on he describes a chest as inscribed 'William and Sarah Kidd, Their Chest'. It was in fact a workbox and inscribed 'William and Sarah Kidd, Their Box': typical examples of errors being repeated. The same author carries on to quote that Nagashima story and the connection with Kidd. We know of course that Kidd had no connection with the bullion story.

Deer Island and Kidd's Treasure

Deer Island, which lies in Penobscot Bay, off the mouth of the Penobscot River on the coast of Maine, USA, was in 1892 the property and summer home of Mr Frederic Law Olmsted. The island had been in the family since 1699 when his ancestor, Cotten Mather Olmsted, was presented with the island by an Indian chief as a token of gratitude, Mr Olmsted having cared for him after the chief was severely wounded by a bear.

At the extreme south end of the island is a cave, the opening of which is upon the sea. The cave is about 10 ft. wide and high, of irregular shape, and extends back into the rock formation some 25 ft. It has evidently been excavated by the ceaseless action of the waves upon a portion of the rock somewhat softer than its surroundings. At high tide the entire cave is under water, but at low tide it can be entered dry-shod, being entirely above sea-level. The bottom of the cave is covered with coarse sand, five or six inches deep, below which is a compact bed of hard blue clay. At low tide the cave was often visited by the family of Mr Olmsted and the other residents of the island.

In 1892, Mr Olmsted observed upon the rock at the inner end of the cave some marks or indentations, something in the form of a rude cross, which seemed to him possibly of artificial origin. If so, it was of ancient date, as its edges were not well defined – rounded and worn, as by the action of the waves and ice. Still, it appeared more regular in form than the other markings upon the walls of the cave, and Mr Olmsted one day suggested to his family, when in the cave, that as stories of Captain Kidd's buried treasures had sometimes located such treasures upon the Maine coast, they should dig at the place below the cross for such hidden wealth.

Purely as a matter of sport, the excavation was commenced: the sand was cleared away, and, to their utter astonishment, a rectangular hole in the clay was discovered, about 15 by 30 inches on the surface and about 15 inches deep. This was filled with sand, and upon the sand being carefully removed, there was plainly to be seen upon the bottom of the hole the marks of a row of bolt heads some three or four inches apart, and extending around the bottom about an inch from its edge.

The appearance was precisely as if an iron box heavily bolted at its joints had been buried in the compact clay for a period long enough to have left a perfect imprint of itself in the clay, and after its removal, the excavation having been filled with sand, the impression had been perfectly preserved. After a perfect facsimile of the bottom of the hole had been taken in plaster of Paris, the excavation was again filled with sand. The clay was so hard that the taking of the cast did not mar its surface. The bottom of the hole and such portions of the sides as had not been marred by the removal of the box were heavily coated with rust, so that everything indicated the former presence of an iron box which had remained buried in the clay long enough at least to become thoroughly rusted on its surface and firmly embedded in the clay matrix.

As there were various legends relative to the presence of Captain Kidd upon the Maine coast, the discovery of the excavation was sufficient to awaken eager interest in the question of the iron box and the person who carried it away.

Thinking back, Mr Olmsted recalled a family story about a trader who used to hunt for furs on the island at the turn of the century; the story went as follows:

About the year 1801 a French-Canadian, named Jacques Cartier, who was one of the employees of John Jacob Astor in his fur trade and who had for several winters traded with the Indians and hunters along the upper waters of the Penobscot River, returned from New York, where he had been to deliver the season's collection of furs, and expressed a desire to purchase from Oliver Cromwell Olmsted, who was then owner by inheritance of Deer Island, either the whole island or the south end, where the cave previously described was located. Mr Olmsted refused both requests, but finally sold him a few acres near the centre of the island, where he built a log cabin and lived for many years with an Indian wife, hunting and fishing occasionally as a diversion but giving up entirely his former method of earning a living.

This trader had for several years previous to 1801 camped upon the south end of Deer Island when collecting his furs, passing up the Penobscot River and its tributaries in a small canoe, and storing his furs in a hut at his camping place until the end of his season, when he sailed with his little cargo for New York. He had always seemed extremely poor, having but a meagre salary from Mr Astor, but when he purchased a portion of the island he seemed to have an abundance of money, sufficient in fact to meet his wants for many years. Occasionally, when under the influence of whiskey, he would speak vaguely of some sudden good fortune which had befallen him, but when sober he always denied ever having made the statement, and seemed much disturbed when asked about the source of his wealth, which led to various suspicions among the few inhabitants of the island as to the honesty of his methods in acquiring it. These suspicions ultimately became so pointed that he suddenly disappeared from the island and never returned. On searching his cabin some fragments of papers were found, torn and partially burned, so that no connected meaning could be determined from them. On one fragment was the signature of John Jacob Astor, and on another in the same handwriting, the words: 'absolute secrecy must be observed because'. These fragments were preserved, however, and were in the possession of Mr Frederic Law Olmsted.

From the story of the trader and from the fragmentary papers, Mr Olmsted fancied that there might be some connection between the mysterious box and the newly acquired wealth of the trader, and that the secret, if one there was, was shared by Mr Astor.

As the trader for many years previous to his sudden good fortune had camped upon the end of the island immediately adjoining the cave, it might readily be conceived that a heavy storm had washed the sand away so as to make the top of the box visible, and that he had found it and taken it with him to New York to Mr Astor, with his boatload of furs. The trader's desire to purchase this particular location in the island harmonised with this suggestion.

Various questions presented themselves regarding this theory. Had the box contained the long-lost treasures of Captain Kidd? If so, to whom did the box and its contents belong? Mr W.M. Evarts, to whom Mr Olmsted applied for an opinion as to the legal part of this question, after careful examination of the evidence gave his views in substance, as follows:

1. That Captain Kidd, in the year 1700, had acquired, by pillage, vast treasures of gold and gems, which he had somewhere concealed prior to his execution in 1701.

2. That if such treasure was concealed upon Deer Island, that island was the absolute property, at that time, of Cotton Mather Olmsted; for while the record title to the island bore date in President Washington's administration in 1794, yet this, as appeared by its tenor, was in affirmation of the title made in 1699, when the island was given to Cotton Mather Olmsted by the Indian chief, Winnepesaukee, and established the ownership of the island in Mr Olmsted when the box, if concealed by Captain Kidd, was buried, and that Frederic Law Olmsted, by inheritance and purchase, had acquired all the rights originally held by his ancestor in that part of the island where the treasure was concealed.

3. That, as owner of such real estate the treasure would belong to him, as affixed to the land, as against the whole world, except possibly the lineal descendants of Captain Kidd, if any there were.

Mr Olmsted learned that, in his early life, Mr Astor kept for many years his first and only bank account with the Manhattan Bank, and as the books of the bank were all preserved, he was able, by a plausible pretext, to secure an examination of Mr Astor's financial transactions from the beginning. His idea, in this search, was to learn if Mr Astor's fortune had increased at the same time as that of the hunter and fur trader Jacques Cartier.

The business of both Mr Astor and the bank was small in those early day, and the entries of the customers' accounts were much more detailed than in our time, when, as a rule, only amounts are recorded. The account commenced in 1798, being one of the first opened, and for several years the total deposits for an entire year did not exceed $4,000. He shipped some of his furs abroad, and others were sold to dealers and manufacturers, and whenever he drew on a customer with a bill of lading, the books of the bank show virtually the whole transaction. Each year showed a modest increase in the volume of business of the thrifty furrier, but the aggregates were only moderate until the year 1801, being the same year that the trader bought off Mr Olmsted a portion of Deer Island, when the volume of bank transactions reached, for the first time, enormous dimensions, springing from an aggregate for the year 1799 of $4,011 to over £500,000 for the year 1801.

Among the entries in the latter year were two of the same date for cheques to Jacques Cartier, the trader: one of $133.50 drawn 'In settlement fur account', and one for $5,000, 'In settlement to date'. Inasmuch as in each previous year the aggregate fur transactions with Mr Cartier had never exceeded $500, the entry of $5,000 seemed inexplicable on any ordinary grounds. The enormous growth of Mr Astor's own transactions seemed equally mysterious. Mr Astor had evidently visited England in 1801, as the bank entries are filled with credits to him of drafts remitted by him from one Roderick Streeter, varying from £10,000 to £40,000, and aggregating, during the year, nearly $495,000. Credits of the same Streeter drafts are made also during the two following years to the amount of over $800,000 more, or a total of over £1,300,000, when the Streeter remittances abruptly cease.

Edwin W. Streeter of London was at that time one of the largest dealers in precious stones in the world and, as in England the same business is often continued in a family for many generations, it occurred to Mr Frederic Law Olmsted who, from the facts already given, had become greatly interested in following the matter to a conclusion, that the Streeter who had made the vast remittances to Mr Astor might be an ancestor of the present London merchant. An inquiry by mail developed the fact that the present Mr Streeter was a great-grandson of Roderick Streeter, and that the business had been continued in the family for five generations. Mr Olmsted thereupon sent a confidential agent to London, who succeeded in getting access to the books of the Streeter firm for the years 1798 to 1802 inclusive. Here was found a detailed statement of the transactions with Mr Astor.

The first item was for £40,000 entered as 'Advances on ancient French and Spanish Gold Coins' deposited by Mr Astor, and later another of £4,218 8*s.* for 'Balance due for the French and Spanish gold coins'. All other entries were for the sale of precious stones, mostly diamonds, rubies and pearls, which in all, with the sums paid for the French and Spanish gold, reached the enormous aggregate previously given. Certain of the gems were purchased outright by Mr Streeter and the others were sold by him as a broker, for the account of Mr Astor, and the proceeds duly remitted during the years 1801–2. The whole account corresponded exactly, item for item, with the various entries of Streeter remittances shown on the books of the Manhattan Bank.

The facts gathered thus far enabled Mr Olmsted to formulate a theory in substance as follows:

That Jacques Cartier had found the box containing the buried treasures of Captain Kidd; that he had taken it to New York and delivered it to Mr Astor; that Mr Astor had bought the contents of the box, or his interest in them, for the cheque of $5,000; that he had taken the contents to England, and had, from their sale, realised the vast sums paid him by Mr Streeter.

Many links in the chain of evidence, however, were still missing, and a great point would be gained if the mysterious box could be traced to the custody of Mr Astor. It seemed reasonable that this box, if ever in the possession of Mr Astor, and if its contents were of such great value, would be retained by him with scrupulous care, and that, if he had imparted the secret to his children, it would still be in their possession. If not, it might have been sold and lost sight of, as a piece of worthless scrap-iron, after the death of the first Mr Astor. Mr Olmsted learned that the last house in which the original John Jacob Astor had lived had been torn down in the year 1893, to be replaced by a superb modern building, and that the old building had been sold to a well known house wrecking firm for an insignificant sum, as the material was worth but little above the cost of tearing down and removal. In the hope that the rusty box had been sold with the other rubbish about the premises, Mr Olmsted inserted the following advertisement in the *New York Tribune*:

A rusty iron box, strongly made and bolted, was by mistake sold in 1893 to a dealer in junk, supposedly in New York or Brooklyn. The dimensions were 15 x 30 x 15 inches. A person for sentimental reasons, wishes to reclaim this box, and will pay to its present owner for the same several times its value as scrapiron. Address F.L. Box 74, N.Y. Tribune.

Within a few days, Mr Olmsted received a letter from Mr Bronson B. Tuttle of Naugatuck, Connecticut, an iron manufacturer, stating that, in a car of scrap-iron bought by him from M. Jacobs of Brooklyn, was an iron box answering the description given in the *Tribune*; that if it was of any value to the advertiser, it would be forwarded on receipt of eighty cents, which was its cost to him at $11 per ton, the price paid for the carload of scrap.

Mr Olmsted at once procured the box and shipped it to Deer Island, where the bolts upon its bottom and the box itself were found to fit perfectly the print in the clay bottom of the cave. The plaster case of the bottom of the cavity, taken when it was first discovered, matched the bottom of the box as perfectly as ever a casting fitted the mould in which it was made. Every peculiarity in the shape of a bolthead, every hammer-mark made in riveting the bolts, as shown in the clay, was reproduced in the iron box. There was no possible question that the box was not the identical one which had been long before buried in the cave.

On the top of the box, too, distinguishable despite the heavy coating of rust, in rude and irregularly formed characters as if made by strokes of a cold chisel or some similar tool, were the letters W.K., the initials of the veritable and eminent pirate, Captain William Kidd. Further inquiry developed the fact that M. Jacobs, the Brooklyn junk dealer, had purchased the box in a large dray-load of scrap-iron, mostly made up of a cooking-range, sash weights, gas, steam and water pipes, etc. from the wrecking firm of Jones & Co., and that Jones & Co. had taken much material from the family mansion occupied by the original John Jacob Astor at the time of his death, when tearing it down to make room for the new buildings.

The indications intensified that the mysterious box contained the long-lost and widely sought treasures of Captain Kidd. One peculiarity of the box was that there had apparently been no way of opening it except by cutting it apart. The top had been firmly riveted in its place, and this fact possibly indicated the reason of its purchase by Mr Astor at the moderate price of $5,000, as the trader who found it had been unable to open it before his arrival in New York, As, however, we have no information of the contract between Mr Astor and Jacques Cartier, the amount named,

$5,000, may have been precisely the percentage agreed upon, which he received upon the profits of his season's business in addition to a salary.

Mr Olmsted had an accurate copy made of all entries in the books of the Manhattan Bank as to the transactions of Mr Astor shown by such books, from 1798 to 1803, and his English agent had similar copies made of all entries in the books of Roderick Streeter for the same period, with copies of many letters passing between the parties. The agent also looked up and reported everything available relative to the career of Captain Kidd.

They discovered that from the great number of vessels which he had destroyed and plundered, with their ascertained cargoes, it was known that the treasure recovered on Gardiner's Island was but an insignificant fraction of what he had captured. It was known that gold and gems of vast value were somewhere concealed – and thence came the endless searches from Key West and Jekyl Island to Halifax for the treasure, which had thus far seemingly escaped human detection and utterly disappeared. In fact, from the little care taken by Captain Kidd as to the plunder hidden on Gardiner's Island, the owners of his ship concluded that to be merely a blind to divert their attention from the vastly greater wealth he had appointed.

However, Olmsted's agent also discovered that after the death sentence had been passed on Kidd, his wife was allowed to see him in Newgate Jail. They were seen to hold a whispered conference, and at its close Kidd was seen to hand her a card, upon which he had written the figures 44106818. This card was taken from her by the guards and never restored. Every effort was made to induce her to tell the meaning of the figures, but she utterly refused, and even claimed not to know herself.

The paper was preserved among the proceedings of the trial, and a photographed copy secured by Mr Olmsted. From the records of the trial, it appeared that Captain Kidd was the only child of his parents; that he had been married for several years; that he had two children, a daughter who died whilst still a child and before the trial, and a son, who survived both his father and mother. It also appeared that this son, ten years after his father's execution, enlisted as a private soldier in the English Army and was killed in the battle near Stirling in 1715. The records of the English War Office showed that the widow of this son applied for a pension under the then existing law, that her affidavit and marriage certificate showed her to have been married to the son of Captain Kidd, and that no child had been born to them; the usual pension was awarded to her and paid until her death in 1744.

These facts settled the question as to any claim upon the treasure by descendants of Captain Kidd. The records of the trial also contained a report by experts upon the card given by Kidd to his wife, to the effect that they had applied to the figures upon it the usual tests for the reader of cipher-writings without avail, and if the figures had a meaning, it was not to be undiscovered. The same conclusion was reached by several people to whom Mr Olmsted showed the copy of the card.

In the summer of 1894, Professor David P. Todd, the astronomer of Amherst College, was visiting the family at Deer Island. He one day amused himself by calculating the latitude and longitude of the home, near the cave, and gave the results to Miss Marion Olmsted. As she was entering the results in her journal, she was struck by the fact that the figures for the latitude, 44° 10′, were the same as the first four figures on the card, 4410, and that the other figures, 6818, were almost the exact longitude west from Greenwich, which was 68° 13′, a difference easily accounted for by a moderate variation in Kidd's chronometer. The latitude, taken by observation of the Pole Star, was absolutely accurate. It appeared as though Kidd had told his wife in this manner where to find his hidden treasure, but that, inasmuch as the authorities had seized the card, she preferred silence towards those who had pursued her husband to his death, and the total loss to everyone of the treasure, rather than by a confession to give it into the hands of his enemies. The very simplicity of the supposed cipher-writing had been its safeguard, since all the experts had sought for some abstruse and occult meaning in the combination of figures.

By a happy thought of Miss Olmsted, another link was thus added to the chain of evidence. With the facts given, the only point seemingly needed to show that that Kidd treasure had come into the possession of Mr Astor was to show that some of the money or gems sold by him had been actually seized by Kidd. Even this, by a happy chance, become possible through the correspondence secured from Mr Streeter of London.

It appeared that in the year 1700, Lord and Lady Dunmore were returning to England from India, when the vessel upon which they had taken passage was fired upon and captured by Kidd. His first order was that every person on board should walk the plank, but several ladies who were passengers pleaded so earnestly for their lives that Kidd finally decided to plunder the cargo and passengers and let the vessel proceed on her way. The ladies were compelled, on peril of their lives, to surrender all their jewellery, and among the articles taken from Lady Dunmore was a pair of superb pearl bracelets, the pearls being set in a somewhat peculiar fashion. Another pair, an exact duplicate of those possessed by Lady Dunmore, had been purchased by Lord Dunmore as a wedding gift to his sister, and the story of the two pairs of bracelets and the loss of Lady Dunmore's pearls, which were of great value, and of her pleading for her life to Kidd, is a matter of history, as well as one of the cherished family traditions.

In 1801, Roderick Streeter wrote to Mr Astor that the then Lady Dunmore, in looking over some gems which he was offering her, had seen a pair of exquisite pearl bracelets which were part of the Astor consignment, and had at once recognised them as the identical pair taken by Kidd nearly one hundred years before. She returned the following day with the family solicitor, bringing the duplicate bracelets; told and verified the story of the loss of one pair by Lady Dunmore; compared the two pairs, showing their almost perfect identicalness, showing certain private marks upon each, and demonstrating beyond question that the pearls offered by Mr Streeter were the identical gems seized by Kidd.

The solicitor demanded their surrender to Lady Dunmore on the grounds that, having been stolen, no property in them could pass even to an innocent purchaser. Mr Streeter then stated that he had asked for delay until he could communicate with the owner of the gems, and asked Mr Astor for instructions. Mr Astor replied, authorising the delivery of the bracelets to Lady Dunmore, and asking Mr Streeter to assure her that the supposed owner was guiltless of wrong in the matter, and was an entirely innocent holder. He repeated the caution, given also in sundry other letters, that to no one was the ownership of the gems sold by Mr Streeter to be revealed. They were to be sold as the property of Streeter, acquired in the regular course of business.

So, by the discovery of the hole in a cave in Maine, after a lapse of nearly two hundred years, was curiously brought to light the apparent origin of the colossal Astor fortune. The records show that during the period (i.e. from 1801) that Mr Astor aggregated over a million dollars, he spent over half of it on the purchase of real estate in New York and subsequently became the owner of some twenty tracts of land in what is now the very heart of the business and residence area of Manhattan.

Mr Olmsted and his agents had spent over two years obtaining the information chronicled so far and the results they summarised as follows:

1. Captain Kidd had sailed along the Maine coast shortly before his arrest, and an iron box, marked with his initials, was afterwards taken from the cave upon the land of Mr Olmsted, and this box afterwards came into Mr Astor's possession.

2. Jacques Cartier had camped for many years while employed by Mr Astor, immediately adjoining the cave where the box was concealed, and his rapid increase in wealth and that of Mr Astor were simultaneous.

3. Mr Astor's great wealth came from the sale, through Mr Streeter, of ancient Spanish and French gold, and of gems, some of which were proved to have been part of the spoils of Captain Kidd, which made it a reasonable presumption that all of such property was of the same character.

4. Captain Kidd was known to have captured and somewhere concealed gold and gems of vast value, and the card given to his wife just before his execution indicated, by a plausible reading, the cave upon Mr Olmsted's land as a place of concealment.

5. The family of Captain Kidd had long been extinct, and no one could successfully contest with Mr Olmsted the ownership of the property concealed upon his land.

Having his evidence thus formulated, Mr Olmsted called upon the descendants of Mr Astor, accompanied by his attorney, and demanded of them:

1. A payment by them to him of the sum of $1,300,000, the amount received of Mr Streeter, with interest from the date of its receipt. The total amount, computed according to the laws of New York in force since 1796, was $5,112,234.80; and Mr Olmsted offered, on condition of immediate cash payment, to deduct the item $34.80. This demand was refused.

2. Mr Olmsted then demanded that the Astor family should convey

to him all the real estate in New York City purchased by their
ancestor with the money received from Mr Streeter, with the
accrued rents and profits from the date of its purchase, and this
demand was likewise refused.

These refusals left Mr Olmsted no other alternative except to resort to
the courts for the establishment of his rights, and an action was accordingly commenced.

The remainder of this interesting story is of no interest to us because
we are only concerned with Kidd and his treasure. As we have seen, it
has been found, or at least one of his caches has – or has it? Aspiring
treasure hunters, whose hearts have sunk at the revelation of the story,
can breathe a sigh of relief, for the whole story was a hoax.

The tale was written in 1894 by Frank Head, a friend of the Olmsteds.
The Olmsteds did in fact own a summer home at Deer Island, Maine.
Many people were taken in and convinced by the story and the Olmsteds
were pestered for many years by friends, acquaintances and strangers
asking for more details and explanations. Frederick L. Olmsted finally
had to send out a circular to newspapers and libraries etc., explaining
that the story was written for the amusement of the author and his friends
only.

The story is included here for two reasons. Firstly, it is the best of the
Kidd yarns and secondly, to demonstrate that, as shown in the 'Edmunds
Expedition' chapter, it is easy to create a 'real' story, throw in a few
genuine facts and figures woven around the known story, get it published,
and it must be true! Anyone can do it.

Trinidad Island and Kid's Millions

Trinidad Island lies at Lat 20° 15'S, Long 29° 20'W, some 700 miles
from the coast of Brazil, in the South Atlantic Ocean. What has it got
to do with Kidd? you ask. Maybe something. Maybe nothing at all! You
can make your own mind up on what follows.

In 1897 a book was published titled *Captain Kid's Millions*. (Why one
'd' I don't know – unless implying that what followed was a half truth!)
It starts off as follows:

A Note by the Present Possessor of the
Manuscripts Here Made Public

This strange history is no mere story for boys, full of pirates, islands, and buccaneers, but the true history of one of the mysteries of the world. It matters not how these papers came into the hands of the writer.

Till now we have been dependant on one Charles Johnson (who wrote early in the eighteenth century) for the history of Captain Kid. This man confesses that he was dependant upon 'chap-books' for his facts. It doubtless pleased Lord Somers to have it reported that Kid was hanged; in times so full of corruption such a report could easily be put abroad. In the second edition of Johnson's book, Kid's history was omitted as a string of falsehoods; in later editions it appeared again.

But till now, his true story, written by himself, has never been given to the world. This is here supplemented by a more ancient manuscript of Elizabeth's time, and in two places by extracts from the diary of a Devonshire girl of whom Kid was enamoured, and who had a child by him, and, lastly, by a statement of one John Varn.

A glance got at Kid's history by surreptitious means a few years ago, led to an abortive expedition to the little known rock of Trinidada, in the South Atlantic, after hidden treasure; this manuscript shows the reason of its failure.

The story relates how Kid in 1695 called in at Madeira. By chance he was recognised by a very old man who said he had a packet of papers for him. He had served with Kid many many years before in Elizabeth's time. Kid didn't know what he was talking about. But the old man insisted the papers were his. When he opened them he found: a long history, a Papal indulgence, a list of the ship's company of the *Golden Lion* and a paper in Spanish, the end of which was in some secret cipher.

The history turned out to be a narration of one James Kid, who Kid could only think was some mysterious ancestor of his. It related how James Kid and his crew in the *Golden Lion* (the year was 1591) decided to bury treasure they had already taken, before going on to sack the Spanish town at Montevideo. They made anchorage in a certain bay in the Magellan Strait. The treasure they secured in a chest, taking an inventory, a copy of which remained in the chest. The value in the chest they estimated at £200,000. The contents included a pair of diamonds, which had been the eyes of a Virgin Mary at the church of Mexillones. The diamonds were the largest they had ever seen.

> With the morning it was resolved that we four should land alone, sending the boat back to the ship, and that we should conceal our treasure with cunning, and so mark the place that none but ourselves should be able to discover it.
>
> Thus at ten of the morn we stood together upon the shores of the little bay, and in silence watched our boat row back to the ship.
>
> 'Now,' says Fernandez, 'let us be about our business, and first to seek a secure place.'
>
> Wherewith we lifted the chest, and having carried it a piece away from the shore, set it down amongst the flowering bushes, and looked around us. Then, after some search, we found what seemed to us a safe place. Where the steep mountain sides began to rise was a natural cleft in the rock, like to a cave with no roof. Entering this, we found that it went back some twenty paces, and that the floor was a fine gravel, and beneath soft earth. Here we dug a hole with a spade and pick which we had brought with us, and here we buried our chest, stamping down the earth and spreading it over again with the gravel. When we had done, no one could discover that the soil had been touched. Then on the rock-side we roughly graved the signe of the crosse and a certaine ancient emblem of masonry to mark the place, and returned towards the beach.

They never got to Montevideo. Their ship was wrecked. Two survived, including James Kid. They were rescued by a Spanish woman. To cut a long story short, Kid and the woman poisoned the other survivor so that they could have each other and the treasure. (There is a lot more to this story but I have cut it down to that which is of interest to us.)

When W. Kid had finished reading James Kid's story, he turned his attention to the Spanish paper. This turned out to be the directions for the recovery of the treasure. It gave the marks and bearings of the Bay of Ice within the Magellan Straits and many other directions. The cipher he could not read.

As Kid was on a roving commission, he decided it was good enough cover to go to the Magellan Straits. There could be pirates there – and treasure!

With his Lieutenant, they found the cleft in the rocks and eventually the marks of the cross and ancient emblem on the rock face. But they found no treasure where they searched. They had more or less given up when they found two skeletons in the brush. There was evidence of a fight and alongside one was a small wooden casket with iron bands. Kid knew this wasn't the treasure he was looking for. He was expecting a large chest. The Lieutenant challenged him on their discovery, calling him a liar and cheat, accusing him of hiding something from him. A row ensured, swords were drawn, and in the fight that followed the Lieutenant was killed. In the casket Kid found a severed hand, shrivelled and brown with a jewelled crucifix and a few rings and loose stones. Kid, disappointed, guessed that to find the real treasure he must solve the Spanish cipher.

He was unaware at this time that the fight had been witnessed by one of his crew, one Jan Polperro.

During the following months Kid turned pirate, due in the main to a very unhappy crew. He reached a point where he decided that his activities, being increased in danger, could mean him losing his papers and cipher.

And thinking of treasure brought to my mind the wild-goose chase in Magellan Strait, and I once more got out my papers and looked at the strange cipher which I could not read. Then a voice said, 'Thou art about to engage in serious matters. This may be lost, and with it thy chance of ever reading it.'

With which I went out on to the stern galley, and tried to think how I might secure it.

Presently I returned to my cabin with a set purpose.

First I got me pen and ink, and carefully writ out, as small as possible, this cipher. I then took a leaf of gold-foil, in which I had a certain drug wrapped, which we carry at sea for the cure of an ailment to which sailors in foreign ports are greatly subject. I now rolled up my little script in as small compass as possible, and covered it with my gold-foil. Then with a lancet I cut the skin of my thigh, and having laid back a portion and staunched the bleeding with salt,

I inserted my little roll and sewed the skin over it; and on the wound
I clapt a plaister.

To cut a long story short again: after attempts to get rid of Polperro
had failed, and various other run ins with the crew, Kid was locked in
his cabin. (Whilst in there he took the ship's position which was: 'About
21 degrees south latitude and about 10 degrees west of the longitude of
Ferro, or 28 degrees from out new position of Greenwich.' (I mention
this because of interest to us is that the meridian they were using for
longitude was Ferro).

Kid was eventually brought out to be tried by the crew. The appointed
Judge said 'William Kid, you are charged with offences against the
Society of Pirates.' When called upon as the accuser, Polperro said, 'I
charge William Kid with murder, with attempting to murder me, and
with concealing the knowledge of treasure from his shipmates.'

The outcome was that Kid and Polperro were allowed to settle their
quarrels by sword. A call of 'Land ho!' stopped the fight. The land turned
out to be three little islets rising out of the ocean. (The Martin Vas rocks,
in the South Atlantic.) They were all astonished, as no land was known
of here. Kid knew that the nearest land was the South American coast,
and that lay about seven hundred miles further west. Later there was
another call of 'Land Ho!' Into sight loomed an island of some size,
again, to them, uncharted land. None on board knew of it. Kid's thoughts
were that as it was no very great distance from the coast, it was like
enough known to South Spanish seamen.

The crew's decision regarding Kid's trial was that both Kid and
Polperro be cast upon the island. This they were. All that Kid was allowed
was food, his Bible (it contained the ancient narrative) and his navigation
book *The Seaman's Secrets* by John Davis. Kid went one way and
Polperro to another part of the island.

Eventually, to while away the time, (the island was uninhabited), Kid
retrieved the cipher concealed under the skin of his thigh. He then put a
lot of effort into solving its secret. It read as follows:

Gowan ge $\triangle$ monl 20½ feigt bon la okipod neen
    yodpt aciun' Hdokum 600

After many months he eventually deciphered it by trial, error and
substitution. The solution reads thus;

Taken to △ land 20½ South Pan de Azucar noon March equin*
Brazil 600.

Kid was still puzzled.

You say, 'Tis still all Greek.' And yet, when one hath little else
with which to pass the time, 'tis relief to have such a nut as this to
crack. And presently I had the kernal – so I thought.

And was amazed and astonished at my thought. Upon the shore
of this very island was hidden this treasure! If this were so, my
Satanic master had in very deed guided his servant – and at this
thought I shuddered, sinner though I was.

The interpretation is this:

We were about this latitude, namely 20 degrees and a half south
of the line. Brazil lay some 600 miles away. 'Twas plain that this
islet was the place referred to.

What the triangle signified I did not then discover; and it caused
me much thought. But I may here put down that the island is called
Trinidada; and this triangle is an ancient symbol of that holy mystery.
It therefore readeth 'Trinity land'.

Now, as to the Pan de Azucar – that was plain to one conversant
with Spanish waters. Wherever your Spaniard findeth a conical rock
or mount, he ever nameth it 'sugar loaf'. There was such an one on
our island, near the south point. Upon the north shore was a still
more strange rock; but that was like a pillar, whereas my 'Pan de
Azucar' was worthy of its name.

'Noon of the march equinox.' This I at once set down as relating
to the shadow of this peak. Was I right? To know this I must wait
patiently until the time given.

The day upon which I finally solved my puzzle was, by my
reckoning which I had kept since landing, February the twenty-first.
I had a month to wait.

Kid guessed that at noon on the March equinox, the shadow of the top
of the peak would show where to dig. He climbed to the top of the peak
and found a cairn of stones. The top stone had engraved on it the same
sign as that on the rock in the Magellan Strait. He was now convinced.

When the day came, he duly dug at the spot revealed by the shadow of the cairn, but to no avail. He subsequently discovered that Polperro had moved the pile of stones, so the true place was lost.

After another fight with Polperro, who was eventually forced over the edge of a cliff, Kid thought he was finally rid of him. Over the months he cursed his memory, in that Polperro's devilish spite had made it impossible he should ever find the treasure that he knew lay beneath the sands somewhere.

To his great terror one night, an earthquake hit the island causing a tidal wave. When all was calm in the morning, Kid wandered down to the beach. It had changed. The tidal wave had cleared a huge amount of sand off the beach. A large flat stone was exposed that drew his attention. He couldn't believe what he saw when he gazed upon it. For there was that ancient symbol. Kid describes it as: 'Like to the shank, stock, and ring of an anchor, being a line, a cross line, and a circle, all joining.' We know it of course as an ankh, the ancient Egyptian symbol of life.

It took him an hour to move the stone but his search was over. Beneath it lay an iron-bound chest. He broke its rusty hinges with a stone and opened it.

Truly the riches of the world lay before me! and were of no more value to me than the sand surrounding them. 'Twas plain to see that it was plunder from the altars of Spanish churches. Pyx, monstrance, [consecration vessels and receptacles] and jewelled cups lay there, with loose stones of untold value; and, opening a little golden box, I found two diamonds of such a size as none ever heard of. Scarcely knowing what I did, I slipped one of these into my pocket. Then, shutting the lid again, I raised the chest from its bed with some difficulty, and at much labour dragged it to my sleeping-place. Then, being worn out with my toil, I fell asleep, and woke not till the sun was well up in the sky.

Next day I hid the casket in a certain place which, by a most strange chance, I had discovered some time before, and which could only be reached at certain times. Here I bestowed this treasure, having once more gazed upon it, and picked out a golden ring set with a blue stone, and which took my fancy. Then I marked the position secretly upon a chart which I had long since made of the island, and I am certain that no man can find the secret thereof.

Thus hath this cursed treasure, stolen from God, been thrice buried;

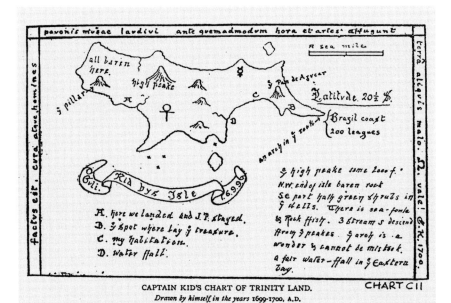

CAPTAIN KID'S CHART OF TRINITY LAND.
Drawn by himself in the years 1699-1700, A.D.

CHART C11

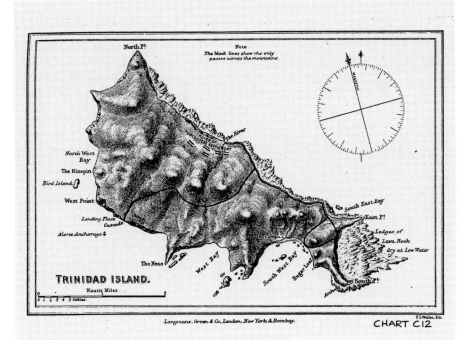

TRINIDAD ISLAND.

CHART C12

having caused the deaths of many people, and never prospered the finders thereof. May it now lie hidden till the great day of judgement, say I William Kid!

It was another fifteen months before Kid was rescued.

There is much more to this story, and is of some historical value, giving a very accurate picture of sea manners, etc., and describes accurately Execution Dock, and the way in which pirates were hanged there.

The story continues into the late nineteenth century and tells of the adventures of a descendant of Kid, one Richard Kedde. It tells of how Kid's papers eventually came to him and of his efforts to solve the chart instructions.

This book, however, is trying to deal with factual evidence on the subject of Kidd. The above story is more than likely to be fiction interwoven with known facts. But the book is after all about treasure islands, and even if the Kid story is not true, it would probably be of interest to you to know the solution to his chart of 'Trinity land'.

The translation of the Latin around the chart makes no sense whatsoever in relation to chart directions, and is not meant to, so we won't include it here. The solution is read from the placement of certain letters in the Latin! The clue lies with the word '*affugunt*'. I quote again in part from the story:

'And you said the Latin meant nothing.'
  'No . . . nothing.'
  'How does it read in English?'
  'Oh! the baldest rot!'

Further on:

'The man who translated it said it was dog-Latin. Now, dog-Latin means bad Latin, and the fellow who wrote it did not even know how to spell the blooming lingo.'
  'How's that?' asked Jefferson.
  'Oh, there's a word here, "*affugunt*", which should be spelt with an "e" instead of an "a".'
  '*Affug* . . . *aff* . . . I can't say it! Why a? Double f comes after a. After it, see?'
  'Holy smoke!' ejaculated Keddy; 'if that should be the key. The

letters that come after the a's.'

Holding the little chart to the light of the fire, he examined the Latin writing.

'What comes after a? I'll try that first.'

Another moment, and he knew that the secret was his. With considerable nervous tremor, he slowly unfolded the mystery; the guide to Kid's treasure was plain . . . too plain to be doubted for a moment. They could now lay their hands on that which had eluded the grasp of expedition after expedition. A chapter in the world's history was closed. This, which had supplied the motive for all the pirate stories, and tales of buried treasure, since novels first began to be written, was now a mystery no longer; and they were rich men.

Word by word, in the light of the camp-fire, he went over the doggerel Latin; for a moment the diphthong of *musae* led him astray, but soon it was all plain. Following his sudden illumination, *factus est* gave him c.

Cura atque homines only supplied a.

Pavonis musae laudivi was richer, bringing out v, e, and u. *Caveu* puzzled him, and, for an instant, he feared lest he had only stumbled upon some other unknown tongue, but the next step decided it.

Ante quemadmodum gave him n and d.

Hora et artes, e and r.

'Cave under!' The secret was out! 'Cave under' – what?

Ah! the mystery of *affugunt* was explained; this word, with the following *terra aliquis malo vale*, brought forth 'fall'.

'Cave under fall.'

And, in the further light of Kid's English, 'fall' as spelt in his directory notes – it could only refer to the 'water-fall' marked D on the chart. This very fall he had himself seen when, from his vantage height, he had surveyed South-West Bay. A cave, if one looked for it, could not easily be hid.

In fact there was no cave at the base of the fall. He had to climb quite high up before he found it – and the treasure.

Trinidad – The True Story

'Trinity Land' is no figment of the imagination of the author of *Kid's Millions*. As I said at the beginning, it is known as Trinidad* Island. Whilst the story of Kid's treasure is probably fiction, the fact is that a treasure is (or was) buried here. The island was the scene of several treasure hunts in the nineteenth century.

The story is as follows:

In the latter part of the nineteenth century, there was, living not far from Newcastle, a retired sea captain. Captain Peters.† He was in command of an East Indiaman engaged in the opium trade in the years 1848 to 1850. At that time the China Seas were infested by pirates, so that his vessel carried a few guns, and a larger crew than is usual in these days. He had four quartermasters, one of whom was a foreigner. The Captain was not sure of his nationality, but thought he was a Russian Finn. On board the vessel the man went under the name of 'the pirate', on account of a deep scar across his cheek, which gave him a somewhat sinister appearance. He was a reserved man, better educated than the ordinary sailor, and possessing a good knowledge of navigation.

The Captain took a liking to him, and showed him kindness on various occasions. This man was attacked by dysentery on the voyage from China to Bombay, and by the time the vessel reached Bombay he was so ill, in spite of the Captain's nursing, that he had to be taken to the hospital. He gradually sank, and when he found that he was dying, he told the Captain, who frequently visited him at the hospital, that he felt very grateful for the kind treatment he had received at the Captain's hands, and that he would prove his gratitude by revealing a secret to him that might make him one of the richest men in England. The Captain said that he appeared very uneasy about this secret, and insisted on the door of the ward being closed so that there might be no listeners. He then asked the Captain to go to his chest and take out from it a parcel. The parcel contained a piece of old tarpaulin with a plan of the island of Trinidad on it.

The man gave him this plan, and told him that at the place indicated

---

* Also known as Trindade or Trinidade Island.
† Some narratives name him as Tom Sinnet

on it – that is, under the mountain known as the Sugarloaf – there was an immense treasure buried, consisting principally of gold and silver plate and ornaments, the plunder of Peruvian churches which certain pirates had concealed there in the year 1821. Much of this plate, he said, came from the Cathedral of Lima, having been carried away from there during the war of independence when the Spaniards were escaping the country, and that among other riches there were several massive golden candlesticks.

The Finn further stated that he was the only survivor of the pirates, as all the others had been captured by the Spaniards and executed in Cuba some years before, and consequently it was probable that no one but himself knew of this secret. He then gave the Captain instructions as to the exact position of the treasure in the bay under the Sugarloaf, and encouraged him to go there and search for it, as it was almost certain that it had not been removed. The quartermaster died shortly afterwards.

On leaving Bombay after the death of his quartermaster, the Captain had intended to land on Trinidad and examine the spot indicated on the pirate's plan. But as he had a rather unruly crew, and was himself crippled with a broken arm, he thought it prudent not to make the attempt then.

On his return to England he told the pirate's story to many people, but of course preserving the secret of the exact position of the hiding place. Nothing, however, seems to have been done towards recovering the treasure until 1880. The Captain persuaded a shipping firm at Newcastle to allow one of their vessels trading to the Brazils to visit the island. It was arranged that the Captain's son should go with the vessel so as to identify the spot and act on his father's behalf. He got onto the island with great difficulty and had to spent a night alone there. On returning he reported that he had discovered the spot described by the pirate, but that a great landslide of red debris had fallen at the site which could not be removed without great labour. He said the place tallied exactly with the information given him and he firmly believed the story to be true and that the treasure was still there.

Now this story, so far, bears a strong family resemblance to many other stories of pirate treasure, mythical or otherwise and, though there can be no doubt that great stores of valuable plunder are still lying hidden away in this fashion on many a West Indian cay and desert ocean island, the dying quartermaster's deposition was hardly enough by itself to warrant the expense of fitting out an expedition for Trinidad. But it was intriguing enough for one man to check it out.

The old sea captain was fated to meet a well known barrister and war correspondent of the London *Times*, one Edward Frederick Knight. On making researches, Knight found that the story was corroborated in many remarkable ways.

In the first place, the archives of Cuba were inspected, and a record was discovered which showed that a gang of pirates who had plundered Spanish vessels sailing from Lima had been hanged at Havana at the time mentioned. Further research convinced Knight of the facts of the treasure. The story of what the Captain's son had found also helped to convince him.

Knight also thought it highly improbable that the Finn had evolved the whole matter from an imaginative brain, especially on his death-bed. Neither could his statements be considered as being the ravings of a sick man, for they were far too circumstantial and compatible with facts.

In the first place, his carefully prepared plan of the island, the minute directions he gave as to the best landing, and his description of the features of the bay on whose shores the treasure was concealed, proved beyond doubt to Knight and others who knew Trinidad that he, or some other informant of his, had landed on that rarely visited islet; and not only landed, but passed some time on it, and carefully surveyed the approaches to the bay. The information shown could not have been obtained from any Pilot-book. The landing recommended by previous visitors is at the other side of the island.

Beyond this, the Finn must have been acquainted with what was taking place in two other distant corners of the world during his professed landing on the island. He knew of the escape of pirates with the cathedral plate of Lima. He was also aware that, shortly afterwards, there were hanged in Cuba the crew of a vessel that had committed acts of piracy on the Peruvian coast. It is scarcely credible that an ordinary seaman – even allowing for the fact that he was superior in education to the average of his fellows – could have pieced these facts together so ingeniously into this plausible story.

The outcome was that before Knight came on the scene, Captain Peters finally managed to interest a group from South Shields in his map. They departed the Tyne in 1885 on the barque *Aurea* led by a Mr Aem. It was at this time that Knight became acquainted with this expedition through newspaper reports in London. Some months later he read another report:

> Further information has been received regarding the unfortunate expedition of the *Aurea*, the vessel charted by a number of Tynesiders for a voyage to the small island of Trinidad, off the coast of Brazil, where it was reported a large amount of treasure was concealed. The last letter is from one of the seamen, a young man named Russell, to his parents in North Shields. Russell states that it is with 'the greatest pleasure' that he has an opportunity of writing, and continues to say that the *Aurea* left the island on 29 April, and, he was sure, the crew were not sorry at leaving. He states that eight seamen were ashore fourteen days, and at the end of that time they were so exhausted with the want of water and provisions and with the scorching heat, that they had all to be carried on board. As a consequence eight of them were laid down with fever, and out of this eight, two seamen died. The expedition was thus unfortunate in more than one respect. The *Aurea*, according to the writer of the letter, was at Trinidad in the West Indies, and was expected to leave for England. Russell says nothing about treasure; the burden of his letter is that the crew left the island with the greatest satisfaction.

In 1888, Knight happened to meet some people involved with the ill-fated *Aurea* expedition. There was talk of another, so he travelled to South Shields and made acquaintance with Mr Aem. Subsequently they made a deal and Mr Aem handed over details of where on the island the treasure lay. And so it was, that in August 1889 Knight, in company of seven 'gentlemen adventurers' and four crew sailed out of Southampton in the cutter-yacht *Alerte*.

About three months later they arrived at Trinidad, having stopped off at the Salvage Islands on the way. Knight had been told of another treasure here. They didn't find anything, but more of that treasure story later.

I will now quote from Knight's narrative on the adventure from when they arrived on the island:

> The pirate in his confession had spoken of a channel he had discovered through this reef, situated under the Sugarloaf, at the eastern extremity of the bay. We now saw that it existed there exactly as he had described it – a broad opening in the line of rocks, through

which a boat could be pulled and beached on the sands.

But, still, it was an awkward place, and it would be impossible to land there on such a day as this was, for immense rollers were sweeping up the shore which would have almost certainly dashed any boat to pieces that ventured among them. We were, however, very satisfied with the success of our expedition so far. We had discovered and taken bearings of the channel, and we knew how to pilot a boat through it, when the weather should be favourable. Our next duty was to descend into the bay and identify the place where the treasure was supposed to be hidden.

It was not long before we had discovered what we considered to be the right spot.

The pirate had described a small gully in the middle of this bay, at the foot of which he and his men had erected three cairns, which should serve as landmarks to those who had the clue, and point the way to the treasure.

Mr P..., and after him Mr A..., had found this gully and the three cairns, just as they had been described. Mr A..., either for the purpose of putting others off the scent, or in order to discover if anything had been concealed beneath them, blew up these cairns with gunpowder and dug into them, so that now we could only see traces of one of them. He had however communicated to me what he understood to be their signification, and how he had been led by them to the first bend in the ravine, at which spot the plunder had been buried under a hollow rock.

We walked up the ravine till we came to a bend, and here, as we had expected, we saw what appeared to be a landslip of red earth, filling up the corner of it, blocking up the mouth of any cave that might exist there.

What followed was three months of digging and clearing the landslip. They never found anything!

As I said at the beginning of this chapter. What's all this got to do with Kidd?

It struck me when reading these stories that there were certain similarities that somehow seemed to fit in with the Kidd/Palmer charts. I would think to myself, 'Well I've read that before!' and 'I've seen that before somewhere!' It could all be mere coincidence, I don't know, but consider the following:

Look at the general outline of Trinidad Island. There are obvious similarities to the Kidd/Palmer charts. Similar features include: small islands and rocks off the north and south coasts, hills running the length of the island, coral ledges and reefs, landing place and anchorage more or less positioned the same, three cairns of stones leading the way, turtles abound here, a cave, the mysterious symbol ʊ appears on the Kid chart, and so on. 'Has to be coincidence,' you say.

Perhaps you are right!

Alan Oscar, the author of *Kid's Millions*, was a very knowledgeable man on maritime matters, and also on Trinidad. Having read all the book thoroughly I was impressed by the accuracy and detail which he gives to sixteenth and seventeenth century piracy, and other matters relating to that era. The accuracy with which he writes about Trinidad shows that he must have spent time there to write with such detail. His book was published in 1897, and he was obviously on the island prior to that date. I would guess 1889, and I would guess that Alan Oscar and E.F. Knight are one and the same. Knight was, after all, a journalist and author of several books including of course *The Cruise of the Alerte*. He died in 1925 after an illustrious career as a war journalist and correspondent.

What I am suggesting is that Knight created a very clever treasure chart for Kid, based on his own experiences. By his research into the Finn's story he showed that he had the ability to delve into historical piracy — and write about it. He penned a very readable yarn.

Could it not be that thirty or so years later, somebody else might have thought it a good idea to create some Kidd charts, and try and cash in on it?

I am leading you back towards the possibility of a hoax. Could all the charts have been found by one man in – what – the space of three years? It really is a monumental coincidence. Were they not fed to a gullible Palmer who was prepared to pay anything for Kidd relics? Was Hill Cutler, Palmer's antique dealer friend, the culprit? Dealing in antiques, he might have had the resources and knowledge to create such maps and expertly secrete them? Who knows!

Trinidad Treasure Stories

Before leaving Trinidad Island, it is apt to relate the other pirate treasure stories associated with it. This is no easy task because of the confusion between similar stories and names. For example. H.T. Wilkins in his book *Treasure Hunting*, relates how a French schooner sailed from Southampton in 1819 to trade in 'black ivory' (slaves). The crew mutinied after the often drunk captain took pot shots at their legs. They dispatched him with a marline spike through his back whilst the crew held him down and he was dumped 'hissing hot' into the sea. The mate followed with a mop full of tar in his mouth! The Jolly Roger was hoisted and off they went 'a-pirating'. They took a rich Portuguese vessel amongst others. The captain eventually ordered them to beat up for an island in the South Atlantic where the loot was buried. Needless to say this was the Ilha da Trinidada. They carried on in their craft, looting and wrecking numerous ships, but met their match when they took on a East Indiaman. She out-fought them and captured the crew. They were taken to Cuba where nineteen were hanged and one somehow got away.

Sixty years later, this man was still alive in a seaman's lodging house in a north of England port. His name was Tom Sinnett (real or assumed, Wilkins was not sure). Sinnett said he could never muster enough brass to buy a boat to go after the treasure but he enjoyed telling the story without giving away the location. He eventually made a treasure chart with proper cross-bearings and it reached the hands of a war correspondent of the London *Times* newspaper, Mr E.F. Knight.

Wilkins' version of the story (I have toned it down) contained his usual style of added colour and embellishments.

Treasure Islands by Rosemary Kingsland relates how the Lima Cathedral treasures were put for safety into ships bound for Spain. One was captured by the pirate Benito de Soto. He buried the treasure in a cave on Trinidad. His ship was itself later captured by Lord Dundonald and they were taken to Cuba where just one crew member escaped execution. After many years he turned up as a quartermaster on a ship trading in opium in the China Seas. He was known as 'the pirate' by the crew and the ship's captain was Captain Peters. 'The pirate', dying in a Bombay hospital in 1850, told the captain his story and gave him a treasure map. The rest we know.

According to *The Book of Buried Treasure* by R.D. Paine, Benito de

Soto was a Spaniard who sailed out of Buenos Aires in 1827 to smuggle slaves. He took over the ship and started on a voyage of piracy. They plundered and burned and slaughtered without mercy, their most nefarious deed being the capture of the British ship *Morning Star*. Benito de Soto met his end as the result of being wrecked in his own ship off the Spanish coast. He was caught in Gibraltar and hanged by the Governor.

There is no mention by Paine of any treasure taken by de Soto being buried on Trinidad. He does relate however that the Lima treasure, or part of it, furnished the foundation of a story belonging to Trinidad. This version is that the pirates who chose this hiding place had been the crew of a fast English schooner in the slave trade. Whilst at sea the crew mutinied and killed the captain by pinning him to the mainmast with a boarding pike. They hoisted the black flag and took a great amount of plunder including a rich Portuguese ship and an East Indiaman. The proceeds were buried on Trinidad. Later, they themselves were taken by a heavily armed merchant vessel. The twenty survivors were taken to Havana and handed over to the Spanish authorities who gleefully hanged nineteen. The one who got away died in bed in England at a very great age, so the story runs, and of course he had a chart.

Benito de Soto's encounter with the *Morning Star* is worth enlarging on. It reminds one of how bloodthirsty pirates were and this action exemplifies everything that caused victims to be filled with dread at the appearance of a pirate ship.

The *Morning Star* was bound from Ceylon to England in 1832 and carried amongst its passengers army officers and their families, also twenty-five invalided soldiers. The pirates opened fire on the unarmed ship, raking it with cannon fire and wounding many on board. Having taken the ship, the captain was decapitated by de Soto. The pirates then brutally raped the women passengers. They and the survivors were thrown into the hold and the hatches fastened. Auger holes were drilled in the ship's bottom and she was left to sink. By a miracle the men managed to force open one of the hatches, the pumps were manned and the leaks plugged.

Benito de Soto was captured in Gibraltar after being recognised by one of his victims and hanged there. (Some accounts say he was sent to Cadiz.) He died better than he lived. Those of his crew who were captured, after execution had their limbs severed and hung on hooks 'as a warning to all other pirates'.

To add confusion to these stories is the fact that the pirate Benito Bonito was, during this same period, harrying the Spanish in the Pacific and burying treasure on Cocos Island. He also plundered the Spanish/Lima treasures and with the similarity in names with de Soto, confusion with a mixture of facts is bound to occur over the centuries.

Another English slave captain (turned pirate) known by the strange name of 'Zulmiro' is alleged to have hidden a treasure of some eight million dollars on Trinidad. He can't have made a big impact on history. I haven't been able to find out anything about this particular pirate and one wonders where this story came from. The same applies to a Spanish pirate named José Santos, who is said to have taken a ship laden with gold, silver, altar vestments and candelabra from Peruvian churches. This was a forty million dollar hoard and is supposedly buried on Trinidad.

If all these stories are true then Trinidad is richer in treasure than Cocos!

Perhaps then in all of this we should be asking first: 'Where lies the truth – not the treasure!'

Chapter 6

Analysing the Evidence

The Charts

Just three pieces of old parchment, but what a lot of time, trouble, inconvenience and money they have cost. The old saying is very true: 'More money has been spent searching for buried treasure than has ever been uncovered.'

'Are they really genuine?' I am often asked. I have to answer that as far as my researches and continuing investigation will allow me – yes they are. I am 99% convinced; it is the remaining 1% that bothers me. I am sure that readers who have got this far will either be totally convinced or will have raised questions of their own; some of those questions will more than likely be amongst those to follow in this chapter.

An awful lot of nonsense about Kidd and the charts has been written over the years, with authors copying previous material and therefore repeating errors and theories. It might make good reading, but it also shows that they have not done their homework or any original research. Some examples I have already mentioned in the 'Kidd Connections' chapter. Recently I came across an article titled 'Captain Kidd's Treasure' in the October 1986 issue of *The Unknown*. The author says we have to regard Mr Palmer's maps as forgeries and that how Mr Palmer came to be in possession of forged maps and fake furniture we can only speculate. I am a firm believer that any author of a factual work must be able to back up his facts and claims. Dismiss the charts if you want to, but you must show on what grounds. That author obviously did not know that the map expert of the time in the British Museum had pronounced the charts genuine. If he had done his homework properly he would *not* have had to speculate on how Palmer came into possession of the furniture and maps. We know exactly how, because I know that Palmer kept detailed records of all his purchases, and these were examined.

An article 'Does Captain Kidd's Treasure Exist?' in the January 1983 issue of *Treasure Hunting* reprints two of the Kidd charts. Proof that they are reprints of earlier (probably Furneaux's) publications lies in the fact that with reference to the 'skull' chest chart, the directions start: 515 SE; if the author had carried out his research properly he would have known that only the last figure 5 can be said to be as originally penned; the figures 51 prior to the 5 are only conjectural as the original chart was almost illegible at this point.

That author also quotes a letter from the then (1972) superintendent of the map room at the British Museum which stated that they could not provide any information on Dr Skelton's assessment of the charts and they had no reports in their files on the matter. I have in my possession a letter from the British Museum and signed by R.A. Skelton, in which he states that the 'third chest' chart (i.e. 'key' chart) shown to him some fourteen or fifteen years previously was drawn on the back of a perfectly genuine will, apparently of the early eighteenth century. His memory must have been playing tricks; he really meant seventeenth century, for another letter from a colleague of his says he can remember Mr Skelton having an opinion that they were authentic seventeenth century charts.

Anthony Howlett recalls seeing a letter (about 1950) on British Museum headed paper containing a report on authenticity tests carried out by the museum on the originals. The report was of course (says Howlett) very cautious, but was to the effect that the parchment and ink were probably of seventeenth century date.

The Library Departments of the British Museum, which included the Map Room, were incorporated into the newly formed British Library in 1973, and they, as they told me, are still receiving a steady stream of enquiries about this *alleged* map (my italics). Even they are confused and uncertain about the business. They said there is no original manuscript of this alleged map as far as they knew: I had to tell them there is – or was. They were very helpful though and added to the mystery by saying:

> The copies reproduced do not bear comparison with other contemporary maps of the period, indeed, some features (such as the lettering) seem to indicate that the charts were drawn much later.
>
> A colleague in the Department of Manuscripts who examined the chart some time ago pointed out:
> a) That the handwriting on the charts does not resemble that of

A sample of Kidd's writing. The infamous 'lodged goods and tresure....' sentence from his letter to Robert Harley. A sample of his signature, below, is also shown.

William Kidd in the Welbeck Harley papers.

b) It is distinctly twentieth century. It is even open to doubt whether they could have been copied from late seventeenth century charts, so uncharacteristic are the cartographic conventions, unit of measurement and representations of scale.

In contrast to that, Furneaux, when carrying out his research, spoke with Skelton who repeated to him his earlier findings: They are genuine seventeenth century charts, conforming in type, parchment, ink and cartography to charts of that period; also, examples of Kidd's handwriting preserved in the Public Records Office conforms to the writing on the charts.

At this point, we should recall some of Howlett's investigations which lasted five years:

Thanks to the great kindness of those managing the Palmer estate, I was given every assistance in checking the matter, and I was granted full access to the (original) charts and all of Palmer's private papers and notes.

First of all, I verified all the details of the discoveries from Palmer's own records and photographs, and made numerous enquiries and checks of my own. I very thoroughly examined the charts themselves, together with enlarged photographs of them, taken by infra-red and ultra-violet light.

In addition, I perused and checked the written opinions of the British Museum, of eminent handwriting experts, cartographers and other leading authorities. Deliberately seeking flaws, I was forced, nevertheless, to recognise the fact that the evidence indicated that the charts were genuine.

It would appear then that we have a contradiction within the British Library (or Museum), twenty or thirty years ago; before the war, the charts were genuine, now it would appear they are suggesting they are not.

This is where part of my 1% uncertainty lies.

It is not so curious that the British Museum have nothing on their files regarding the charts, even though the copies of the charts that I possess, including the 'Yunnan' parchment, all carry the 'B.M.' imprint; the fact is that the work done was a private commission.

Few people are aware that the chart reproductions commonly seen are *not* of the original charts. The great problem with the originals was their illegibility; not only had the ink faded and the parchment become badly discoloured with age, but, particularly in the case of the 'key' chart, the parchment was apparently a palimpsest and there was a certain amount of confusing 'bleed through' of the original writing underneath.

Palmer had had the originals photographed in the 1930s and obviously all kinds of filters had been tried to bring up the details, but without much real success.

Mr Skelton was privately commissioned to obtain the best results possible from the Palmer originals. Both infra-red and ultra-violet photography was tried, as well as numerous enlargements using filters, but the results were still somewhat confusing and difficult to interpret for a non-cartographer layman. Skelton therefore had the maps redrawn by a skilled cartographer (he may have even done this work himself) in an endeavour to reproduce the originals as faithfully as possible. The bureau map was reproduced on the same scale as the original, but the 'skull' chart, 'key' chart, and 'Yunnan' parchment were with a x2 magnification.

In other words, the copies we have were constructed by means of an accurate tracing of a photographic enlargement (x2) of the original.

Notes accompany each drawing referring to conjectural markings and writings which – supported by certain extrinsic evidence – is the cartographer's interpretation of what he thinks they should be.

Therefore, if one has these Skelton reproductions, one has the best possible copies available today. The above also explains why – as it was a private commission – the British Museum possesses no copies of these charts. They have, understandably, become a little irritated over the years by people who mistakenly think they have.

The 'key' chart drawing you see on page 226 is the *only* true reproduction in every detail of the Skelton drawing. You will not have seen it before. On previously reproduced copies (probably the Furneaux reproductions) there are three areas which show faint lines and what can only be described as squiggles. It is very difficult to distinguish what they might be. Only on the Skelton original (of which I have a copy) are these marks more clearly shown. I have traced over and re-defined these lines to make them more distinct and legible. I can vouch that with reference to the original, they are an exact copy.

As now shown, therefore, these re-defined areas could represent exactly what was penned at the time the chart was drawn and had merely faded with age – as other features have. *Or*, they could of course be palimpsest marks. Until we can get hold of the original chart parchment and have it tested with today's technology, we will never know. So it is up to you to make up your own mind if you think they might show any more clues. Skelton's notes that accompany his reproduction of the chart are as follows:

The original of this chart has become badly discoloured with age and is now partially illegible. This copy was constructed by means of an accurate tracing of a photographic enlargement (magnification x2) of the original, verified by reference to the original and to enlarged photographs thereof taken under infra-red and ultra-violet light.

Notes

(1) The following markings, indicated in a lighter colour on this copy, are only conjectural and are probably the result of the penetration through the parchment of ink writing on the other side:

(a) The markings between the words 'Rocks' and 'Smugglers

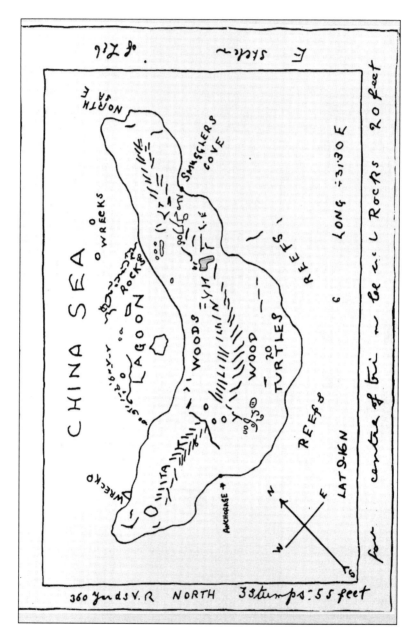

The 'key' chart re-defined with reference to the 'skeleton' original.

Cove';

(b) The shaded area about 1½ in. to the left of 'Smugglers Cove';

(c) The markings to the left of the words 'Wood' and 'Turtles'.

(2) The incomplete reading of the longitude is uncertain.

(3) The writing in the bottom right-hand margins is partially illegible. The following are conjectural readings, supported by certain extrinsic evidence:

(a) Bottom margin: 'four . . . centre of triangle on to Rocks 20 feet';

(b) Right-hand margin: ' . . . E . . . Stakes . . . of Lake'

Similar notes by Skelton accompany his 'skull' chart reproduction. They are:

The Chart from the 'Skull' Chest

The original of this chart has become discoloured with age and it is not easily legible. This copy was constructed by means of an accurate tracing of a photographic enlargement (magnification x2) of the original, verified by reference to the original and to enlarged photographs thereof taken under infra-red and ultra-violet light.

Note.

In the line of numerals and letters reading '515 S E AND BY 50 N', the numerals '51' in the group '515' are only conjectural, the original document is almost illegible at this point.

A similar note accompanies his 'bureau' chart reproduction;

The Map from the Adventure Galley Bureau

The original of this map has become discoloured with age and, by reason of its lack of clarity, is not suitable for direct photographic reproduction. This copy was photographed from an accurate tracing (same scale as the original) made direct from the original map.

The Yunnan Island Parchment

This is different in that no island outline is shown, just obvious recovery instructions having arrived at the spot marked 'X'. Little can be added to the story on p. 18 except the following:

In about 1936 or 1937, Mr Hill Cutler, the antique dealer of Eastbourne who occasionally acted as Mr Palmer's agent, attended an auction sale of the effects of a recently deceased barrister of Hampden Park, Willingdon, in Sussex. Here he purchased the very old oak-framed mirror, 15 inches square, with the skull-and-crossbones (the skull containing two paste stones in the eyes) and the initials 'W.K.' carved on the frame. The story connected with this mirror was that it had been looted from a ship wrecked off Beachy Head, near Eastbourne, about the turn of the century.

Palmer was a little sceptical as to whether there was a genuine Kidd association and he apparently had some suspicions of the mirror generally. But by this time, in view of his previous discoveries of the charts, he was loath to risk the possibility of overlooking any alleged Kidd relic. He therefore bought the mirror from Hill Cutler.

The alleged history of the mirror is entirely uncorroborated. Howlett's view is that it is too vague and picturesque: Palmer himself was, Howlett believed, dubious about the historical authenticity, and it is not without significance that the parchment was not subjected to any scientific tests as in the case of the charts.

Howlett was also not too happy about Hill Cutler's association in the matter. It was a personal suspicion, which, as he admits, could well be unfounded. However, Cutler did once sell Palmer an item which was purported to have belonged to Prince Rupert of the Rhine and, as Howlett personally discovered after having taken expert opinions, was clearly a fake.

We may also recall at this point that Palmer came into possession of the Morgan 'skull' chest through Cutler.

Howlett is of the view that this parchment should only be accepted with extreme caution, and if genuine that it may possibly refer to a cache on some island other than the one described in Kidd's charts.

I for once am inclined not to agree with my learned friend. Assuming once again the charts are genuine, they all obviously depict the same island in the China Sea. The Yunnan parchment is the only document to name the *South* China Sea, and the latitude of 9°16′ N on the 'key' chart can be said to run right through the South China Seas. I believe therefore that the Yunnan parchment is linked with the other charts and must be used in conjunction with them. As stated previously in the chapter on this document, I interpret '4th NƐat' to mean '4th North and at'. That being the case then:

a) It is significant to me that on the bureau chart, compass *North* points directly to the 'X'.

b) On the 'skull' chart, compass North points directly to the *fourth* dot.

c) On the 'key' chart, compass North points directly to a conspicuous looking valley (Valley runs *North*) and 3 stumps.

d) Even John S's Rough Map has compass North pointing directly to the 'X'.

I would guess that having arrived at the spot, dot, or 'X', which could be a cave, the Yunnan document tells you exactly where to dig for treasure in that cave. (See also p. 259.)

Another interpretation for '4th' could be (with reference to the 'skull' chart) that it refers to the fourth cache buried and applies to the fourth dot – counting from the Anchorage – with an 'X' alongside it. If the 'X' implies a burying place then it could be that this cache was buried on the way back to the coast where one might expect to find a cliff and cave. This theory does not however explain what the letter 'N' might mean. It cannot mean 'North' in this context because this dot does not lie north of any of the other feature points.

There are two other observations I can make regarding this document:

1) The writing can be said to be of the same style as that around the border of the 'key' chart.

2) It could relate to *two* caches. We have assumed that the word 'cave' as penned is just that, but the 'e' is not an 'e' as typically written elsewhere but Ɛ as in 'NƐat'. The document could therefore be meant to read: 'at back of cav *and* in cliff under ledge.' The fact that 'cave' is spelt without an 'e' is not unusual for three hundred years ago.

Part of my 1% uncertainty lies with this parchment, but only because Palmer did not have it tested; the chances are it is perfectly genuine. I am inclined to believe it is genuine as it makes sense and fits in with the other charts. As a forgery or hoax, it does not make sense; it would be too complicated.

I lean towards the belief that this document – assuming it was indeed written by Kidd – confirms that it was penned early on in his career, thereby confirming that the charts come from that same time. The reason is the writing. In his later life, Kidd's writing style was stylish, neat and consistent in style. This is evident from the letters he wrote in Newgate gaol. Although he was often ill and suffering, he still wrote a neat letter. He was about fifty years of age at this time. In 1669 he was twenty-four years old, immature in his writing without a personalised style yet to be recognised as his own. This shows in the Yunnan parchment which is definitely untidy with no consistency. His curled 'C' in China and Cave are very similar to those penned in later life, but is not yet consistent – look at the 'C' in Cliff for example. The 'd' in ledge has yet to develop into his consistent curled back 'd' as in his signature (see page 223). In his later writings this curled 'd' stands out and is always the same. His 't's are definitely childlike on the parchment with none of the sophisticated style of his 't's in later life. The same can be said of the letter 'f'. It is written in two totally different styles: see the words of 'of' and 'left'. I believe these observations show without a doubt that the Yunnan parchment was penned when Kidd was a young man.

Skelton's notes regarding his reproduction of this document are as follows;

The 'Yunnan Island' Parchment

The original of this document has become discoloured with age. This copy was constructed by means of an accurate tracing of a photographic enlargement (magnification x2) of the original, verified by reference to the original document.

Elusive or False?

The name 'Yunnan' remains a mystery to me. This inland region of China does not appear to have an island named after it. Searches in the Map Library of the British Museum, the Hydrographic Department of the National Maritime Museum and the Hydrographic Department of the Ministry of Defence, have all failed to find a Yunnan Island on seventeenth century and current charts. My colleague in the States, Philip Masters, who is a maritime historian has searched on my behalf in the equivalent libraries over there. Whilst he has found some islands with similar sounding names, they are not the right shape or size. Of interest though is that on one of the old French Indochina charts that he sent me, I spotted an island remarkably similar in shape to that we are looking for. Because of the scale, detail is not too clear, but the shape looks about right also the size, and most important, the 'lie' of the island is right. Unfortunately its latitude and longitude is nothing like that on the Kidd chart. However, it is in the South China Sea area and looks interesting enough to pursue further.

John S's Rough Map

While the horn mugs themselves are probably genuine, forget the engravings – all that is except the island outline.

It would appear that, assuming the island engraving is genuine, then that drawing must be the first and original engraving on the mug. The majority of the other engravings were obviously added at a much later date. For example, the pocket pistols: their butt shape and over and under lock, makes them late eighteenth or early nineteenth century, definitely not earlier. The ships shown – on the left a barque and right a brigantine – are without a shadow of a doubt mid-nineteenth century. This is evident from the triangular head sails, dolphin stricker under the bowsprit, gaff and bow shape. (My thanks to Mr R.B. Knight, owner of the Workbox, for these observations and comments.)

One might expect to find a skull and crossbones, as depicted on the mugs, in the eighteenth or nineteenth centuries, but almost certainly not as early as the seventeenth. To explain our reasoning for this we have to delve a little into the history of pirate flags.

The Jolly Roger

The term 'Jolly Roger' appears to have embraced pirate flags in general, but the flag was also known as 'The Jack' and 'Old Roger'. No one knows the origin of the name 'Jolly Roger' but it is thought to have come from the French *joli rouge* (pretty red), the term used by the French buccaneers. Another possibility is that is comes from the eastern 'Ali Raja' meaning 'King of the Sea'. The notorious eastern seas pirates known as the chiefs of Cannonore went by this title and the English pronunciation was 'Olly Roger'.

Some early pirates used a red flag with the 'death's head' in white. Although the black flag with skull and crossed bones underneath has come to embody the symbol of piracy, you will see from the illustrations that that design is but one of many. Because of the reluctance of the pirate fraternity to place their deeds on record, we have very little evidence of the actual flag colours and design. Historians and artists tended to draw what they thought the flag looked like from contemporary descriptions. For example: 'A flag was hoisted called "Old Roger" . . . in the middle of it an anatomy [skeleton] with an hourglass in one hand, and a dart in the heart with three drops of blood proceeding from it in the other.' This description is taken from an old account of John Quench, a pirate executed at Boston in 1704.

The earliest pictures of pirate flags I have come across are in Charles Johnson's *A General History of the Pirate*, first published in 1724. The engraving shows Captain Bartholomew Roberts with his two ships *The Royal Fortune* and *Ranger*. At least two pirate flags are shown. One clearly shows his favourite design, that of a large effigy of himself standing, each foot on a human skull. Under one skull are the letters ABA and under the other AMH. These abbreviations stood for 'A Barbadian's Head' and 'A Martinican's Head'. The design was a reminder of the two occasions he was treated roughly by a ship from Barbados and by the inhabitants of Martinique. (He later hanged the Governor of Martinique from the yardarm.)

Another account of Roberts' exploits reads: 'His sloop went in with drums beating, trumpets sounding, English colours flying, and the pirate flag at the topmast with death's head and cutlass.' Roberts was prolific in flag design. Those labelled 'A', 'B' and 'C' in the illustrations are all attributed to him – and he had variations on a theme of these. We can date these flag designs fairly accurately to around the 1720s.

One of the first recorded uses of the 'death's head' symbol was in 1700 by the French pirate Emanuel Wynne. He flew 'a sable [black] ensign with cross-bones, death's head, and an hourglass'. It seems the hourglass was to signify to an intended victim that time was running out and he had best surrender. Sometimes the terms of engagement were presented differently. Some crews made use of both red and black flags.

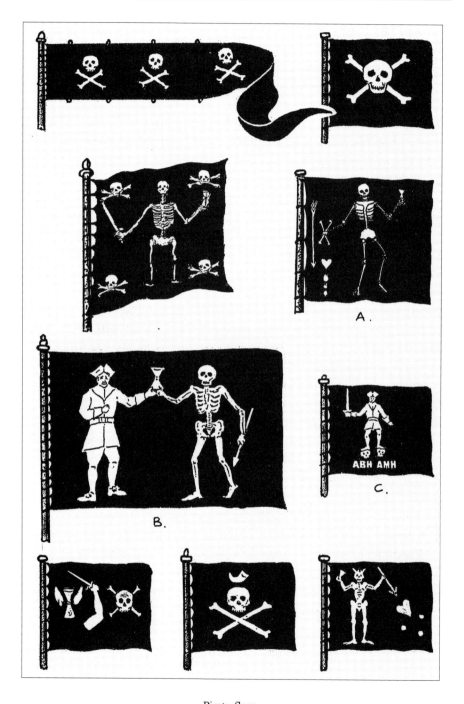

Pirate flags

It was the practice first to run up the Jolly Roger, signifying an offer of quarter. If this was not accepted and the victim chose to fight, then the red (or Bloody) flag was hoisted indicating that the offer was withdrawn. We will recall here that Kidd flew a red broad pennant when he tried to take the *Sceptre*.

During this same period, the pirate Edward Lowe is reported 'to have, in July 1723, taken a new ship for himself, naming himself Admiral, and sporting a new black flag with a red skeleton upon it.'

This early part of the eighteenth century seems to have been the birth of a great variety of flag designs. Most were similar, some pirate captains obviously copying others and adding a touch of their own. There were yellow flags with black skeletons, red flags with a yellow hourglass with pair of wings, even a white ensign with no effigies but the words 'For God and Liberty' embroidered on it. This was attributed to the priest turned pirate, Caraccioli. There could be a skull with a cutlass, or even crossed cutlasses. A severed arm holding a scimitar – daggers – hearts – bones – they were all used in many different designs and variations.

What I would like to make clear, besides giving you a useful background in pirate flags – is that the skull and crossed bones design we are interested in, namely that on the mugs and on the Morgan chest, is not typical of the seventeenth century. My research has yet to disclose any instance of this design being used during Kidd's lifetime. That of course does not mean to say it never was used then!

Kidd's Island?

For reasons explained in the earlier chapter on these mugs I am assuming the island depicted is the same as that on the other charts. You will probably react differently – they are nothing like the same, you will say. No, they are not, but you must remember two things:

1) The charts were drawn at least twenty-three years after Kidd visited the island in (we assume) 1669; he only had his memory to go by – no aerial photographs – he remembered certain features and possibly exaggerated them.

2) John S did the same. His island is different because he remembered it differently, but he did not forget certain features. Ask yourself

this: if you had stepped on an island briefly twenty-three years ago, would you be able to remember exactly what it looked like? Even more difficult, could you draw it? Remember also, the wording does say *rough* map.

I have reason to believe that of the two island shapes that we have, John S's outline is a lot closer to the shape of the actual island, but more of this theory later.

The Bureau and Chests

I am led to believe that the bureau came originally from America, and that the opinion of a knowledgable antique dealer, also the Victoria and Albert Museum, is that the bureau cannot date from before 1740. It must be noted that these opinions were based on viewing photographs of the bureau.

As this item bore a brass plate inscribed 'Captain Kidd, *Adventure Galley* 1669', and if we are to believe it was in fact used by Kidd, then we must accept that the bureau is in fact from the seventeenth century but was altered in the mid-eighteenth century perhaps to 'modernise' it.

An obvious question to be asked here is: If Kidd did not get the *Adventure Galley* until 1695, how could the bureau be inscribed as it is with the date 1669? It is suspicious, and here lies another part of my 1% uncertainty. The disbelievers will say the plate was added afterwards, to suit the date on the chart: maybe, but why and by whom? The answer could be that it was an engraver's mistake, he meant to put 1699. On the other hand, according to H.T. Wilkins, Kidd *did* have a previous ship of the same name. He unfortunately does not make it clear if his statement is as a result of historical research or if he postulates that Kidd must have had a ship of the same name because of the bureau inscription. It was of course by no means unusual for a later ship to be named after an earlier one.

If the bureau came from America, i.e. originally from Sarah Kidd, then either Kidd or his wife could have secreted the chart in it. Although the chart is dated 1669 by (we assume) Kidd, the fact that Sarah W is on it is proof that Kidd did not draw it in 1669 because he did not meet his wife until many years later. The chart was drawn therefore sometime *after* his marriage in 1691, and 1669 is probably when he visited the island.

There seems to be no doubt that the chests and workbox are genuine. Kidd would have had at least two sea chests: There is no reason to suppose that the Hardy and Morgan chests did not originally belong to Kidd; on the other hand, we have no proof that they did. It is a fair assumption that the bureau really was Kidd's because the chart found in it had his and his wife's names on it. Whilst the pedigree that comes with the Hardy chest is impressive, the carving on the lid – 'Capn Kidd his chest' and date '1669', does not mean a thing; they could have been added at any time. The same applies to the Morgan 'skull' chest: the plate engraved with the monogram 'K' and skull and crossbones could have been added at any time to any old chest. We have already seen that the skull and crossbones features typically on eighteenth and nineteenth century pirate flags, so we should view this chest with added suspicion. We should also ask ourselves the question: if Kidd believed himself innocent of piracy charges, would he raise unnecessary suspicions by having pirate banners on his furniture? It is highly unlikely, so here we have another part of my 1% uncertainty.

Whilst the bible in the chest could be acceptable – pirate crews were sometimes sworn in on the bible – the plaster skull is suspicious. I do not know of any authentic instance where a skull was used for swearing in the crew. No doubt a reader will enlighten me.

Kidd's Ditty Box

I have mentioned earlier that Anthony Howlett had a Kidd chest, given him by Mrs Dick, which he refers to as 'Kidd's ditty box'. He told me it was about 2 ft. by 18 ins. with a brass key plate inscribed 'Willm Kidd, Leith Scotland'. Just an old chest he said, nothing special, no secret compartments. I had not seen this chest at this stage and was looking forward to examining it when I spent some time with him.

Something most odd struck me about the chest as soon as I saw it. My remarks left Mr Howlett with a puzzled and faraway look and he probably wishes I never saw it, because of the time and effort it will now take him to have it examined professionally and possibly X-rayed.

The chest measures 17 x 10¾ x 8½ inches, appears to be of oak construction and has been treated for woodworm. The inside of the chest is lined, unusually, with the pages of a book, stuck to the sides, bottom and inside lid. The pages are from seventeenth century books: *Nobility and Gentry, which are, or lately were, related unto the North-Riding of Yorkshire With their Seats and Titles by which they are, or have been known*, and from a similar work relating to the West Riding, and from *Isles and Territories Belonging to His Majesty in America*. Also, affixed to the inside back near the top is a silver shilling of Charles II dated 1668. On the inside bottom is a ledge about ½ inch wide and 1 inch deep where possibly another (false) bottom rested.

My remarks were made regarding the outside bottom of the chest. This was also lined with pages of the same book as appeared inside. Why would anyone go to the unnecessary trouble of lining the outside, especially the bottom where it gets most wear? I could only guess that it was covering and hiding something else. The thought had not occurred before to Mr Howlett.

Somebody, probably Palmer, has already attempted to prise the bottom off, but nobody has thought to have a look behind the lining. I am probably wrong, but neither of us will be really happy until our curiosity is satisfied. I don't know that we would want to find another chart: that would really put another twist to my story!

The lining almost certainly confirms this chest, at least, to be seventeenth century. The shilling appears to have always been attached to the chest and, minted in 1668, is only one year earlier than the date on the bureau chart.

What is also interesting about this chest is that it is the only one probably to have been with Kidd all his seafaring life, from when as a lad he left the shores of Scotland. He would have kept what personal belongings he had in it. The chest apparently came from a Scottish descendant of Kidd, who sold this and other relics of his ancestor before he emigrated to South Africa.

The Oriental Chest

There is evidence of another chest linked to Kidd. In 1934 Hubert Palmer came into possession of a splendid, ornate, oriental chest. The description was given as: red lac on teak wood, heavy and brass bound with studs, 4 feet 3 inches long, 2 feet high and 1 foot 10 inches wide. It has three drawers and stands on a teak pedestal 6 inches high. The pedigree that

The Kidd chest owned by Anthony Howlett shown open and upside down with lining on bottom. Also a close-up of the key escutcheon.

came with the chest attests that it was once the property of Henry
Cristophe, the Negro Napoleon King of Haiti.

The link with Kidd is a brass plate attached to the chest (it is not clear
where). On it is engraved; 'Capt Wm Kidd, His chest From ye Q Mt'.
Christophe lived over a hundred years after Kidd's death, so the chest
obviously changed hands after it was taken out of the *Quedah Merchant*
(Q Mt).

Palmer gave the chest his usual thorough examination, but found
no hidden compartments or charts. It is not known where this chest is
today.

How Probable the Improbable?

Don't you think it strange that all these chests and other effects of Kidd
should end up with one man? What else did Palmer have in his museum
of pirate relics that once supposedly belonged to Kidd? I can list them
as follows:

1) Gold ring with miniature portrait of Kidd set in it. Palmer himself
   wore this. It came from a Miss Kyd or Kydd of Scottish descent.

2) Silver shoe buckles worn by Kidd at his trial.

3) Kidd's cutlass, with gold wire grip, brass horns head handle and
   blade engraved with birds and faces.

4) Pair of flintlock pistols.

5) Small pewter snuffbox. Lid engraved on inside 'William Kidd,
   1698'. Bought off a schoolmaster Palmer knew in Sussex; his
   grandfather bought it in Leith.

6) Small clay pipe stand made of oak. Top engraved 'Adventure.
   W.K. 1697'.

7) Cutlass with ivory grip. Presented to Kidd by William III. Engraved: 'William Kidd, Captn. Bristol 1697'.

8) Kidd's silver baldrick (shoulder sash). A curious wax impression
   on the leather reads 'Baldrick buckle worn by Wm. Kidd, executed
   London'. On the back is the name 'Sarah Kyd'. This was also
   obtained from the Miss Kyd mentioned above.

9) Pieces of Kidd's black flag.

10) Oak box containing bible with inscription 'Kidd's Family Bible'.

11) Wall mirror in oak frame made of wood from the *Adventure Galley*.

12) Oil painting of Kidd. Frame also made of wood from the *Adventure Galley*.

I have my doubts that the frame was in fact made out of wood from the *Adventure Galley*. The painting was done from a sketch made during Kidd's trial. The *Adventure Galley* had been abandoned by Kidd three years before in 1698. His new ship (the *Quedah Merchant*) was known as the *Adventure Prize*. When this painting was finally framed, the *Adventure Galley* had long gone.

The question may be raised that, as Kidd spent most of his life abroad, are we really expected to believe it possible that all these effects of his could end up in a seaside town in England? We have already asked a similar question of the chests. It is feasible to find maybe one chest and hidden map, but two, three or four? Isn't it stretching coincidence a bit too far?

But the arguments for are equal to the improbabilities. All of Kidd's chests, personal belongings and effects arrived in England together. They were shipped back with him after his arrest. The exception is the workbox in which the 'key' chart was found. That would have been amongst Sarah Kidd's possessions and so ignored by the authorities.

Kidd was visited in Newgate by relatives to whom he probably gave some of his personal things when he knew he was to hang. This would explain how the ring, sword sash and belt and other items stayed in the Kidd, or Kydd, family. It was usual for the pirates' ill-gotten gains of gold, silver, gems, etc. to be auctioned off with the proceeds going to the Crown. If there was no one to claim his personal effects such as his chests they would be auctioned off as well – if they hadn't been 'lifted' beforehand. We will never know for sure how Kidd's chests were distributed, but they stayed in the British Isles. Palmer's antique dealer was on the lookout for anything piratical and in particular anything to do with Kidd. Palmer himself advertised far and wide.

So if you believe the charts are genuine, then you have to believe that Palmer was indeed very lucky to come by the chests the way he did!

Interpreting the Charts

If you are fortunate enough to identify correctly the island – bearing in mind that you do not know that you have until you have found the treasure – your problems start all over again, this time trying to decipher and follow the instructions and directions given to find the spot or spots 'X'.

The directions could relate to 1, 2, 3, or 4 caches. Referring to the 'skull' chart, one cache could be ?5 paces (or yards) SE, another 50 paces North, another 36 paces NE and the fourth another 36 paces further on. To follow this theory one of course has to have a starting point – problem number 1.

Perhaps it is significant that 'Rocks' are mentioned on both charts and that they – wherever they are – are the starting point.

Before attempting to fill in the gaps in the margin around the 'key' chart, one needs very carefully to study the handwriting; the style sometimes varies even for the same letter. Having said that, I repeat that I do not believe that what appears to be 'le' in the bottom margin of the 'key' chart is the end of the word 'triangle'; it would make that word too long. It makes more sense if it is the start of the word 'leads'. The top of what can only really be an 's' in the same configuration means that the word must surely be 'leads'. The next word cannot really be anything other than 'to'. This bottom margin instruction could therefore read:

'fourth, centre of triangle leads to rocks 20 feet'

I cannot see that 'fou' can be anything other than 'fourth'. This word seems to have some importance, 4th also appears on the Yunnan parchment.

So in conjunction with the 'skull' chart, perhaps the instructions so far mean:

'*360 yards* from the *Anchorage* is a Valley *Running North*, there you

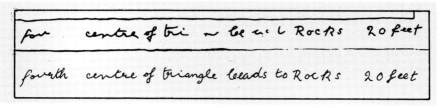

A likely interpretation of the bottom margin inscription on the 'key' chart.

will find *3 stumps 55 feet* apart, the *fourth* cache is *?5* paces *SE* from the *Rocks* that are *20 feet* from the point of the *triangle* of *stumps*.'

The italicised words and figures are those that actually appear on the charts.

Of course the remaining instructions on the side margin leave us with problem number 2: what are they for? Some people have said the word starting with an 's' is 'shelter' or 'skeleton' followed by 'of Leb' or 'L16'. Nobody has been able to make any sense out of what is there.

Having studied the writing very carefully, I don't believe 'shelter' or 'skeleton' to be correct. I believe it to be two words – 'Sh clearing'.

I have tried many combinations of letters and words to try and make sense of what I believe is 'of L and C'. To keep within the context, anything other then 'Ledge' and 'Cave' doesn't make sense. These words are of course significant to the Yunnan parchment. A possibility then for the third margin could be:

'Now [or 'also'] go *E*ast to *Sh clearing* dig at back of *Ledge and Cave*.'

The last couple of words could also read:

'at back of Ledge and 6ft deep' or '6ft away'.

On the other hand, all the above could be totally wrong!

'20 TURTLES' has always been another bit of a problem. If the author of the charts noticed turtles on the island, why mention that on a treasure map and to what purpose? Mention immovable landmarks such as trees and woods, maybe, but turtles? I don't go along with the 'turn turtle' theory, i.e. turn the map upside down. The only other plausible explanation could be that TURTLES just happens to be the word spelled out of an abbreviation for something else. For example:

'Treasure Under Rocks Triangle Lies East Stumps'. It is food for thought and included to confuse you even further.

The odd shaped triangular projection drawn under the word 'WRECK' (top left hand corner of chart) has been another puzzle. It is not a promontory of land as it has been added after the coast was drawn. I believe it was the chart-creator's way of showing an opening in the cliff and it is my guess that a cave is in the cliff here. It could have a connection with the 'Yunnan' parchment, who knows?

Dots and Crosses

The four 'dots' on the 'skull' chart could refer to cairns or piles of rocks, and the four directions refer one to each pile. It is doubtful but I am trying to show you all the options to demonstrate the next problem (number 3).

I am inclined to believe the directions initially give the precise layout of the triangle. Why whoever drew them should state their size I do not know, because presumably the 3 stumps (or whatever) would be there on their return anyway.

As stated earlier, the '51' in the instruction '515 SE', is purely conjectural. I think it was misleading of Skelton to put it in. In the notes accompanying the original redrawing he admits that the document is almost illegible at this point. Something *was* there, but I cannot believe it was *two* figures missing. Three figures means at the least it is 105 paces or yards and that does not tie in with the other three sets of two figures. 515 paces is about a quarter of a mile; it just does not fit in with instructions for a small island. The first two characters could be 'ST', and the instruction meant to read: 'Step 5 [paces] South East'. Or even 'S15', meaning the same thing but '15 paces'.

However, if '?5 SE' were to read '35 SE', we have an interesting revelation: see diagram 1, below.

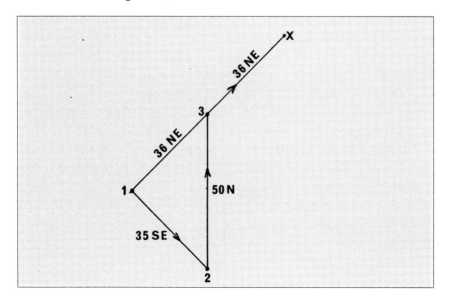

Diagram 1.

Having followed the instructions 35 SE then 50 N, the third side of the triangle, i.e. 1 to 3, measures almost exactly 36 and *exactly* NE. Perhaps the additional instruction 36 NE takes us to the spot marked 'X'.

If a previous interpretation is correct, i.e. 'centre of triangle leads to rocks 20 feet', then perhaps we are looking at two sites: see diagram 2, below.

Should this interpretation be correct, we are of course still left with the problem of the third side margin instructions, unless they refer to a third cache. But if this is the triangle construction, what do the 55 feet refer to? We have previously assumed they measure the sides of the triangle. The whole problem, as you see, multiplies rather than reduces.

Putting that problem aside for the moment (thank goodness), the triangle of three small circles on the 'key' chart point to a conspicuous looking 'dot'. It could be significant because there is what looks like a 'K' above it and, furthermore, a little more to the left what appears to be the letters 'TA'. Could this mean 'Treasure at K'? Just another one of the many possibilities! On the other hand, the 'TA' and 'K' could be coincidental marks and the dot a palimpsest mark.

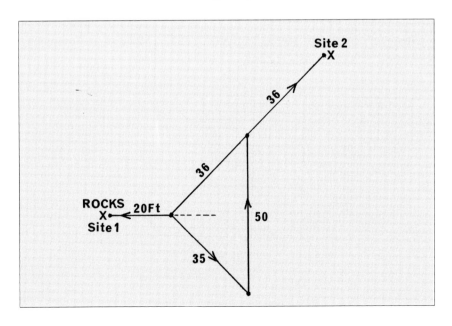

Diagram 2.

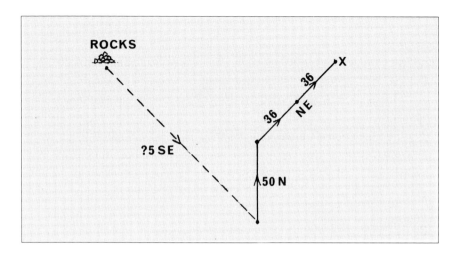

Diagram 3.

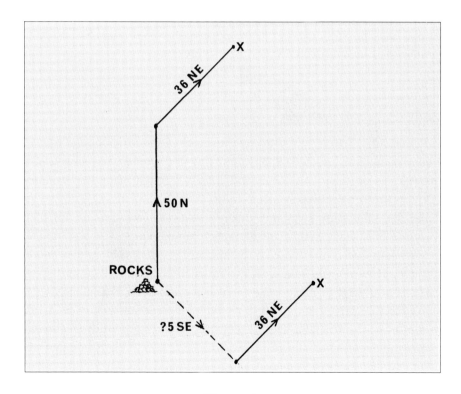

Diagram 4.

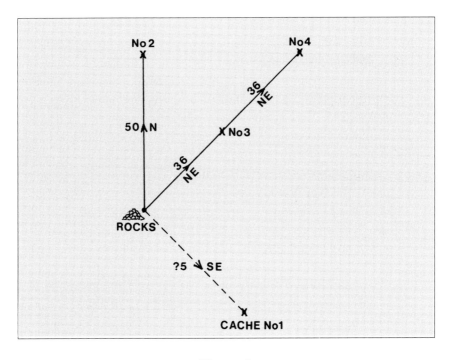

Diagram 5.

Perhaps the 'fourth' and '4th' refer to a 4th cache buried on the island, I cannot imagine another explanation. But the bureau chart shows just one 'X', as do the 'skull' chart and John S's rough map. The Yunnan Island parchment obviously refers to one hiding place only. We have to make our minds up as to how many caches we are looking for and therefore how many sets of instructions, one or four.

Choosing one is not the easy option; in fact the problem gets more difficult. How do you relate all the instructions to one location? You can't, if you want to make sense. If you try and keep it simple: having arrived in the valley running north we look for three stumps 55 feet apart in the form of a triangle, and 20 feet from the centre (or 20 feet from, and in the direction of, the point) we will find rocks. This is our starting point and the skull chart instructions are to be measured from this point. You can of course arrive at one point as in Diagram 3, previous page.

But why go the trouble of giving three different directions? Why not just one compass heading and distance direct to the spot? Also, instead of 36NE, 36NE, why not 72NE? The latter point is I believe important; if Kidd had left instructions for one cache then of course he would have put 72 NE. The fact that he didn't can only mean a) there are two caches 36 paces apart on the same line or b) the distance 36 is measured once from two different points. We could therefore have the possibility shown in diagram 4, p. 245.

We have cleverly used up the instructions, but to two spots 'X' not four.

If there are four separate caches then there must be four separate sets of instructions. The 'key' chart shows the way to one, possibly two (third margin instructions) caches, but more probably shows the way to the starting point. I cannot see that there are four sets of instructions on this chart. This is what I assume the 'skull' chart is for: the two must be used together.

To utilise the four sets of figures on the 'skull' chart by relating them separately each to one cache, then they can only be measured from one point. We assume again the starting point is the rocks. A fifth option then is in Diagram 5, p. 246.

Richard Knight's story made me think of another possibility. Three chests could be buried together and the Yunnan Parchment tells you where the fourth and final chest is.

Skull Chart – Further Interpretations

There is nothing to tell us what the figures refer to. Are they feet, paces, yards or degrees? The only clue could be in the way 'AND BY 50N' is written. This term is typically nautical, meaning a compass heading. If that is the case then the figures are degrees.

So to test your patience further and with reference to chart Diagram 6 (p. 248): you will see that a line with its starting point at the 'Anchorage' and drawn 50° from north, will pass exactly through the fourth lower 'dot' adjacent to the 'X'. Similarly, a line drawn at 36° from the north, i.e. north-east, will pass exactly through the third 'dot' down adjacent to the ℧ sign.

If we apply the same angles and use the same starting point to the 'key' chart (See Diagram 7), the 50° line passes almost exactly through the lower 'stump' of the triangle and the 36° line passes exactly through

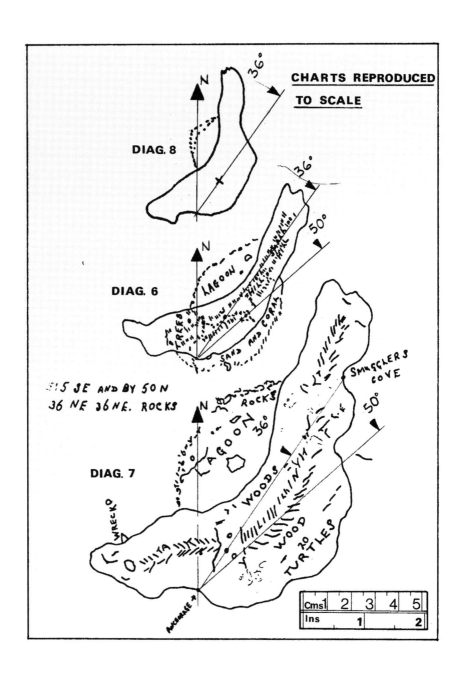

the centre 'stump'. It is interesting to note that if this line is projected on, it will intersect the 'dot' at Smugglers Cove.

Having discovered these interesting facts, what do we do with them? In fact they do not appear to open up a new avenue of discovery at all. Three significant dots on a straight line at 36°NE must surely mean something. Apparently not and must be coincidental or a hoax. If a hoax then again the instigator has boobed. It is easy to line three dots up on a map but, in actual practice, to be on an island and then by eye be able to line up three transit points from one end of the island to the other is highly improbable. The island would have to be very small or very flat to allow for that sort of line of sight. Both charts show that line passing through hills and valleys.

On the other hand, could this be the explanation of the puzzling '36 NE 36 NE'? Having arrived at Location 1, you take the same bearing to Location 2. Location 2 is obviously Smugglers Cove, because the intersect point is the coast. Location 1 we can assume is the centre of the triangle and must correspond with the dot ʊ on the 'skull' chart.

Applying the 36° line to the 'bureau' chart (Diagram 8), from where one would place the Anchorage, further increases the probability that we have discovered the interpretation and significance of '36 NE'. As you can see, the line passes exactly through the centre of the 'X'.

We are assuming the figures represent degrees, so we must apply the same theory to the first part of the instructions, i.e. '?5 SE'. This is where the theory doesn't add up because any line in the south-east quadrant will take you out to sea. The first line instructions must therefore be measured from some point inland and the figures are a measure of distance. The second line instructions define the compass heading from the starting point, i.e. the Anchorage.

If '50 N' is to be used as an inland instruction then are we to ignore the 50° line that happens to pass through the 'X' dot? Perhaps it is coincidental that this dot lies 50° from north. The 'bureau' chart is showing just one 'X' 'marks the spot' at 36° NE, so perhaps the 50° lines does not have any meaning when measured from the Anchorage, and is not to be interpreted this way.

A more plausible interpretation of these figures is that they could be transit lines. Supportive evidence for this is as follows:

With reference to the 'key' chart (Diagram 9, p. 250), if you draw a

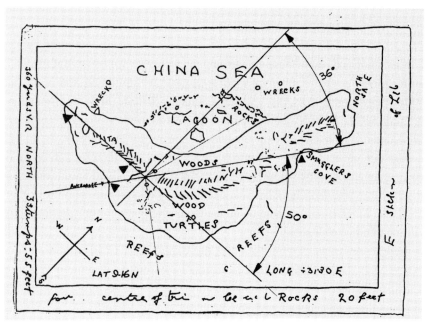

Diagram 9.

line from the centre triangle circle (bisected by the line 36 NE from the Anchorage) and project it through the conspicuous dot[*] directly west. That line intersects exactly another conspicuous 'dot' at the end of the island. The angle separating these two lines just happens to be 50°.

As we have already seen, a line drawn between the dot at the Anchorage and that at Smugglers Cove intersects exactly the centre triangle circle. It also measure exactly 36° East of North.

Surely it cannot be coincidental that these lines provide us with angles exactly as mentioned on the 'skull' chart? It has to be that one or both show the way to the triangle at least!

Further support evidence is suggested by the fact that if you transfer these findings to the 'skull' chart (Diagram 10) the 50° line passes through three conspicuous dots, including the one to the east that has an 'X' adjacent to it. The dot marked thus ☉ we can assume is showing where the triangle of stumps lie.

---

[*] see also bottom paragraph, p. 258

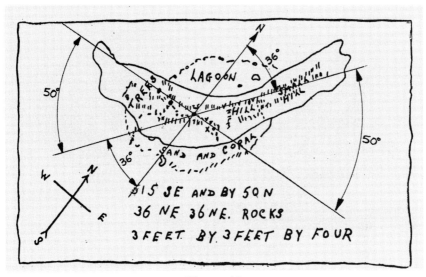

Diagram 10.

So having identified the significance of '50N' and '36NE', we are still left with '?5SE and another '36NE'.

Another point to consider is that as the stumps are visible above ground mark, then you only need one bearing to guide you there. In other words, if you walk on a bearing 36° NE from the Anchorage, you will come to the centre stump; you do not need another transit. So the 50° line must be pointing you somewhere else. Obviously pointing you to the other treasure sites, you say. But think about it! If you are at the centre triangle stump, with compass in hand, and you want to show the way to a cache to the west on the 50 line, you would mark it down as follows: '4 S of W', possibly '266SW' or even '94W'. When taking a bearing in the opposite direction, you would have marked it down as '86E' or '4 N of E'.

Perhaps half of a figure 8 is missing, having disappeared over a period of three hundred years. What is 36NE should read 86NE. It makes more sense. The figure is a convenient summation of 36 ± 50, but who knows! The problems, you see, just don't go away.

The above of course all adds evidence to the hoax theory. It also goes towards part of my 1% uncertainty. If we are on the right trail regarding the 35NE and 50N lines, i.e. they are transit lines, the directions would

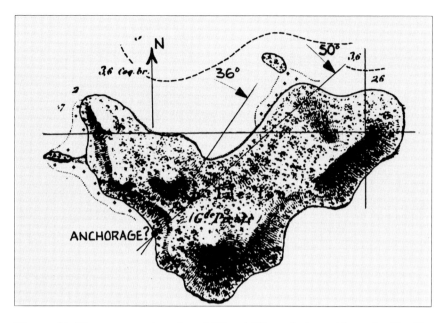

Diagram 11: These two transit angles of 36° and 50° are further evidence that Hon Tre Lon cannot be the island. All the Kidd charts show these lines leaving the coast on the eastern side or southern coast of the island. You can see from the diagram that both these transits exit the island on the north coast

not have been put down as they have been. The hoaxer forgot to imagine himself on the island to visualise how it would have been done.

Having examined most – if not all – of the possible solutions to the instructions, my thoughts and conclusions are as follows:

1. The triangle of stumps or rocks are obviously the key to where any treasure is. That being so, the triangle centre lies on a heading of 36° NE from the Anchorage. At 55 feet in a south-easterly direction from the stump bisected by the 36° line you will find another stump; 55 feet north of this brings us the third stump creating the triangle. The treasure lies under rocks 20 feet from the centre of the triangle. A further treasure lies at Smugglers Cove in a cave. This is the meaning of '36 NE 36 NE' and where the Yunnan parchment directions are to be used.

OR

2. Having found the triangle of stumps or rocks, any one of the possibilities shown in Diagrams 1–5 could apply, as then all the

instructions are used. However, we do not know if the 'key' chart third margin contains any further instructions.

3. The ӧ sign must add some importance to the dot bisected by the 36° line. It is no mere squiggle but purposely drawn that way, otherwise in its place would possibly be another set of parallel lines such as those that appear either side of it. I have already mentioned that this sign could represent a well. Another possibility is a trench or hole in the ground, i.e. where the (main) treasure is buried, or even a cave.

Chapter 7

This Be Where it Lies

The Secret Uncovered

I have been looking at these charts, off and on, for over fifteen years. They have been pinned up on my study wall in front of my desk for a long time. I was hoping that perhaps in my 'off beat' moments I might draw some new inspiration or thoughts from them, or maybe find that elusive 'breakthrough'. Well I finally did!

The solution came when one day I decided to put myself in the creator's shoes (again!). If I had buried a treasure or treasures, what information would I have to write down to make sure I could locate them again? First of all we have to find the island. If it is remote, or one of many in a group, then a latitude and longitude are essential. We have already discussed at length the problems associated with the latitude and longitude shown for our island. Having arrived at the island I don't need to refer to anything else because I've been there before and know where I buried my treasure. So why write it down? This is where a lot of controversy comes in regarding pirate treasure maps. You don't need one! Certainly not if you have just one cache. You are not likely to forget where it is, even more so if you intend returning within a short space of time, say a year.

Now if I have, say, three caches, then it might be a wise move to put something down on paper to remind me where they are. So I would want an island drawing showing me where. I would mark the hiding places with the traditional 'X' (or 'T'). If I was showing compass bearings I would need a starting point. Distances would need to include direction and method of measuring, for example '35 feet NE', or '70 yds SE'.

If the distances involved were too great then transits would be required with an angle. The transit points must of course be visible on the land for line of sight. I would also need to know where along that line our cache is.

So the above information should appear somewhere on the charts, hidden or disguised or shared amongst them. Let us assume it does. Now let us look at the information that is there that we do not need. For example, we know the island is in the China Sea: why give it away? We don't need to know there are turtles there, or even that there are twenty! Why show wrecks to the north? Why show woods, or where 'Smugglers Cove' is. It is all useless information and of no help in locating the spots marked 'X'.

Or is it!

I looked more closely at the 'wrecks', and this is when I realised this 'useless information' is there for a reason. A study of Chart 13 reveals all.

A line drawn between the two outer wreck circles (11) and (9) is exactly horizontal to the chart border. Bisect this line and draw a line 90° vertically down it and it passes through three 'O's. The first 'O' in 'WOODS', the second 'O' in 'WOOD' followed by the 'O' in '20'. Keep projecting this line and it is in line with the vertical part of the letter 'T'. Notice also how a further projection takes us through the centre of the word 'triangle' in the border. Remember the (my) interpretation of the legend is 'Centre of triangle leads to rocks'. In other words, the word 'triangle' is positioned here purposely. It is emphasising the importance of the centre of the triangle. It probably hasn't escaped you now that a vertical extension of this line passes through the top of the 'A' in 'CHINA'. That is why the word 'China' is there, or positioned where it is. It is showing you (and reminding the creator), that a line drawn from this 'A' to the 'a' in 'triangle' marks the exact centre of *the* triangle. The wreck circles (11) and (9) are there to fix the position of the triangle base and *this* is the triangle referred to in the bottom margin instructions.

An equilateral triangle (all sides equal) would put the apex just below the 'T'. I would guess the apex is meant to be the 'T'. There is a lot of factual evidence to support this as I will show later.

Assuming we have indeed found the true reason for the wreck circles, let us use the other two circles the same way. The one above the 'L' in 'LAGOON' (12) has been underlined to show its importance as a base point for two more triangles. You can see that the equilateral triangles constructed each point to obvious areas of interest to us. The triangle to the left apexes on the 50° transit line where 'TA K' appears (Treasure at K?). The other triangle apexes close to the 36° line and close to what could be a 'T'. This location appears to coincide with a small 'T' on the 'skull' chart (between the two hills, right hand side). There also appears to be a track shown here going down to the coast. The assumed triangle of stumps then could be a confusing blind, the triangle referred to on the chart being the one we have found.

More geometrical evidence supporting my theory is as follows:

Look at part of the instructions on the 'skull' chart – '36 NE 36 NE ROCKS'. As we have seen, an angle of 36° measured from the Anchorage (3) transits with the centre stump and Smugglers Cove (3) (2) (8). Now measure another 36° as instructed (72° total), and we bisect the triangle centre line exactly at 'T' (1). This is where the rocks are. 'TUR' means 'Treasure Under Rocks'. The remainder of the instructions on the 'key' chart could read '20 feet to the East, Sh (south) clearing'. The 'LES' in 'TURTLES' then could mean 'Look (or lies) East Side'. Twenty feet away here one assumes is another treasure.

On the other hand the point 'T' could mark where there is a turtle shaped boulder (see sequel at end of chapter) or a boulder marked like a turtle's back. At an angle of 50° to the north and 20 feet away lies the treasure. The '20' *is* shown on the triangle centre line and approximately 50° north. Could this be the meaning of '50 N' on the 'skull' chart and '*Centre* of triangle leads to rocks 20 feet' on the 'key' chart?

Obviously there can be no giant triangle drawn out on the land – the base is anyway in the sea – so this geometrical construction is showing us where the boulder or rocks are. A treasure is buried under the rocks and 20 feet away to the east or north. The 'skull' chart as you know has a conspicuous 'X' and dot at the bottom of the island. This corresponds to the 'T' position (1) on the 'key' chart. Both 50° transit lines (Diagrams 10 and 11) also pass through the same locations on both charts.

Further confirmation – if you want it – can be obtained as follows:

The 36° NE line passes through point (2) on the 'key' chart (centre of the three stumps) and corresponding point ʊ on the 'skull' chart (Diagram 10). The conspicuous dot to the right of the 'X' on this chart is exactly 90° from the north measured from the dot. Measure the equivalent 90° on the 'key' chart from point (2) and you once again intersect (1) (T) or the spot marked 'X'.

If the 'T' is significant in that *here* lies the treasure, and if there are three or four caches, then one would suppose there are more 'T's to be found. We of course know there are. Let us look more closely at the pen strokes depicting the slope of a hill at the left hand end of the island. They are all more or less parallel as expected but two are different in that a stroke has been purposely added to the top of each at right angles. So what has been thought could be meant to read 'T at K', probably is meant to read 'T at T', thereby again confirming our position 'T' (1). Another possibility of course is that the two 'T's signify two treasure sites which correspond with the two dots at the same position on the 'skull' chart.

Another interesting fact is that the Anchorage and first wreck circle (11) are exactly in line vertically. Using the Anchorage as centre, an arc scribed from (11) also bisects the triangle centre line at 'T'. The same thing happens if you scribe an arc from (11) again but this time using as centre the wreck point (10).

The promontory (13) top left hand corner, has always been something of a puzzle. I don't believe it is high land jutting out to sea. It is more likely to be another compass centre point or geometrical transit point. A figure that is in fact a '6', located off the coast, bottom of the chart (14) has also puzzled me. It is after all a bit conspicuous out there all on its own. But if you draw an line from here to point (13), it just happens to bisect the triangle centre line at 'T'. I can't find any other reason for point (14). It could of course be – just a mark! Point (13) does also confirm the triangle apex point (7). A compass with its centre at (13) and radius 'T' (1) will scribe an arc passing through this apex. So there are at least 5 constructed lines that all pass through the same point 'T' (1). Do you think it could all be a coincidence? I think not.

A point here about drawing accuracy. Any criticism you may have regarding angles not exact or bisected points etc. not exactly in line are unfounded. You have to realise that the charts were drawn approximately three hundred years ago. In that time the material they were drawn on will have moved, stretched or shrunk, or possibly all three. Today's reproduction of them is therefore bound to vary slightly from the original.

Let us now look at the two other smaller triangles.

Note how the apex point (5) happens to fall on the 50° transit line (2) (6) (4). Note how the vertical line drawn from the Anchorage passed through the letter 'T'. Is this significant, supporting the 'Treasure at K' theory? In other words, somewhere on this hill or ridge, positioned as shown by the apex point (5), there is a sign in the form of a 'K', and this is where to dig.

What is the significance of the dot (8) at Smugglers Cove besides the fact that it lies on the 36° transit line? You can see from the diagram what it is. Using this point as a centre, a line with radius passing through the wreck circle (9) also passes exactly through the apex (7) of the right hand triangle.

Using the same centre and radius to triangles base point (12), a scribed arc will once again pass through point (1) at the bottom of the 'T'. I cannot yet see the significance (if any) of mentioning 'Smugglers Cove'. It doesn't show up as a feature of the 'skull' chart. A few of the 'O's as we have seen are there for a reason other than what might seem the obvious, and an arc centre (9) does go through the 'O' in COVE (17) and the intersection point (7), but that could be a coincidence.

Another point of interest is that occurring at (18), between what could be a 'G' and 'E' (Go East?). It just happens to be exactly vertically in line with wreck point (9). I am not sure why. Perhaps it is a coincidence. A similar vertical line from wreck point (11) is of significance in that it goes direct to the Anchorage point but I cannot see that this point (18) is important. However, with it as a centre, a radius (Going East) to the 'O' (17) in COVE does take an arc almost through the triangle apex (7). Similarly, an arc radius to the 'O' (19) in NORTH does – yes – go exactly through the 'T' (1). (I haven't shown these arcs because there are enough already converging on the intersections and it gets confusing). Although lines of geometry seem to confirm point (7) and that triangle as being possibly of some importance, I am not happy with it because I may have been subconsciously looking for a triangle and confirmation of it to fit that area, because of what could be a 'T' there. I would have been much happier if the triangle and arcs had pin-pointed the 'T' (20), because this looks as if it has been intentionally scribed as a 'T'.

You can anyway now see that all of the 'useless information' is required for the construction and confirmation of the triangle apexes.

There are one or two other mysterious points or dots. Take number (6) for example. It lies on the 50° transit line (2) to (4) and therefore looks to be of some importance. However, when I checked with the enlarged photographic copy I have of the original chart, the 'dot' is in fact a mark like a figure 6. The photocopy reduction in size has made the curled part look as if it is filled in. So it is not a dot at all.

Another conspicuous dot (15) lies in the right hand border. It is lost in reproduction on a lot of copies and is positioned with verification to the original chart. However, I couldn't tie it in with anything other than the fact that it just happens to be in line horizontally with the dot (16) between the 'V' and 'R' in the opposite border. It could of course be a palimpsest mark, or they (15 and 16) might have been used by the draughtsman to line up the paper horizontally.

So to sum up, we have three precisely positioned areas of definite interest. In fact no, we can make that four! We are forgetting the 'Yunnan Parchment' instructions. Remember '4th North and at'? Refer back to our chart diagram 13. You can see that a line drawn north from the 'T' position (1) (this being the main triangle) points to what looks like a large 'V' on its side. What looks like a letter 'T' appears just to the right of it. Is this where the caVe is and fourth treasure? I believe so. There are of course a lot of what could be faded marks here (see chart page 226) which could be of significance making this an area of positive interest.

The geometrical solution so far described of course explains the unconventional way the charts are drawn, i.e. not on a compass north/south axis. From a geometrical drawing construction point of view, it is much easier to draw the main triangle and everything else on a conventional horizontal plane. The compass rose was put in afterwards. This therefore must have been the first chart drawn and explains why the other three charts are drawn in the same unconventional manner.

There is a curious sequel to the fact that '20 TURTLES' is of major importance. A person came into our shop recently asking for advice on metal detectors. He was not from this country and it soon emerged that he was not interested in an ordinary detector. He is in the business of hunting mainly land-buried treasures and he wanted something that goes deep on large objects – chests for example. We obviously had a mutual interest and had a long talk. I showed him a copy of the 'key' chart without giving away the solution. To see what comments he might have, I said, 'It doesn't make much sense, does it, to mention that there were 20 Turtles there?' His immediate response was, 'That is where the treasure is buried!' I must admit I was momentarily speechless. I had spent nearly fifteen years working it out and he did it in fifteen seconds! He obviously had a different explanation and solution to mine and it is this: turtles come in from the sea and lay their (golden) eggs (buried) in the sand. He also said that it has been known that a turtle-back shaped boulder will be chiselled into squares, similar to a turtle and measurements cut into them. This boulder will be on the beach in the vicinity of the treasure.

If we are both right, the one confirms the other.

It just goes to show, you can keep learning new things about these charts and treasure hunting!

Progress and Patience

Anyone who is astute will recognise my own progress in the book in my attempts to solve the chart's instructions.

I have been researching and writing this book off and on for over fifteen years and of course attempting to solve the charts at the same time. This might help the reader understand why my thoughts and reasoning earlier on in the book might differ in places to my thinking later on. Newly discovered revelations or ideas on certain aspects would change previous thinking. When I decided I was wrong on a particular tack I would start again and try a different direction investigating other possibilities and lines of thought. But I didn't erase previous thoughts, errors and work that I could see later was probably incorrect. I have left it as it was the way I was working through it. If I had not, then you would have had just this chapter on the solution and not all the work that led up to it. The reason was to give you a look at *all* the possible solutions. To get your mind working. To see if you can come up with any possible solutions that I have not covered.

This chapter is the culmination of all those years of work, puzzling and pondering. I am confident that the centre 'T' in 'TURTLES' marks the spot 'X' and that my solution is the real and only one. It is logical, is geometrically correct and makes sense to me, but then, I am not perfect . . . !

I am confident I have shown you where the chests are. Now all you have to do is find the island. Well let's be fair, I have to leave you something to do yourself, don't I?'

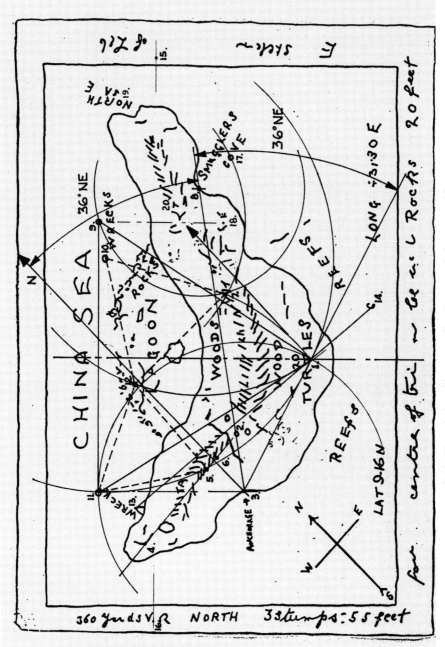

C.13. The solution. Shown smaller than actual size, see p.15.

Finding the Island by Focusing on Features

If, having got this far, you have decided that *nobody* has yet found the right island, then where is it? To try and find it ourselves we have to make some important assumptions as follows:

1) The serious contenders, i.e. Furneaux and Knight, despite their work got it wrong, and anyway, obviously they cannot *both* be right.

2) Knight, whilst getting it wrong, was on the right track, i.e. the China Sea.

3) Latitude is correct to within ±1°.

4) They got it wrong because the actual island shape could be quite different to that shown.

5) The island has on it a valley running due north.

6) There are, or were, reefs north and south of the island.

7) The island cannot be more than a few miles across.

The topographical features on the charts give us important clues. We must put ourselves in Kidd's shoes three hundred years ago, and imagine we are on his ship at anchor where the ANCHORAGE is shown, or perhaps standing in the valley. With reference to his charts then, his observations were as follows:

1) There is good anchorage and a cove on the south side of the island.

2) There is a hill to the left, also to the right with yet another at the far end of the island.

3) There are reefs east and south-east of the island.

4) There are reefs on the opposite side of the island with rocks and/or a small island.

5) There is also a rock or small island off the south-eastern coast of the island.

6) There is a valley running north, open to a plain or the sea at its south end.

7) The island has trees.

8) There are one, possibly two, coves on the east coast.

9) At the other end of the island there is a valley running down to Smugglers Cove.

10) There are cliffs (Yunnan Parchment) either on the coast or inland.

11) We are in the *South* China Sea.

12) We are at latitude 9° 16′ North.

13) The island is at the most a few miles long.

I have examined all the possible and probably islands in a band 2° wide and the width of the China Seas. Some of them are shown in this book. Those that are not were either far too small or had none of the qualifying features required. With one main exception I have ignored all the islands in the Gulf of Thailand (or Siam) north of the line of latitude of 9° 16′. We cannot be said to be in the South China Sea here of course, this is the Gulf of Thailand; certainly anything north of this line is getting further away from the China Seas. The area south of this line could have been known as the South China Sea in Kidd's time. It has to have been because there are no suitable island candidates in the China Sea to the east of Vietnam; this leaves us only with the south end of the Gulf of Thailand, i.e. on or south of latitude 9° 16′.

The exception I have made lies exactly on this line and is Poulo Panjang Island (on modern charts it is shown as Hon Tho Chau).

With reference to the chart showing this island, (p. 47) let us imagine we are in the bay south-west of the island, having been on the island and buried our treasure. What observations could we note down?

1) There is good anchorage here (drawing of anchor shown in the cove signifying good anchorage).

2) There is a hill to the left, another to the right with yet another at the far end of the island.

3) There are reefs to the south.

4) Small islands off the opposite end of the island.

5) Small islands south and south-east of the island.

6) There is a valley running north between two hills.

7) The island has trees.

8) There are two coves on the east side of the island.

9) There is a valley running down to one of these coves.

10) We are at latitude 9° 16′ North.

11) The island is 2–3 miles long.

As you can see, the similarity in features is quite remarkable. There are of course questionable differences:

1) No lagoon on the far side of the island; a sandy bay is all that is shown here.

2) The small island south-east and just off shore. This was probably joined to the mainland a few hundred years ago and would have created Smugglers Cove.

3) No obvious cliffs, a question we cannot really answer until on the island.

4) A stream is shown originating near the centre of the island. The 'skull' chart shows a symbol ($\triangle$) in the middle of the island. I have always thought it could be a representation of a well and cannot imagine what else it could be. I am either right or very wrong!

5) How do we relate the north of Kidd's chart to Poulo Panjang north?

This final point is an interesting one and has been a big stumbling block but could be cleared up quite simply:

The 'key' chart emphasised the fact that there is a valley running north. Kidd, or whoever drew the map, remembered that when he was in the valley, his compass showed it to lie due north. Having drawn the island as best he could from memory, he had to show north, so he showed it in the direction of the valley. In other words, the island plan came first with compass north added after to suit. (See also page 259.)

Bearing in mind that you do not have the benefit of a birdseye view of the island, how would you have drawn Poulo Panjang maybe many years later? It would not be easy. See the sketch maps p. 266. It is easy to see from the sketches how, on redrawing, an island outline can change completely. The all important drawing is of course the first one. How accurately three hundred years ago did the draughtsman reproduce the actual shape? It was probably highly inaccurate; subsequent copies or redrawings are therefore bound to be further still from the true shape.

This then demonstrates to the reader another way he should be looking at the problem of identification, i.e. from the known features and bearing in mind the inaccuracy of cartography three hundred years ago, also the fact that the island was probably drawn from memory.

We can see now why John S's island shape should not be dismissed out of hand. The map sketches p. 267. show why.

In conclusion then, and bearing in mind our previous assumptions and conclusions, personally at the moment, I would plump for Poulo Panjang as being Kidd's island. One of its main qualifying points must be the fact that it lies exactly at 9° 16′ North, and we know latitude could be measured very accurately in the seventeenth century.

The *China Sea Pilot* (Admiralty instructions for sailors) includes the following amongst its information about Poulo Panjang:

> It is of a nearly uniform elevation of 545 ft. and has the appearance of a table-land from every direction. The island is inhabited on the western side which also affords shelter with a good anchorage in a depth of 16 fathoms. Isle du Pic (Peak Island) lies about 2 cables off the southern side with foul ground between. [1 cable = 1/10 nautical mile or 608 feet.] The passage between the island and two islets east-north-east are obstructed by coral. The closest islet is 200 ft. high, the furthest 150 ft. high.

No island has as many qualifying features, I know, because I have examined *all* of them. If Kidd's island is in the South China Sea, this has to be the one.

I am still inclined to believe Richard Knight's island of Hon Tre Lon is not Kidd's island. I would love him to prove me wrong, but it is far too north in the Gulf of Thailand to be considered anywhere near the South China Sea. Anyway, why would Kidd, a westerner, go all this way up the Gulf so close to the coast? It just does not make sense. He is going closer to danger all the time. Acceptable to local pirates maybe but would you have chosen an island here to bury a fortune?

We will recall from the 'Where' chapter that Wilkins and Palmer, also Howlett in his magazine article, favoured the Sequeiras Islands, particularly after one of them appeared to have been identified as Kidd's island by a Captain Orchard. Wilkins refers to this gentleman as 'This British Seaman who navigated a cruiser in the World War' (First) and implied that he was in the Navy at the end of the century by referring to 'our

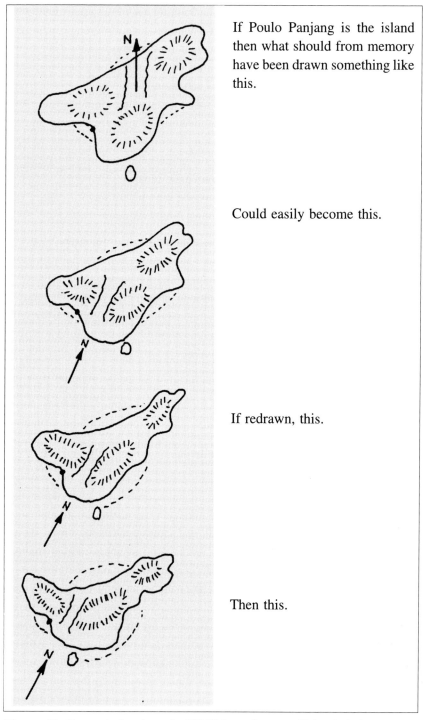

If Poulo Panjang is the island then what should from memory have been drawn something like this.

Could easily become this.

If redrawn, this.

Then this.

Diagram 12: Demonstrating how the Kidd/Palmer charts could be depicting Poulo Panjang island.

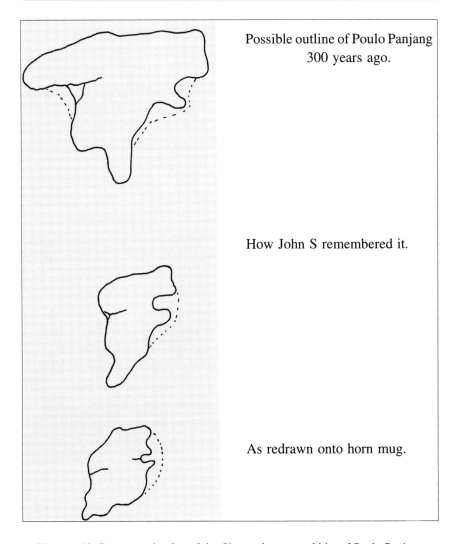

Possible outline of Poulo Panjang 300 years ago.

How John S remembered it.

As redrawn onto horn mug.

Diagram 13: Demonstrating how John S's rough map could be of Poulo Panjang.

own naval patrol'. He also refers to him as a British Captain in1896 when he sighted them (the Sequeiras islands).

An investigation into British seamen and naval records reveals that Commander Orchard RNR (1874–1941) was an apprentice up to 1894 and 2nd mate in 1896. During this period he served with the Douglas Steamship Co Ltd on the SS *Andelana*. He was in the RN Reserve from 1906. So in 1896 he would have been twenty-two years old and certainly not a captain. When he first saw Palmer's charts he would have been about sixty years old and trying to recall events of about thirty-nine years previous.

We should not therefore rely too much on Wilkins' account.

If you are convinced the charts are genuine, then in my opinion Poulo Panjang must be the number one contender, but only from a practical point of view. That is, it more or less fits the bill as mentioned, and of course it lies at 9° 16′ North.

From a realistic view, although unknown, it is highly unlikely that Kidd was ever in this region. Depending which way you go, it is some 14,000 sailing miles west of the traditional pirate hunting grounds. If you went east, it is still some 10,000 miles. There were no Panama or Suez Canals in those days. But if you believe in the charts, then somebody was there.

I wouldn't completely ignore out of hand some other islands in the West Pacific Ocean, namely the Ngulu group at 8° 16′ N, 137° 40′ E. Although way off the track, they are closer than the Gulf of Thailand. We are assuming of course that the longitude figure on the chart of '?31.30E', was originally meant to read '137 30E'. It is a distinct possibility. This area of the East Indies is more likely to have been visited by Kidd than the South China Seas. The description of the island (Ngulu) includes woods and reefs (see p. 45). These are shown on the charts. The island outline is vaguely similar, and we have seen how and why the outline of an island drawn three hundred years ago can be very different to its real shape. These islands are very remote – ideal for hiding a treasure.

Going Bananas?

Most of the comments and points for discussion in this chapter so far are based on the assumption that the island we are looking for is of a different shape today than that depicted on the charts. But we must of course also face up to the possibility that the shape of the island today is still more or less as depicted on the three charts and has changed little in three hundred years. That being the case, then we are still looking for a distinct 'banana' shaped island with a lagoon on the north side and reefs on the south-east side.

Do not therefore let my thoughts and theories detract you from this point. I am, in this book, merely making you aware of all the possibilities. Having said that, if you assume the island has changed little – what do you do about John S's Rough Map? Nothing like the shape of the others but has a lagoon!

Not simple, is it?

Until the island is found, we will never know which theory is correct.

At Long Last

Let us come back to the longitude problem one last time. It seems that the more time I spend trying to solve it, the harder it gets. I was still working on it up to the time the manuscript had to go to the publishers. It seems almost insurmountable.

My final thoughts on it were that the mark in front of the '31.30' (if indeed it is 31.30) is a capital letter Kidd used to signify the meridian used. It looks to me remarkably like a 'G', confirming Greenwich as the meridian, the back of the letter having disappeared. But as we know, we are high and dry in the Sudan at this position. The same theory raises the possibility of a 'H' or 'A', Hierro or the Azores. However, it doesn't matter how you use these meridians in conjunction with 31° 30′ and relating them each to Greenwich, you will still not arrive at a satisfactory answer. Even assuming the figures are 81° 30′ doesn't help.

So if the contending islands so far named are wrong, we still have a major stumbling block to overcome.

Chapter 8

To Conclude and Final Thoughts

Was Someone Kidding?

Well, there you have it, I wonder what you make of it all. Do you think it all true, or just a good yarn and thanks for buying the book? No, everything you have read is true. I will not make such a bold statement as to say it is all here, but I would like to think of this as the definitive work on the Kidd/Palmer charts. Nowhere else will you find all this information together and almost certainly there is nothing more to divulge about these charts. You have *all* the information here in this volume.

Why four charts,* all different? you may ask: surely only one is required? Are all the charts needed, together with the 'Yunnan Parchment' to find the treasure? Doesn't the 'key' chart show the way, the others not being necessary? You have to decide for yourself but someone has gone to a lot of trouble to put specific different information, directions and clues on five different documents, all relating to the same island. We have already discounted the hoax theory, so why – unless all the documents *are* necessary.

To believe in these charts, one has first of all to overcome the 'China Sea' obstacle. Nowhere in the accounts of his known life is there any reference to Kidd visiting this part of the globe. The last ten years of his life are fairly well documented, so we know where he was during this period. Twenty-two years prior to that, in 1669, he would have been about twenty-four years of age, too young probably to have his own command but not too young to have accumulated loot of his own as part of his share as a crew member. Perhaps the charts show where he buried

---

* The three shown plus the Hardy chest chart

this loot. But then you ask the question, 'Why in the South China Sea, so far from home?' We therefore have to look at the possibility that the charts show the way not to Kidd's treasure but that of somebody else. Kidd was merely one of the gang that helped bury it.

It has also been suggested that Kidd came into possession of these charts – by fair means or foul – and that he never was in the China Seas. That makes sense when you consider that most piratical activities involving westerners took part in the Caribbean and West Indies area, thousands of miles away across the Pacific. Yet the 'bureau' chart says 'China Sea' and is signed and dated by Kidd. The same applies to the 'Yunnan' parchment, this time specifying the *South* China Sea. I am inclined therefore to believe that Kidd *was* there. He carefully observed where a treasure was buried and noted these observations, hoping that perhaps one day he would be in a position to go back for it. Having said that, I still find it difficult to believe that a Westerner or European would bury a treasure in or anywhere near what was the Gulf of Siam – it is a long way to go back to retrieve it.

We must now be aware of course of the possibility that if it was not Kidd's treasure, then whoever it did belong to may have been back for it. Bear in mind then that you could devote a lot of time, energy and money to solving these charts and finding the island – as indeed there already has been – and that if you have correctly identified the island and somehow got there, the hole you uncover under the spot marked 'X' could be empty.

The theories expounded and conclusions reached are obviously my own. I believe that to attempt to solve these charts you have to approach the problem from a common sense point of view. Imagine yourself in the shoes of the creator of them three hundred years ago and be *practical*.

I would be pleased if the book has exercised your mind to the extent that it has strayed off at a tangent towards other possible solutions and explanations; it just proves how intriguing these charts are and that there are possibilities other than those I have shown.

Two other points should be born in mind when contemplating the genuineness of these charts and the possibility of a treasure cache.

1) A chest full of bullion would be heavy, probably between 100 and 200 lbs. Think about it: having struggled ashore with one or more of these in a small boat on possibly more than one trip, you are not going

to carry them very far, are you? Don't forget, when retrieved, it's the same journey back.

2) One also has to look at the mentality of pirates in those times. They turned to piracy because they wanted money. After capturing a prize they usually divided the loot there and then and usually quickly lost it gambling or at a port where innkeepers and ladies of doubtful virtue soon showed them how to spend it. This was all the pirate lived for. He knew he might have a short life so he made the most of it. Under the conditions they lived and worked, almost without exception, all they looked forward to was a good time at the next port of call.

The idea of burying their hard won booty on a deserted island was alien to their way of life. They would have little opportunity to do that and it would have been even more difficult to keep the hiding place a secret from the rest of the crew. What little they didn't spent they kept as their nest egg.

Considering the amount of treasure taken during the age of piracy, very little was buried for later recovery. He who buried the chests was not going to forget where, so there was no need to write the location down. It may though have been necessary to do that at a later date if they realised they might not be able to get back for a while. Some were bound to have been killed or died before they could go back but it was the exception rather than the rule for booty to be buried by pirates for later recovery.

Some Notable Treasure Hunts

Those hoards that we know about and that are waiting to be found are really very few and include the following legendary but real pirate treasures: Roberton's pirate treasure on Agrihan (formerly Grigan) in the Mariana Islands; Bonito's hoard, and others, on Cocos Island; the Alvarez church treasure of Pisco on the Tuamotu Archipelago, Central Pacific; Benito de Soto's treasure, Trinidad Island off Argentina, and so on.

Searches for concealed treasures are seldom successful. I know of only three cases in which treasure has been found. Considerable mystery surrounds two of the discoveries, not surprisingly, for people who find treasure are loath to talk or write about their achievement.

The first relates to the treasure cache made by Blackbeard Teach, the famous pirate who constructed a brick-lined chamber on the beach at Plum Island, Beaufort County, North Carolina, in 1716. He lived nearby and the tradition of his deposit lingered amongst his descendants. It seems that some knowledge of its exact location was preserved locally, for on Christmas Day 1928, two fishermen walking on the beach stumbled upon a freshly excavated brick-lined vault. Its sandy floor was marked by the imprint of an iron-bound chest. The story is told by Charles B. Driscoll in his book *Doubloons*, published in 1931.

The other story is even more mysterious. In 1935 the English explorer and archaeologist, Frederick Mitchell-Hedges, dug up five chests containing treasure in the floor of a cave on the island of Roatan in the Gulf of Honduras. Roatan is believed to have been used as a haven by Sir Henry Morgan who looted the city of Panama in 1671. Lord Kilbracken, who told the story of his visit to the island in the *London Evening Standard* in March 1965, went in search of the chest Mitchell-Hedges was reported to have left behind, having been unable to carry all five away. His daughter had told Kilbracken that he had reburied the chest in the cliff-face. Kilbracken easily identified the narrow entrance. In its floor gaped a square, grave-like hole. But he failed to find the other chest.

The three pirate treasures reputed to have been concealed in the Cocos Islands off the coast of Costa Rica have not been found despite visits by a number of people armed with the proverbial sea-stained charts. It seems that the separate clues to each famed cache have become so interwoven as to defy description, and the island has suffered several landslides which have destroyed the land-marks. An organised expedition has had some luck though. Effectively planned and prepared, a few French students went illegally to the island in the mid-sixties; they found two chests in a cave and came away with two thousand gold coins and thirty gold bars.

The Herculean Task in the Seychelles

Another fairly recent treasure hunt has ended in tragedy: Olivier de Vasseur (also known as the Buzzard) was a French pirate hanged for his crimes on Reunion Island in 1730. He had made two rich captures, a Portuguese vessel, the *Vierge du Cap*, carrying the Viceroy and Archbishop of Goa, and an Arab ship conveying a princess on her way to marry in Zanzibar. Before Vasseur died he is supposed to have flung a roll of parchment into the crowd crying, 'Find my treasure he who can.' Besides a treasure map, the parchment contained a series of clues to an amazing and elaborate puzzle based on the twelve labours of Hercules and the achievements of Perseus. These had to be solved before the location of the treasure would be revealed. An Englishman, Reginald Cruise-Wilkins, came into possession of the map in the late forties and was to spent the next twenty-eight years on the Seychelles, digging for and solving the clues. Each clue had to be solved before the next step of the search could be embarked on. By 1977 he had solved nearly all the clues which led, he believed, to a chamber underwater. It was on a part of the beach covered at high tide and he had to dam the sea back to carry out excavations. Sadly he died that year. His son carries on the search to this day. However, two brothers on the same island believe *they* have found the treasure site, not in the sea but in caves in the jungle. They have produced drawings and photographs of the jewelled encrusted cross of Goa, which they say could weigh as much as 400 lbs. The hiding place will stay a secret, they say, until they have the right backing.

The Tuamotos Islands Treasure

Failure met another group in 1931 when an English expedition went to the Tuamotos Islands in the mid-Pacific. The concealment of treasure there seems well authenticated. In 1849 a gang of thieves looted the church at Pisco, a town on the coast of Peru which housed a wealth of golden ingots, church ornaments and rich jewels, part of the treasure stolen from the Incas. The thieves fled across the Pacific with their £3,000,000 of treasure, intending to reach Australia. Realising they would be unable to account for its ownership, they landed on a tiny atoll in the Tuamotos group of islands and dropped their loot into a pear-shaped pool.

They all met untimely deaths in Australia, but not before one passed the clues for the recovery of the treasure to a man named Charles Edward Howe who, armed with the map, spent seventeen years searching on the wrong atoll before he located the right one. He returned to Australia to obtain partners and disappeared, never to be heard of again. His map came into the possession of the Englishman George Hamilton who, with five other adventurers, sailed to the islands. They located the pool easily and felt something hard by probing its depths. But attempts to recover the treasure were foiled by its monstrous guardians, the giant octopus and moray-eels which came from the sea by a tidal inlet. Presumably the treasures of Pisco still lie in the depths of the pool. Hamilton told the story in his book *The Treasure of the Tuamotos*, published in 1938.

Some people are just plain lucky. About ten years ago a ten-year-old boy digging in his garden in Burgos, north Spain, uncovered a large chest. When prised open it was found to contain rare pieces of gold, silver, pearls, gold figures and other objects of great value. It is thought to be loot buried over two hundred years ago by pirates. The chest apparently weighs hundreds of pounds and the value of its contents has been put at nearly a million pounds.

The Salvage Islands Treasure

One of the books read during my research (*Islands Time Forgot*) carried a statement that I have not been able to corroborate or disprove.

> Cocos Island in the Pacific and Long Island near New York have been mentioned as Kidd's treasure islands. One of Kidd's crew however, made a statement fixing one of the Salvages as the correct spot.

These islands – there are three – lie at Lat 30° 5′ N and Long 16° W.

The treasure hunt story that follows, although very little known, is told not only because of the possible Kidd connection but because our own Royal Navy took an interest in it. I came across it during research before I found mention of it in E.F. Knight's story of Trinidad.

Writing a book of this sort has meant consulting many old books. To get as close to the source as possible then the older the book the better. Consequently one tends to buy anything and everything that comes on the market that could relate to your subject. One such book was called *Sea Drift*, by Rear-Admiral Hercules Robinson, published in 1858.

The story goes like this:

In 1813, a 'respectable looking foreign seaman', after an interview with the Secretary of the Admiralty in Portsmouth, was granted an audience with the Admiral. The outcome was that a fortnight later, Robinson was sent for by the Commander-in-Chief Sir Richard Bickerton. He was given some papers and a letter from the Secretary.

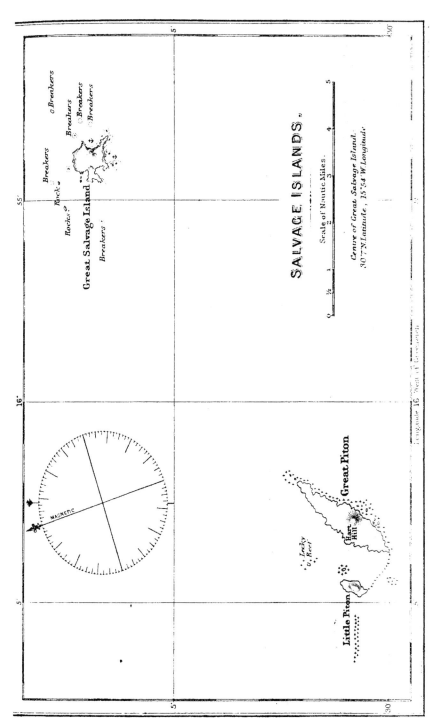

C14. The Salvage Islands

The enclosed, which are left open for perusal, will explain to you the purpose of sending the man to Madeira. I believe there is not the least truth in the story, and that the treasure, island and all, are visionary. But Lord Liverpool and Mr Vansittart think it worth while to make a trial of the thing, as it can be done without any great inconvenience; will you, therefore, have the goodness to let the man be sent in the first King's ship likely to touch at Madeira. The packet may be left unsealed that the captain may know the history of the people, and the object of their voyage.'

Robinson was introduced to the foreign seaman whose name was Christian Cruise.

I charged him to tell no person what he knew or what was his business, that he was to mess with my coxswain, and be borne for victuals but not for wages, and that no duty would be required from him. He replied, that was all he desired, that he was willing to give his time and would ask for no renumeration if nothing resulted from his intelligence. A few days found us standing down channel, and another week at anchor in Funchal Roads at Madeira. I took occasion during our passage to examine and cross-question Christian Cruise, and compare his verbal with his written testimony. The substance of both was, that some years before he had been sent to the hospital of Santa Cruz, in yellow fever, with a Spanish sailor, who had served for three or four voyages in the Dutch merchant ship in which Cruise was employed. He was in a raging fever, but notwithstanding recovered. The Spaniard, though less violently ill, sank under a gradual decay, in which medical aid was unavailing. The Spaniard moreover, had a 'mind diseased', and told Cruise he had something to disclose which troubled him, and which accordingly a few days before his death he related as follows:

He said that in 1804, he was returning in a Spanish ship from South America to Cadiz, with a cargo of produce and about two millions of dollars in chests, that when within a few days sail of Cadiz they boarded a neutral, who told them that their four galleons had been taken by a Squadron of English frigates – war being declared – and that a cordon of cruisers from Trafalgar to Cape Finisterre would make it impossible for any vessel to reach Cadiz, or any other Spanish port. What was to be done? Returning to South America was out of the question, and they (or rather the captain) resolved to try back for the West Indies, run for the north part of the Spanish Main or some neutral island, and have a chance thus of saving at least the treasure with which he was entrusted. Keeping out of the probable track of cruisers they reached a few degrees to the southward of Madeira, where they hoped to meet the trade winds.

They eventually found themselves close off a cluster of small uninhabited islands, fifty leagues to the southward of Madeira, and nearly in its longitude, the name of which the narrator did not know. The centre island, about three miles round, was high, flat, and green at top, but clearly uninhabited; the temptation was irresistible, here was a place where anything might be hidden; why run risks to avoid the English in order to benefit their captain and their owners? Why not serve themselves? (The crew were mutinous, having preferred running the risk of attempting Cadiz.)

The captain was accordingly knocked on the head or stabbed with their ready knives and carried below, and the ship hauled in to what appeared the anchorage, on the south side of the island. There they found a snug little bay in which they brought up, landed the chests of dollars, and cut a deep trench in the white sand above high water mark, buried the treasure and covered it over, and some feet above the chests they deposited in a box the body of their murdered captain. They then put to sea, resolving to keep well to the southward, and try to make the Spanish Main or a neutral island, run the ship on shore and set her on fire, agree on some plausible lie, and with the portion of money they resolved to retain on their persons, they were to purchase a small vessel, and under English or other colours, to revisit their hoard and carry it off at once or in portions.

They passed Tobago, and in their clumsy ignorant navigation ran over, blowing hard, an uninhabited quay, on which the ship went to pieces, and only two lives were saved. They got (I know not how) to Santa Cruz or St Thomas; one died, and the story of the other is being now related. The name of the ship, the owners, the port she sailed from, the exact date, or various other particulars by which the truth might be discovered, were not told to Christian Cruise, or not remembered.

Robinson tried to find discrepancies and flaws in Cruise's story. Could he not, he asked himself, have some interested object in fabricating this story? Why did he not tell it before? Was not the cold-blooded murder inconceivable barbarity, and the burying of the body over the treasure too dramatic and buccaneer-like; or might not the Spaniard have lied from love of lying and mystifying his simple shipmate, or might he not have been raving?

Robinson satisfied himself on the answers to these questions. He had the strongest conviction of the honesty of Cruise and didn't think he could be deceived as to his character. As to his withholding of the information for four or five years, it had to be remembered that the war with Denmark was on at that time. Regarding the murder, well, that was a way of life for a lot of the crews looking to make easy money. Burying a body over the treasure is straight from the tales of pirates and buccaneers. Blackbeard, for example, considered it expedient when he buried any treasure, to cut the throat of a Spaniard and place the body over the deposit, that the ghost might guard it. Robinson pressed this point and was relieved when Cruise said that he understood the object was, that in case any person should find the marks of their proceedings and dig to discover what they had been about, they might come to the body and go no further. Lastly, as to whether or not the Spaniard might have been raving. Cruise replied, 'Certainly not, he was quite clear in his mind, his conscience might be troubled, but his head not disturbed.'

Robinson, then, believed the story. On arrival at Madeira he spoke with the Consul-General and inquired if anything had ever been picked up at the Salvages. He was informed that some years before, one Jose de Lisboa had gone a poor man to gather barilla (a type of seaweed) and returned a rich one. Apparently he had discovered in the taffrail of a foreign ship wrecked there, two boxes of dollars!

Accordingly, one fine morning a few days later, found Robinson's ship off the great Salvage. On hauling round the east point there was the sandy bay with the white beach and the little level spot above high water mark, just as they expected to find it. Cruise, when asked his opinion, replied, 'No doubt, Sir, it must be the place.'

Robinson entrusted his officers with the story, pledging them to secrecy. They were to tell the men that they were in search of the body of a murdered sailor, who was supposed to be buried somewhere about the high water mark. Fifty of the sixty of the ship's crew were landed and provided with all the shovels they had. The rest were provided with a boarding pike. To encourage them they were told that the discoverer of the coffin would have a reward of 100 dollars.

> It was a red-letter day for our poor fellows, to whom any chase is enjoyment, and it may be well supposed with what glee they entered upon so novel a pursuit. In one respect however, our embarrassment was extreme, the white sand extended round the bay, and an area of many acres intervened between the high-water mark and the foot of the cliff, which a month would not turn up. We selected the centre of the beach and went beyond high-water mark to where I thought the breaking of the sea and the drainage through the sand might terminate, and where a man would be most likely to drop his burden; and then we dug a deep hole, but with no greater success than finding some broken shells and rounded pebbles! Our men in the meanwhile were probing with their boarding pikes in all directions and digging in every promising spot. This went on for several hours, till I was dead beat, and I became not only discouraged but a little ashamed of my wild-goose chase.

They found no treasure.

Robinson resolved to go back one day and persuaded his officers to keep the secret. However, it was not until after he was out of the Service, in 1856, that he found himself back there, on board the yacht *Dream*. This was of course a private venture, with two colleagues and a crew of six.

On arriving, the weather was rough, but they managed to get a boat ashore with the guns and landed in a little cove to the westward of Prometheus Bay. The barilla gatherers had erected two huts, a water reservoir and a path up the cliff. Having shot a lot of rabbits and birds, they returned to the yacht. The weather worsened and as there was no chance of landing the tools and equipment, they decided to weather the storm out by going to Teneriffe. One night, while wining and dining in a hotel in Santa Cruz, the landlord told them a story. Robinson made a note of it the way the landlord told it, as follows:

> You see Sir, this is how it was . . . A ship was fitted out by a company at Liverpool, some years ago, to search for treasure at the

Salvage Islands, which was said to be buried there in two ship's coppers and some casks by pirates, who used to plunder outward bound Indiamen and make the crews 'walk the plank'. Well, one day they were chased by an English man-of-war, who pitched into them and sunk them, as they would not heave to. One man only was saved, who was treated so kindly by the captain of the ship-of-war that he told him where the treasure was hid and gave him the marks on the rock to find it out. Well, the story somehow or other gets to Liverpool, and out comes the *John Wesley* to the Great Salvage to search. They remained there digging for two or three months, and said they found nothing; and then they came here for water. They got their water on board and returned to the island, and then came a report that they found money to the amount £40,000, which they carried out the Straits and landed at Marseilles; but whether this was true or false I am sure I can't say, and so the matter passed over. One morning after this, a boat comes here with four starving men, who had to be carried up to my house, and they said they had belonged to a ship which fitted out at Liverpool after the *John Wesley*'s return. Whether because the *John Wesley* had found some, and they thought they would find the rest (two millions sterling was supposed to be hidden), or that as the *John Wesley* failed, and left the chance to others, they would try, I don't know, but out they came in good earnest, with wooden houses, miners, and miners tools, and then they landed with six months provisions and two boats and set to work. They dug, and dug, and dug, till their hearts ached, and they got down to the bare rock, but found nothing except a dead body buried under the sand and a few boards and a copper coin – a penny piece – of the reign of George III, marked with a sort of index on the back, and on the face the four points of the compass with the letter N at every point. Well, they had eaten their six months provisions in two, and were hard up, and so they launched their boat and found their way here; and as they had had nothing for several days but a handful of starched peas, they were regularly done up and so thin and weak that I tucked up the chief man under my arm like a child and carried him up to my house. He was a sharpish hand, the others uncommon stupid. He shewed me the copper coin, and I offered him a goodish bit of money for it, but he said he would not take £100 for it, as he thought it pointed out something, if only he could find out what. When they landed here they certainly had found nothing, for they did not bring a dollar amongst them; and I don't think the *John Wesley* had found anything, or they could keep it so close. Now this is all I can tell. I think there is something in it, but dear knows how much.

A few days later saw them back at the Salvages. This time they landed on the Great Pitton (the other island in the group, about nine miles from the Great Salvage). After exploring here, they had reconnoitred all the likely spots which seemed to fit the description of Cruise's bay. But the unsettled weather still did not allow the yacht to anchor close. They also quickly realised that even if they found the treasure, it would be extremely difficult for them to bring even part of it to the yacht. The outcome was that Robinson was outvoted by his partners. They thought it folly to remain and hope that the conditions would improve. It was probably nearer the truth that his partners had lost some of their enthusiasm, after hearing at Santa Cruz that some, if not all, of the treasure had already been found.

Robinson didn't believe the treasure had been found. For a start, £40,000 is hardly the same as two million in dollars. Robinson in fact disputed the figure of two million. He states that $500,000 to $600,000 was the usual go for a rich trader. It is possible the ship was overloaded and at a push maybe $1,000,000 worth of silver stowed aboard. Robinson also points out that the dollars, if in silver, would have weighed about 120 tons, and would have been contained in some 1,200 boxes. It would have occupied a pit 20 feet long, 10 feet wide and 10 feet deep. Besides the feat of digging such a pit, it would have taken the crew three days just to unload such a hoard, and this assuming smooth calm water. There is also the point regarding the skeleton found. It may of course have been some poor fisherman who ended his days there. On the other hand, nobody knew if they dug below the remains!

However, home they came. His partners suggested that if they could get at the truth regarding what, if anything, had been found by the *John Wesley*, they might try again. But they all went their ways and nothing more was done.

That is the complete story of the Salvage Islands treasure. I spoke earlier about getting as close to the source as possible when doing research, and you won't get any closer than that.

Rear-Admiral Hercules Robinson firmly believed the story narrated by Christian Cruise. That treasure could still be there! His book makes no reference to Kidd's treasure though. Perhaps he wasn't aware of any link – if indeed there is any!

The book that contains the Kidd reference contains another example of misrepresentation of facts. It relates how Robinson reported that Portuguese fishermen had found two chests of silver dollars some time before he arrived. Having read that, prospective treasure hunters could be put off going there. 'The treasures been found! Why bother?' But as we have seen, the dollars found were taken out of a ship wrecked on the island, not buried in it.

Besides the reasons given at the beginning of this chapter, this story is included because there are a lot of truths, probabilities and facts to support it. The same of course applies to the Trinidad treasure story. (Note also the similarities between them.) To the best of my knowledge there is no factual evidence that either treasure has been found. Earlier failures, as we have seen, have been due to: lack of the right weather; lack of the right information; confusing rumours and different stories about different expeditions, all getting mixed up together; lack of time; and lack of the right equipment.

You have the real, true, factual stories here in this book, straight from the source. I might add at this stage that the technology is now available and I have the time, so, if anyone would like to sponsor an expedition?!!

The big difference here of course is that unlike the case of the Kidd charts and story, we know where the islands are and we have a damned good idea where to look.

But I must repeat a previous warning: the treasure (s) may have already been recovered (although I doubt it). If you have dug either up, you are not going to tell anyone about it, are you?

The Christian Cruise treasure is not the only one that is supposed to be buried on the Salvages. In more recent times than Kidd's, a pirate ship intercepted a treasure-laden vessel from Mexico, it is thought early in the last century. Some of the crew were burying part of the treasure on Little Pitton when a gale blew up, marooning them there. It is supposed that they eventually died of thirst as their ship had to clear the islands and couldn't get back. The ship was itself wrecked on the Saharan coast. The crew were taken prisoner by the Arabs. One of the men wrote an account of their adventures and drew a plan of the island. This eventually somehow found its way into the Madrid Library archives and a lawyer found the transcript. Subsequently a small expedition dug up Little Pitton and the narrator of this story said, 'I saw his trenches when I went there with my father not long afterwards. My father carried on the work for two months with sixty Spaniards as labourers, but without finding anything.' This search was carried out sometime before the First World War.

Modern Treasure Hunting

Treasure hunting on a different scale carries on today. I mentioned earlier in the book that I am familiar with metal detecting. This has been a hobby for over sixteen years and I have been selling them for about ten of those years. These days I tend to specialise in underwater detecting, both wading and using SCUBA. At the last count I have found well over a hundred rings, the majority just by wading. Whilst diving on a shipwreck site there is nothing quite like the thrill of getting a signal and digging a silver dollar out of the mud or sand.

Land detectorists do not like to be called treasure hunters because it conjures up the wrong image. The majority are perfectly happy being out for the day, enjoying the fresh air and experiencing the thrill of the find and the thrill of the unknown, not knowing if it is going to be a ring, or an old penny, or maybe an ancient artefact. I have a notice on a framed collection of rings I have found. It says, 'To seek is to find is to wonder.' I often wonder what stories lie behind the loss and what the owner was like. The thrill for me with detecting and diving is that you never know what you might find.

Responsible detectorists adhere to a strict code of conduct but unfortunately there are 'pirates' and 'cowboys' with detectors. They detect on protected sites, even at night (they are known as 'Nighthawks'). It is a fact that treasures that could be called the nation's heritage have found their way abroad illegally through these people. The actions of these few tend to give the majority and the hobby a bad name.

I digress. Being a diver and detectorist I have over the years produced test reports on new underwater detectors for *The Searcher*, a magazine that specialises in detecting. This in turn means that you tend to get a bit of a reputation and it is assumed that you are an expert on the subject. Consequently I am approached for advice and sometimes to search for lost items of value for members of the public, whether it be a ring thrown away during a lovers' tiff or a Rolex watch lost for many years in a pond. I had to travel over a hundred miles to that location and will never forget the look on the owner's face when I held up the treasured watch, the gold wet and glistening.

I was recently approached by a European gentleman who has information referring to several treasures. He wants my help in locating them. We are not talking about the odd ring or two here but very real bullion treasures. Over many years, by various means, he has come into possession of the whereabouts of several treasures both modern – Second World War – and old pirate treasures. He has the maps and I have the expertise and access to the technology that will find these caches. The perfect partnership! He is back in his country now obtaining the evidence I said I required before we complete the deal.

It may seem strange to you that modern treasures have not been recovered. There are usually the same two reasons as for the old treasures not being recovered, namely: those in the know have died or been killed; or, for whatever reason, they cannot go back to the site. For example, during the war some people *had* to leave their country and at the end of the war for political reasons they couldn't go back. So the gold perhaps buried to finance partisans or clandestine operations, or maybe siphoned off from the war chest, is still there.

So you see, treasure hunting goes on today, for pirate treasure and treasures more modern. The treasures waiting to be found most certainly exceed those already discovered.

These days hoards tend to be found by chance, usually by metal detectorists. One frequently reads of Treasure Trove inquests to establish the legal owners of important finds made of gold and/or silver. Conventional detectors are much improved these days over their counterparts of twenty years or even ten years ago. Some even use microprocessors now and circuitry that very accurately discriminates between ferrous and non-ferrous metals. You can pay up to £1,000 for the best conventional hobby detectors. These are designed to find coin size objects deep down to about 15 inches. It might not sound much but it's one hell of a hole to dig!

To find larger objects such as chests, specialist detectors have been developed and are continually being improved on with advancing technology. Powerful 'two-box' detectors are available. The transmit and receive units are separated by a rod-handle and it can be carried by one person or in the wide scan mode two operators 35 feet apart can search large areas fast. These detectors are designed to locate large deep objects – like an iron chest or metal pipes or ore veins. Depending on the ground mineralisation and target size, objects may be detected as deep as 20 feet. The latest pulse detectors claim to find chests at over 25 feet and larger caches down to 40 feet. Also available now are hand-held laser guided digital infrared scanners. Point one of these at the ground or side of a hill or cliff, and the scanner will be able to determine temperature changes caused by buried metals, caves, mine shafts etc. There are 'differential induction magnetometers' designed to find deep iron targets (iron-bound chests for example) or shipwrecks underwater. There are pulse detectors for small coin size objects, underwater detectors, and so on. As I said, if you know the location, the technology is available to find whatever is hidden there. Combine this 'state of the art' equipment with proper research and your chances of finding *your* treasure are considerably increased.

Final Comments

Furneaux, after his TV programme 'Three Characters in Search of a Treasure' was screened, received many letters offering help and advice ranging from the zany to the practical. I wouldn't welcome the zany, but I would welcome any practical comments you may have on the book, also genuine and authentic information, particularly from my readers in America and Canada. Somebody may know something which on its own may not appear worth anything, but which when linked with information from another source could be important and hitherto unknown by me.

Regarding Kidd's association with Nova Scotia, I am sure there is more to learn and research carries on into this aspect of Kidd's life. It takes a lot of time and patience to find out information from the other side of the Atlantic and it could go on for years, but we have to stop somewhere or there would be no book.

Dowsing

My final thoughts on this business are on the subject of dowsing (I did say that I was fascinated by the unexplained). I have no practical experience on the art; all I know about it is what I have read. A lot of people, I am told, have had a certain amount of success dowsing maps. Now I have an open mind on the subject, and I know Furneaux had the two main charts dowsed by Mr H.A. Snowden in 1975, a person very knowledgable on the subject. Snowden said that the results of the map dowsing were very encouraging because they were done on different days with a rod, also the pendulum, and a positive reaction to gold and silver was obtained at the same location in every case.

I thought that if dowsing is something to be believed, then any other person skilled in the art should arrive at the same location. I decided to put it to the test. I sent a copy of the 'key' chart to the late John Bowman who was an acknowledged expert on dowsing and used his skills to help in locating possible metal detecting sights. He had never seen the chart before nor knew anything about Mr Snowden and what he had done. A lot of the information on the chart was purposely obliterated.

The results speak for themselves (see charts drawings p. 288). I was amazed at how close the results of two independent dowsers could be to each other. It is also intriguing that the locations pin-pointed are in the vicinity of the valley and triangle.

The charts have to be genuine. Even allowing for my 1% uncertainty, the probabilities far outweigh the uncertainties. I do not believe Richard Knight has found it; I would be very surprised but happy if he has. I believe treasure is waiting to be found, even if it is not Kidd's. You have all you need in this book to find it yourself.

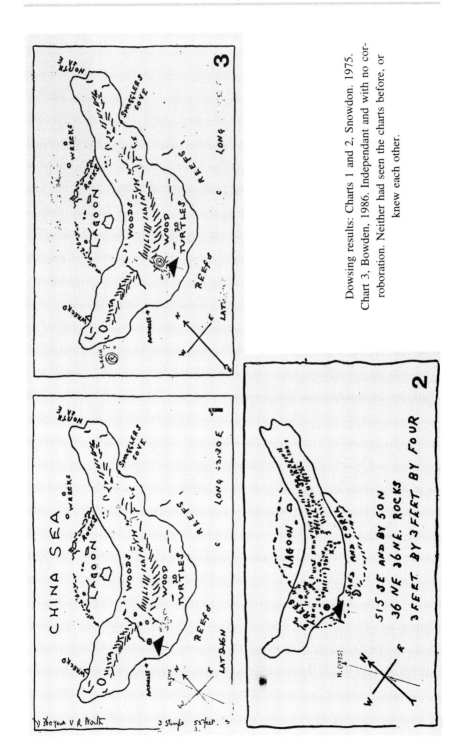

Dowsing results: Charts 1 and 2, Snowdon. 1975. Chart 3, Bowden, 1986. Independant and with no corroboration. Neither had seen the charts before, or knew each other.

Bibliography

Badrick, A.S.T., 'Does Captain Kidd's Treasure Exist', *Treasure Hunting Magazine*

Brooks, G., *Trial of Captain Kidd*

Carse, R., *The Age of Piracy*

Crooker, W.S., *The Oak Island Quest*

Crowell, B., *Atlantic Treasure Troves*

Esquemeling, *The Buccaneers of America*

Furneaux, R., *Money Pit, The Mystery of Oak Island*

Gilbert, H., *The Book of Pirates*

Gosse, P., *The History of Piracy*

Groushko, M., *Treasures Lost, Found and Undiscovered*

Groushko, M., *Lost Treasures of the World*

Hamilton, G., *The Treasure of the Tuamatos*

Harris, R.V., *The Oak Island Mystery*

Haydock, T., *Treasure Trove*

Head, F.H., 'A Notable Lawsuit' from *Studies in Early American History*

Howlett, A.D., 'The Mystery of Captain Kidd's Treasure', *Wide World Magazine*

Hinrichs, D.M., *The Fateful Voyage of Captain Kidd*

Irvine, L., *Castaway*

Jameson, J.F., *Privateering and Piracy in the Colonial Period*

Johnson, C., *Lives of the Most Notorious Pirates*

Kingsland, R., *Treasure Islands*

Knight, E.F., *The Cruise of the 'Alerte'*

Lubbock, B., *The Blackwall Frigates*

Mitchell, D., *Pirates*

Nesmith, R.I., *Dig for Pirate Treasure*

Norvill, R., *The Treasure Seekers*

Paine, R.D., *The Book of Buried Treasure*

Platt and Wright, *Treasure Islands*

Rankin, H.F., *The Golden Age of Piracy*

Ritchie, R.C., *Captain Kidd and the War against the Pirates*

Roberts, G., *Richard Knight's Treasure*

Robinson, Rear Admiral H., *Sea Drift*

Roden, H., *Treasure Seekers*

Snow, E.R., *True Tales of Buried Treasure*

Stommel, H., *Lost Islands*

Verrill, A.H., *The Real Story of the Pirate*
Wilkins, H.T., *Captain Kidd and his Skeleton Island*
Wilkins, H.T., *A Modern Treasure Hunter*
Wilkins, H.T., *Modern Buried Treasure Hunters*
Wilkins, H.T., *Treasure Hunting*
Wilson, D., *The World Atlas of Treasure*
Winston, A., *No Purchase, No Pay*
Buried and Sunken Treasure (Marshall Cavendish)
The Pirates (Time Life Books)